US Senate

Senator Tom Coburn M.D.

Wastebook 2014

Table of Contents

Introduction..2

Wastebook 2014

1. Paid Vacations for Bureaucrats Gone Wild..4
2. Swedish Massages for Rascally Rabbits...8
3. Army Creates Free First-Person Shooter the Intelligence Community Worries Could Train Terrorists.....................8
4. Mountain Lions on a Treadmill..9
5. Anti-Terror Grant Buys State-of-the-Art SWAT Equipment for Safest Small Town in America..........................10
6. OPM Pays Contractor To "Flush" Security Clearance Investigations "like a dead goldfish"..............................10
7. Spouses Stab Voodoo Dolls More Often When "Hangry", Study Reveals.........................11
8. Scientists Hope Gambling Monkeys Unlock Secrets of Free Will..................................11
9. Subsidies for Sports Stadiums Leave Taxpayers Holding the Bill..................................12
10. Teen Zombie Sings, Tries to Get a Date to the Dance..13
11. Watching Grass Grow...14
12. NIH Asks if Moms Love Dogs as Much as Kids...14
13. Taxpayers Help NY Brewery Build Beer Farm...15
14. Colorado Orchestra Targets Youth with Stoner Symphony...16
15. U.S. Coast Guard Party Patrols..16
16. Chronicling Vermont's Radical Hippie Movement in the 1970's..................................18
17. USDA's "Perfect Poop Pak" Smells Like Government Waste......................................18
18. Synchronized Swimming for Sea Monkeys...19
19. Penn State Shame Study Asks How To Boost Morale After Scandal...........................20
20. Promoting U.S. Culture Around the Globe with Nose Flutists, State Department Idol..................................20
21. Free "High-End" Gym Memberships for DHS Bureaucrats...22
22. Golf Testing, Elementary School Experiments Aboard the International Space Station..................................22
23. NASA's Tower of Pork Protected by Politician..24
24. Congress Blocks Closure of Unneeded "Sheep Station"..25
25. Spray Parks and "Splashpads" Help Beat The Summer Heat.....................................26
26. Roosevelt and Elvis Make a Hallucinatory Pilgrimage to Graceland............................27
27. New Bridge Demolished for Using $3,271 Worth of Canadian Steel............................28
28. Exploding Claims of "Sleep Apnea" Threaten to Bankrupt VA Disability Program.........29
29. Pentagon to Spend $1 Billion to Destroy $16 Billion in Unneeded Ammunition.............29
30. NASA Wonders How Humans Will React to Meeting Space Aliens.............................30
31. Bruce Lee Dance Play Panned As Promoting Racial Stereotypes................................30

32. Road through "Ghost Mall" Hopes to Scare Up Business...31
33. Postal Service Pays Thousands to Ship Soda to Alaska for Hundreds..32
34. Taxpayers Sing the Blues for the Grammy's Museum...33
35. Voicemails From the Future Warn of Post Apocalyptic World...34
36. The Funny Ways Government Wastes Your Money: Laughing Classes..35
37. FAA Upgrades Low-Traffic Airport Serving High-End Ski Resort..35
38. FEMA Overlooks Flood Victims, Rebuilds Golf Course Instead..35
39. Disney Polynesian Resort Gets Makeover..36
40. Space Agency Hunts for the Lost Tomb of Genghis Khan..37
41. Abandoned Pennsylvania Mall Wants to be the East Coast Hollywood..37
42. Wineries Get Help Selling Beer, Chile-Infused Wine..38
43. Roaches, Mice, and Feces in Public Housing Funded by Uncle Sam, Slum Lord........................39
44. DHS Buys Too Many Cars and Lets Them Sit Underused..39
45. Costs Skyrocket for "Birds in Space" Replica...40
46. DOD Tries to Build Real-Life "Iron Man" Suit..40
47. Drug Enforcement Administration Celebrates Itself With Own Museum..41
48. Missile Defense Misses the Target..42
49. Virgin Island Ferries Sit Unused for Nearly a Year..43
50. Jonas Bonus: Rich and Famous Rent Out Their Pads Tax Free..44
51. State Department Tweets @ Terrorists..45
52. Border Patrol Builds Over-Priced Houses for Temporary Workers...46
53. NASA Goes to Comic-Con, Explores the Marvel Universe..47
54. Army Corps Buildings in Afghanistan Keep Burning to the Ground..48
55. Airport Tree-Trimming Project Turns into 27-Hole Golf Course Renovation..................................49
56. Earmark-Funded High-Speed Ferry Sinks Alaska Community..51
57. The Selling of an Airport to Nowhere...51
58. NASA Study Predicts the Collapse of Human Civilization...52
59. Facebook for Fossil Enthusiasts...52
60. Gamers Tune in to Radio Show About Video Game Music..53
61. Two Dozen Teachers Travel to Germany for Classes on Bach, Baroque Dancing Lessons.....53
62. Funding to Reduce Road Crashes Used to Restore Non-Working Lighthouse............................54
63. "Gateway to Blues" Museum Funded Over Deteriorating Bridges...54
64. Study Shows How Buddhism Explains the Science of Meditation...55
65. "Get Fruved:" Social Media Campaign Featuring Students Dressed as Fruits and Vegetables.............55
66. USDA Holds Contest to Build Wooden Skyscraper..56
67. Social Security IT Project Wastes Hundreds of Millions..56
68. Feds Waste Millions Trying to Convince Afghans to Grow Soybeans They Won't Eat..............57
69. Corporate Welfare for Mega Farmers...57
70. Snowmobile Race Part of NSF Zero Emissions Challenge..58
71. Unwanted, Unneeded and Unused Ice House..58
72. Virtual Food Fight Smartphone Game..59
73. Prescription for Higher Medicare Bills...59
74. Boutique Hotel Offers Luxury Spa Services, Afternoon Tea, and Upscale Nightcaps.................60
75. Transportation Dollars Fund Media Campaign to Raise Austin Taxes..61
76. NASA Loses Hundreds of Electronic Devices Each Month...62
77. Huge EPA Warehouse for Paper Reports Thwarts Recycling Efforts..62
78. Food Stamps Get Traded for Cash and Drugs, Go to People Who Hide Their Income.............62
79. DOD Pays 16 Times the Going Price for Helicopter Parts...63

80. Injured ICE Employees Cleared to Work, Stay on Workers Comp Instead..63
81. DOD Sends 16 Planes to the Scrap Heap for $32,000..64
82. Unbuilt Eisenhower Memorial Burning Through Cash...65
83. Butterfly Farm Flies Away with Federal Funds..66
84. Transit Security Grant for "Feel Good" Ads That Promote Local Tax Increase...66
85. Identity Thieves Steal Billions Each Year with Bogus Tax Returns..67
86. Feds Study Science Festival Attendance..67
87. Five Decades of Controversy for Beleaguered Government Program..68
88. Navy Sends Hundreds of Magazines to Congress to Promote Green Initiatives...69
89. NSF Studies Why Wikipedia is Sexist..69
90. Main Town Rebuilds 38 "Speed Humps" to Slow Traffic Through Neighborhood..69
91. DOJ Buys Premium LinkedIn Account to Promote Jobs During Hiring Freeze..70
92. Taxpayers Charged to Promote Hillary Clinton's $14 Million Book in Europe...70
93. FAA Spending to Study What to Do With a FAA-Violating Municipal...71
94. Texting Drunks Asking Them Not to Drink..71
95. We All Scream for Federally Funded Ice Cream..72
96. NASA's Near-Earth Object Program: The Comet that Keeps Chasing Its Tail..72
97. Medicaid Provider Taxes...72
98. Earmark Spends Taxpayer Money to Send Coal to Germany...73
99. Marketing Money for Little-Used Wisconsin Airport...73
100. Farmers Get Grant to Produce "Worm Power" Compost...73

Endnotes..74

WASTEBOOK 2014

EBOLA IN AMERICA. **SECURITY BREACHES AT THE WHITE HOUSE.** WAVES OF UNACCOMPANIED MINORS AND OTHERS POURING ACROSS OUR NATION'S BORDERS. **THE RUSSIAN RED ARMY ON THE MOVE, MARCHING INTO PEACEFUL, DEMOCRATIC NATIONS.** IRAQ IN TURMOIL WITH OIL FIELDS PUMPING MILLIONS OF DOLLARS A DAY INTO THE JIHADIST ACTIVITIES OF RADICAL ISLAMIC TERRORISTS. **OUR NATION'S HEROES BEING KILLED, NOT BY ENEMY COMBATANTS, BUT BY THE VERY VETERANS' HEALTH SYSTEM SET UP TO CARE FOR THEM.** AND THERE IS THAT GOVERNMENT HEALTH CARE WEBSITE THAT STILL DOES NOT WORK.

The world increasingly appears to be in disarray with the chaos, confusion and uncertainty growing ever closer. All the while, the leadership in our nation's capital is ever more distant, disconnected, and absent.

The current Congress is "on track to be one of the least productive" in 60 years.[1] Fewer laws were passed over the last two years than by any Congress in half a century or more, and most of the bills passed had little consequence. While a "lame duck" session is scheduled, the harsh reality is the last two entire years were an extended "lame duck," producing little meaningful results.

The problem is not just what Washington isn't doing, but what it is doing.

Instead of working together to solve these challenges, the politicians are more focused on getting re-elected than conducting the business they were elected to address in the first place. Nearly every major, minor and routine decision facing the nation was punted to next year when Congress abruptly adjourned on September 18 to hit the campaign trail— "the earliest departure by the Congress for the elections since 1960."[2]

Congress' role is not just passing bills. It is also responsible for conducting oversight to hold the executive branch accountable, which it is failing to do. In fact, Congress actually forced federal agencies to waste billions of dollars for purely parochial, political purposes. Mississippi lawmakers, for example, attached a rider to a larger bill requiring NASA to build a $350 million launch pad tower, which was moth balled as soon as it was completed because the rockets it was designed to test were scrapped years ago. Likewise, when USDA attempted to close an unneeded sheep research station in Idaho costing nearly $2 million every year to operate, politicians in the region stepped in to keep it open.

Washington politicians are more focused on their own political futures than the future of our country. And with no one watching over the vast bureaucracy, the problem again isn't just what Washington isn't doing, but what it is doing.

Much like Congress, thousands of federal employees who weren't doing their jobs properly have been sent home and paid to do nothing— many for years! Some committed crimes. Others engaged in misconduct. Collectively they brought shame and dishonor to public service. Instead of being fired, they were given paid vacations at a cost of $20 million.

While the IRS was politically targeting Tea Party groups by putting the nonprofits under excessive scrutiny, the agency readily handed over $4 billion to identity thieves because it neglected to spot thousands of bogus tax returns.

The firm that gave the green light to grant security clearances to both notorious NSA leaker Edward Snowden and Aaron Alexis, who shot and killed 12 people at the Washington Navy Yard,[3] received another $124 million to conduct background checks the Department of Justice found to be fraudulent. As a result, thousands of ineligible individuals may now have access to top secret information.

The U.S. Coast Guard reduced drug and migrant interdictions while providing free patrols to keep party crashers away from posh private events on yachts and beaches along some of the country's most exclusive waterfront estates.

The President asked Congress to provide $1.1 billion in emergency funding for Immigration and Customs Enforcement (ICE)[4] to deal with the thousands of unaccompanied children illegally crossing the border this year.[5] Yet, ICE was paying $1 million in workers' compensation to employees who were not working, even though they had been cleared to return to duty.[6]

The pleas for assistance from hundreds of families whose homes were damaged by the "storm of the century" in Austin, Texas, were ignored by the Federal Emergency Management Agency, which instead spent hundreds of thousands of dollars to help clean up local golf courses.

The director of the National Institutes for Health claims a vaccine for Ebola "probably" would have been developed by now if not for the stagnant funding for the agency,[7] which has a $30 billion annual budget.[8] Yet NIH did come up with the money to pay to give Swedish massages for rabbits.

NASA no longer has the ability to send astronauts into space. The agency now pays Russia $70 million per passenger for a round trip fare to the international space station where the "design and creation of better golf clubs" is among the studies being conducted.

These are among the 100 silly, unnecessary, and low priority projects in this year's Wastebook exposing Washington's upside down priorities that tally up to $25 billion.

Only someone with too much of someone else's money and not enough accountability for how it was being spent could come up with some of the zany projects the government paid for this year, like laughing classes for college students (no joke!) or a play about brain eating zombies for children. The National Science Foundation (NSF) taught monkeys how to play video games and gamble. USDA got into the business of butterfly farming. The Department of Interior even paid people to watch grass to see how quickly it grows. The State Department spent money to dispel the perception abroad that Americans are fat and rude.[9] But the real shock and awe may have been the $1 billion price tag the Pentagon paid to destroy $16 billion worth of ammunition, enough to pay a full years' salary for over 54,000 Army privates.

Despite all of this obvious waste, Washington politicians celebrated ending the fiscal year with a deficit under half-a-trillion dollars for the first time since 2008[10], as if adding $486 billion[11] to a national debt quickly approaching $18 trillion is an actual accomplishment deserving praise. Citing this decline without context "is misleading, since it follows an almost 800 percent increase that brought deficits to record high levels," says the Committee for a Responsible Federal Budget. The non-partisan group notes the debt continued to rise during this period and deficits are projected to grow larger, eventually exceeding $1 trillion annually once again in the near future.

This report, the fifth annual Wastebook, gives a snapshot of just a fraction of the countless frivolous projects the government funded in the past twelve months with borrowed money and your tax dollars. Every year taxpayers, regardless of their personal political leanings, raise their eyebrows and shake their heads in disbelief at how billions of dollars that could be been better spent—or not spent at all—were squandered. Then they ask, "but what are you doing about it?"

While I have offered hundreds of amendments to stop stupid spending, most have been soundly defeated. Perhaps there is no better example of Congress's upside down priorities than the Senate overwhelmingly rejected an amendment to defund the infamous bridge to nowhere in Alaska.[12] Under the current Senate leadership, amendments are no longer even permitted, ending any hope of actually cutting waste through the legislative process.

Yet, victories are occurring despite the actions and lack of actions taken by Congress.

That bridge may have been approved by Congress, but it was never built because of the public outraged it sparked. Other projects that made headlines after being featured in Wastebook met a similar fate. An airport in Oklahoma that averaged just one flight per month was landing nearly half-a-million in federal subsidies a year was closed after appearing in Wastebook.[13] A day after Wastebook called out Beverly Hills for selling its federal Community Development Block grants, the Department of Housing and Urban Development instructed the jurisdiction to cease the practice.[14] NSF canceled a climate change musical showcased in Wastebook.[15]

Some spending decisions are reversed before they can even make it into print to avoid embarrassment. A day after my office inquired about a life size inflatable foosball game the State Department ordered in September, for example, the purchase was canceled.[16]

What I have learned from these experiences is Washington will never change itself. But even if the politicians won't stop stupid spending, taxpayers always have the last word.

As you read through the entries presented in this report, ask yourself: Is each of these a true national priority or could the money have been better spent on a more urgent need or not spent at all in order to reduce the burden of debt being left to be paid off by our children and grandchildren?

Sincerely,

Tom A. Coburn, M.D.
U.S. Senator

Paid Vacations for Bureaucrats Gone Wild

$19 million[101]

CHARGING BOOZE AND PERSONAL TRIPS ON THE OFFICE CREDIT CARD. PASSING OUT ON THE JOB AFTER A LATE NIGHT PARTYING. WASTING MOST OF THE WORK DAY SURFING FOR SMUT ON OFFICE COMPUTERS. MAKING UNWANTED SEXUAL ADVANCES. USING AN OFFICE LAPTOP TO SEND EXPLICIT IMAGES.

Any one of these outrageous behaviors would be reason enough for most to be fired... unless, of course, you are on the federal government's payroll, in which case you might instead get a paid vacation lasting months or even years.

Rather than disciplining employees who are underperforming or even engaging in criminal mischief, federal bureaucrats place troublesome employees on "administrative leave," where they continue to get paid but are essentially relieved of their duties including having to report to work or do work. A federal employment attorney calls administrative leave "the government's dirty little secret."[17]

Officially, administrative leave is an "excused absence"[18] with pay and continuation of other benefits, such as health insurance, life insurance, and retirement plans, that is not charged as annual leave or vacation. In 2014, eleven federal agencies spent at least $50 million paying the salaries of government employees on administrative leave status, one-third of which was for disciplinary reasons.[19]

Administrative leave is not just a discipline tool as agencies utilize administrative leave for any number of purposes. Some receive administrative leave for more noble purposes, such as organ donation or volunteering. Others get paid time off to recover from an overseas trip, to attend a conference, to conduct union activities, or to go to a parade.[20] Some administrators abuse it to remove and isolate whistleblowers.[21] The Pentagon's police chief encouraged employees to take administrative leave to go golfing.[22] Several agencies even allow paid leave to attend Mardi Gras.[23] These federal employees are literally being paid to party!

The "predominant reason" for "large amounts of paid administration leave," however, is personnel matters, such as misconduct, criminal matters, or security concerns.[24] The Government Accountability Office (GAO) found these types of personnel matters accounted for roughly one-third of administrative leave charged, or $19 million.[25] GAO found inconsistencies between what different agencies considered administrative leave as well as inaccuracies in the Office of Personnel Management data.[26]

While administrative leave is intended to be used sparingly for limited periods of time,[27] for many it has become a paid vacation lasting months and even years.[28] More than 1,000 federal employees were on paid leave for at least six months and hundreds were given paid absences from work for a year or more.[29] Nearly 60,000 federal employees received paid leave for an entire month or more over a two year period in addition to vacation time and paid holidays.[30]

For those federal employees put on paid leave for criminal activities this year, like criminally negligent homicide, and sexual abuse, crime does pay.

Some put on administration leave in 2014 engaged in nefarious and illegal behaviors that undermine the very confidence in our government.

An office within the most controversial government agency, the IRS, used its power to harass and impede political opposition for years and the director avoided taking any responsibility and also avoided any real discipline by being put on paid leave for months before retiring with a generous government pension.[31] The CIA's chief of Iran operations was put on paid administrative leave for creating "an abusive and hostile work environment that put a crucial division in disarray."[32] A Secret Service agent responsible for protecting the President on an overseas trip was put on leave after being found passed out in a hotel hallway after a late night of partying.[33] The former acting Inspector General (IG) at the Department of Homeland Security was placed on administrative leave in April after a bipartisan Senate investigation found he had "jeopardized the independence" of the IG's office.[34] Two senior officials within the IG office of the Department of Commerce were placed on paid administrative leave after threatening subordinates with negative performance reviews unless they signed "agreements not to disparage" the office upon leaving.[35]

After a never ending series of scandals, the Department of Veterans Affairs had no shortage of excuses to place misbehaving staff on paid leave this year. Veterans across the country were revealed to be dying as a direct result of bureaucratic negligence. Agency managers orchestrated premeditated cover-ups, even punishing those who refused to go along with the scheme to manipulate data to secure performance bonuses while veterans went months without care, resulting in hundreds of unnecessary deaths over the last several years. Those responsible went largely unpunished and were instead placed on paid leave.

Other VA employees were put on paid administrative leave for sexually abusing a female patient,[36] causing a fatal car crash as a result of driving drunk,[37] sexting on government computers,[38] paying for booze and personal items on government charge cards,[39] taking a patient being treated for addiction to a crack house and hooking him up with drugs,[40] and failing to do their jobs.[41]

Congress responded to the growing public backlash against the mistreatment being suffered by our nation's heroes by passing a bill to make it easier to terminate poorly performing VA employees. The President signed the act into law on August 7,[42] warning "if you engage in an unethical practice, if you cover up a serious problem, you should be fired. Period. It shouldn't be that difficult."[43] Yet months later, the VA has yet to fire any of the employees responsible for the deaths, scandals, and cover-ups. They continue to be paid to do nothing.[44]

Paid leave doesn't just penalize taxpayers, it also punishes the dedicated civil servants who get stuck picking up the slack. There are also consequences for those who seeking government assistance or services. At the VA, for example, one absent employee who was put on paid leave was expected to process at least three veterans' benefits cases per day.[45] A co-worker said she became frustrated because he wasn't present to do his job yet she still had "to approve his timecards," while "they desperately needed" a full time staffer "to help relieve a backlog in rating veterans and getting benefits to them."

But the VA is not the only abuser of administrative leave.

Out of 67,000 Social Security Administration (SSA) employees, nearly 10,000 were on administrative leave for ten days or more during the first six months of the year costing nearly $40 million, and no one knows why.[46] The reason for all the paid absences is unknown as SSA does not record why employees are on administrative leave.[47]

Paid leave doesn't just penalize taxpayers, it also punishes the dedicated civil servants who get stuck picking up the slack.

The Department of Homeland Security (DHS) spent at least $4.3 million to pay employees not to work this year.[48] The department had 237 employees on administrative leave for more than 10 days in 2014 as of August.[49] Of these, 205 were on administrative leave status due to misconduct.[50]

The U.S. Postal Service (USPS) had 1,553 employees on administrative leave for more than 10 days as of July 2014, for a cost exceeding $3 million

To be fair, administrative leave in select cases can sometimes be justifiable. It can also take time to fairly adjudicate situations where facts may be murky and not all employees on administrative leave are found guilty of wrongdoing.

But only in Washington would an employee not doing their job be punished by being paid not do their job for months or even years.

Bureaucrats Gone Wild "Punished" with Paid Vacations

The following is just a snapshot of some government bureaucrats gone wild, who continued to be receive paychecks this year—often without having any assignments or even having to show up for work—after engaging in unacceptable and sometimes criminal conduct.

1. Secret Service agent responsible for protecting the President during overseas trip found drunk and passed out in hotel hallway after a late night of partying.

Three Secret Service agents "responsible for protecting President Obama" during his visit to Amsterdam in March 2014 were placed on paid administrative leave after a late night of partying on the eve of the President's arrival.[51] One of the agents was found "passed out drunk in a hallway and later had to be lifted into his room by several hotel employees" and "claimed to have no memory of the events."[52] The other two agents, one of whom was the "team leader" on the trip, "were deemed complicit" because they did not "intervene" or "tamp down his behavior."[53] The agents were "temporarily replaced by other agents in the country until additional agents could be flown in to meet up with Obama's entourage at his next destination, Brussels."[54] All three are GS-13-level agents,[55] which means they are paid an annual salary of at least $72,000.[56] The misconduct violated Secret Service rules barring agents from drinking alcohol ten hours before an assignment. These rules were "adopted in the wake of a damaging scandal in Cartagena, Colombia, in April 2012, when a dozen agents and officers had been drinking heavily and had brought prostitutes back to their hotel rooms before the president's arrival for an economic summit."[57] The Amsterdam incident "came less than three weeks after the traffic accident in Miami, which led to the two officers involved being sent home."[58]

2. EPA employee who admits to viewing porn for up to six hours a day over the past four years paid $120,000 a year with performance bonuses.

An Environmental Protection Agency (EPA) employee who admits spending up to six hours every day viewing pornography on government computers during work hours collected a $120,000 annual salary and with performance bonuses.[59] When a special agent from the EPA Office of Inspector General went to interview the employee about his behavior, he was "actively viewing pornography on his government-issued computer. The employee confessed to spending, on average, between two and six hours per day viewing pornography while at work. The OIG's investigation determined that the employee downloaded and viewed more than 7,000 pornographic files during duty hours. This investigation has been referred to and accepted by the DOJ for prosecution."[60] A high ranking EPA official admitted at a House Oversight and Government Reform hearing in May, "I'm not personally doing anything about it."[61] The chairman of the committee, Congressman Darrell Issa, questioned "how much pornography would it take for an EPA employee to lose their job?"[62] Rather than being fired, the employee received "performance awards, merit based prizes, during the months he was found to be surfing porn at taxpayer expense," according to an EPA official.[63]

3. VA execs covered up veterans' deaths and patient delays to secure performance bonuses for themselves.

Public outrage over a scheme by executives at Department of Veterans Affairs (VA) clinics to get paid bonuses by manipulating wait times and patients' deaths cost the job of one employee at the department-- the Secretary. A whistleblower revealed the Phoenix VA Health Care System was concealing long delays for care and maintaining a secret list of patient wait that claimed the lives of as many as 40 veterans. A series of audits and investigations found VA administrators from coast to coast were "gaming the system" by "producing phony appointment data" to cover-up the thousands of veterans waiting months to see a doctor.[64] Those within the agency who attempted to speak out against the culture of corruption were punished, but those involved in the scheme have yet to be held accountable. Three executives at the Phoenix VA were put on administrative leave in May "until further notice," including the director and associate director.[65] Each continues to receive their full salary, for the director that amounts to nearly $170,000 annually,[66] or $85,000 since being put on leave.

4. IRS official who oversaw office that targeted Tea Party groups misled about her role in scandal.

A Treasury Inspector General for Tax Administration (TIGTA) report issued in May found over a four year period the IRS singled out Tea Party and other conservative organizations applying for tax-exempt status "based upon their names or policy positions" and delayed approval of those requests while demanding "unnecessary" and "burdensome" information.[67] President Obama called the political targeting by the IRS "outrageous," stating "I have got no patience with it, I will not tolerate it," asserting "they have to be held fully accountable."[68] Lois Lerner, the director of the IRS tax-exempt organizations division responsible for the actions, tried to pin the actions, which she called "absolutely inappropriate," on "lower-level workers" who "picked groups for extra scrutiny according to whether they had 'tea party' or 'patriot' in their names." TIGTA's investigation, however, concluded the targeting of these groups began in 2010 and blamed "ineffective management."[69] Two years of Lerner's emails were somehow lost by the IRS and her computer's hard drive was destroyed.[70] E-mails unearthed by investigators, show Lerner was "directly involved in targeting conservative nonprofit groups for special scrutiny beginning at the height of the 2010 midterm election season."[71] She was placed on paid administrative leave in May and voluntarily retired from the IRS in September.[72] With an annual salary of about $185,000,[73] she collected nearly $50,000 during the four months she was paid on administrative leave. "Retiring before the Treasury Department can fire her allows Lerner to keep her pension" which will be "more than $50,900 per year."[74]

5. VA employee hooks up patient being treated for addiction with drugs and prostitute.

A VA drug addiction treatment specialist busted for taking a patient to a crack house to help him score illegal drugs and solicit a prostitute was also found "guilty of patient abuse, misuse of government vehicles, filing false overtime requests and multiple ethics violations" is still employed at Central Alabama Veterans Health Care System.[75] The initial incident occurred in March 1, 2013 according to a VA investigative report that concluded the employee "interfered" with the patient's "medical treatment plan" and "endorsed" his addictions, and exposed him to a "dangerous environment."[76]

6. Senior officials at the Commerce Department Office of Inspector General try to gag subordinates with threats of negative job reviews.

Two senior officials at the Department of Commerce Office of Inspector General were placed on paid administrative leave after threatening subordinates with negative performance reviews if they refused to sign a gag order upon leaving the office.[77] The two "were escorted from the building and prohibited from physical and electronic access to the department," but remained on the Commerce Department's payroll.

7. Administrators overlooked pandemonium in scandal plagued office.

After a seemingly never ending list of scandals, the director and chief of staff of the Central Alabama Veterans Health Care System were placed on paid administrative leave in August 2014.[78] The problems include falsifying "appointment records to mask how long veterans wait for appointments and not reading hundreds of X-rays. Employees at the center have also been accused of taking a patient being treated for addiction to a crack house to buy drugs,"[79] sexually abusing a female patient,[80] and causing a fatal car crash as a result of driving drunk.[81] The Director, James Talton, had implied that "all employees involved in the falsification were terminated," when they were instead "relieved of their duties" while continuing to be paid employees of the VA.

8. VA employee driving drunk indicted for homicide in fatal car crash.

A vocational rehabilitation specialist in the mental health department at the Central Alabama Veterans Administration Health Center System (CAVHCS) was indicted for "criminally negligent homicide" for a fatal car crash that occurred last year while he was driving drunk.[82] The employee, whose job requires him to drive a government vehicle, was off duty at the time. He was speeding when his car ran off the road and "the vehicle flipped several times before landing on its roof." A passenger was killed in the accident. The driver "was arrested for driving under the influence of alcohol." The case was "referred to human resources, but as of Sept. 2, that individual was still employed by and working at CAVHCS more than a year after the accident."[83]

9. VA employee charged with sexually abusing female veteran.

An employee of the Veterans Affairs Southeast Network was placed on administrative leave after being charged with "first-degree sexual abuse" for fondling the breast of a female patient who is a veteran.[84] The preliminary hearing was held August 21 after twice being delayed by the VA employee's attorney.[85] The employee "will only be tried if he's first indicted by a grand jury," which does not meet again until January or February of next year. In the meantime, the employee continues to be paid.[86]

10. NIH police offer pulls a loaded gun on motorist during a fit of road rage.

A police officer for the National Institutes of Health was placed on paid administrative leave in June after pulling a loaded gun on a motorist during a fit of road rage.[87] The motorist told state police he was forced into the officer's lane on the interstate when he "pulled out a black Glock 19 and loaded the magazine" as "a terrified motorist in the next lane desperately tried to get away."[88]

11. Monitoring of Iran's nuclear program potentially compromised by CIA's official's mismanagement.

The chief of the CIA's Iran operations was put on paid administrative leave in March "after an internal investigation found he had created an abusive and hostile work environment that put a crucial division in disarray."[89] The division, which is crucial to monitoring Iran's nuclear program, "was in open rebellion" due to the official's "management style, with several key employees demanding transfers.[90] Internal surveys have long revealed CIA employees believe the agency is "beset by bad management, where misjudgments by senior officials go unpunished."[91] An Inspector General report found "perceptions of poor management, and a lack of accountability for poor management, comprised five of the top 10 reasons why people leave or consider leaving CIA and were the most frequent topic of concern among those who volunteered comments."[92]

12. VA employee used government computers for sexting, showed up for work when he wanted, took unnecessary junkets, and charged personal items to taxpayers.

An employee admitted he was "out of control" sexting his friends from VA computers and working when and where he pleased was put on paid leave March 11, two weeks after a February 24 report detailed his behaviors. On July 25, he "was allowed to resign before he could be disciplined for wasting government time and money."[93] The employee, assigned to an office in Nashville, took 34 trips to Washington, D.C. as well as junkets to Florida and New Jersey. He "worked at his own time and pace" so "he could conduct personal business during the workday. By his own admission, he took advantage of the lack of supervision."[94] The OIG chronicled how the employee eluded punishment time and time again and instead talked his supervisors into improperly creating a new (and higher-paying) job for him in Washington, DC.[95] He misused a government travel charge card "to entertain female companions, withdraw cash when not on travel, charge over $170 at a Target store for personal items, buy liquor from his hotel room minibar, and for his personal commutes to visit family."[96] In total, the employee's excessive travels cost more than $109,000.[97] On at least 20 instances, he was absent without leave "as a result of his previous night's activities, and admitted his misconduct negatively affected his performance."[98] His absences from his job had real consequences for veterans as well as his co-workers. He "was expected to process a minimum cumulative average number of 3.5 weighted cases per day," but "he did not,"[99] despite the backlog processing veterans benefits. This employee also "downloaded and installed unapproved software to his VA-issued laptop for the purpose of sexting—defined as the sending of sexually explicit photos, images, text messages, or emails using a mobile device."[100]

2. Swedish Massages for Rascally Rabbits

$387,000

The real lucky rabbit's foot may be attached to one of the bunnies receiving Swedish massages courtesy of taxpayers.

A group of rabbits received daily rub downs from a "mechanical device that simulates the long, flowing strokes used in Swedish massages."[118] The National Center for Complementary and Alternative Medicine of the National Institutes of Health provided $387,000 for the two year project which ended in April 2014.[119]

The massages were given after subjecting the rabbits to exercise to measure its impact on recovery. To conduct the experiment, 18 "New Zealand White rabbits were instrumented" with "nerve cuffs for stimulation of hindlimb" leg muscles.[120] The rabbits were "anesthetized and secured supine with one foot attached to a foot pedal."[121]

Following the work outs, researchers compared post-exercise recovery time for those receiving immediate massages, delayed massages, or no massages at all.[122] The lucky bunnies received massages four times a day[123] that lasted 30 minutes immediately following exercise.[124] These rabbits not only got the most massages, they also recovered quicker from the exercises.

"We tried to mimic Swedish massage because anecdotally, it's the most popular technique used by athletes," said Thomas Best, the project leader and co-medical director of the Ohio State University Sports Medicine Center.[125]

The researchers "acknowledge that the injury created in our animal model may not be completely analogous to the injury produced in humans with eccentric exercise."[126] They do note, however, that studies do exist to support the use of massage to treat human muscle aches and pains.[127]

If the researchers were seeking to learn how to identify the most optimal application of massage therapy to treat human muscle aches and injuries, then perhaps they should have observed human subjects. Instead, this study seems to have chased tax dollars down a rabbit hole. Taxpayer dollars that could have supported potentially more transformative research were instead spent on exercise and massage equipment for rabbits. As for the rabbits, they were eventually euthanized,[128] so while well massaged, those feet were not so lucky after all.

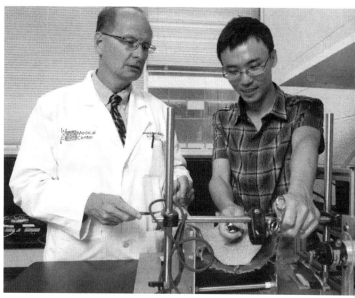

Researchers designed work out equipment to exercise rabbits as well as a Swedish massage machine give rabbit rubdowns.[129]

3. Army Creates Free First-Person Shooter the Intelligence Community Worries Could Train Terrorists

$414,000

War is not a game – unless you're playing *America's Army*, a free, online first-person-shooter game developed, produced and promoted by the U.S. Army.

The Army first released the video game in 2002, and has updated it every year since as part of its enlistment efforts.[130] It features ultra-realism in weaponry, tactics and leadership, but, "[u]nlike commercial games designed to make big money, the aim of this taxpayer-funded project is to generate Army recruits."[131]

According to the Congressional Research Service, the Army spent $414,000 in 2014, which it says were used for "community and forum management, as well as server host and statistical report fees."[132] Yet, taxpayers have spent far more than that in past years. As of 2009, the Army had spent at least $33 million to develop and update *America's Army*, though the project was originally budgeted to cost only a total of $7 million.[133]

But while it may help recruit and train U.S. soldiers, some intelligence officials worry it could also be aiding jihadists and mass murderers. A top secret National Security Agency report from 2007 – and later leaked by Edward Snowden – identified *America's Army* as one of several combat simulation games which terrorists can use to train for missions. It is so realistic, "the army no longer needs to use it for recruitment, they use it for training," the report noted, adding, "The Lebanese Hizballah has taken this concept and the same basic game design and made its own version of the game called Special Forces 2 (SF2), which its press section acknowledges is used for recruitment and training in order to prepare their youth to 'fight the enemy', a radicalizing medium; the ultimate goal is to become a suicide martyr."[134]

The report indicates that terrorists could use games like this to practice skills, noting, for example, that some of the 9-11 pilots had never flown a real plane, and had only trained using Microsoft's Flight Simulator.[135] "These games offer realistic weapons training ... military operations and tactics, photorealistic land navigation and terrain familiarization, and leadership skills," the report said. "When the mission is expensive, risky, or dangerous, it is often a wiser idea to exercise virtually, rather than really blow an operative up assembling a bomb or exposing a sleeper agent to law enforcement scrutiny."[136]

In September the Army rolled out its most recent update to the game, RFI-4, which allows players compete in a deadly version of capture-the-flag called "Intercept" featuring missile components rather than a flag.[137]

"Intercept is the latest and one of the finest America's Army: Proving Grounds maps ever developed," the Army boasted on its Facebook page devoted to the game. It noted that the update was designed "with mission re-playability as the primary focus."[138]

Realistic scenes from America's Army

4 Mountain Lions on a Treadmill

$856,000

"People just didn't believe you could get a mountain lion on a treadmill, and it took me three years to find a facility that was willing to try," exclaimed Terrie Williams, a University of California-Santa Cruz professor.[139]

What people won't have a hard time believing is the federal government would pay to put the big cats on a treadmill. Not so long ago, after all, the National Science Foundation (NSF) paid $560,000 to run a shrimp on a tiny treadmill.[140] In fact, the federal government has raced animals, large and small on a treadmill from monkeys,[141] to rats,[142] and even cows[143] and goats.[144]

In this study funded with an $856,000 NSF grant, three captive mountain lions were taught to use a treadmill.[145] It took eight months of training before the cats were "comfortable on the treadmill."[146]

The study, which also monitored wild mountain lions with a special collar, determined the "power of the pounce" and the energy consumption of the cat's hunting techniques. Before the researchers "could interpret the data from collars deployed on wild mountain lions, however, they first had to perform calibration studies with mountain lions in captivity. This meant, among other things, training mountain lions to walk and run on a treadmill and measuring their oxygen consumption at different activity levels. Those studies took a bit longer than planned."[147]

The treadmill study found "mountain lions do not have the aerobic capacity for sustained, high-energy activity.[148]

"They are power animals. They have a slow routine walking speed and use a burst of speed and the force of the pounce to knock down or overpower their prey," Williams explains.

"In addition to the treadmill studies, the captive cats were videotaped wearing the collars while doing a wide range of activities in a large outdoor enclosure. This provided a library of collar acceleration signatures specific for different behaviors, from resting and grooming to running and pouncing."[149]

A "state-of-the-art" collar—called the Species Movement, Acceleration, and Radio Tracking (SMART) wildlife collar— was designed by a graduate student for the studies in the wild. The high tech collar includes a GPS unit, accelerometers, and a magnetometer "to provide detailed data on where an animal is and what it is doing."[150]

The researchers say the "insights are likely to greatly inform public knowledge and opinion of large mammal behavior and conservation."[151]

The NSF funds were also spent on "outreach," which included attending conferences and developing an interactive website.[152]

While support for basic science is not itself wasteful, federal research agencies should better prioritize how tax dollars are directed to ensure adequate support for more pressing scientific endeavors. With Congress racking up deficits and leaving nearly an $18 trillion debt for the next generation, scarce resources should be used to pay down the debt or on higher priorities, such as emerging biological threats that could pounce on anyone of us.

A mountain lion that has been trained to run on the testing treadmill.

5. Anti-Terror Grant Buys State-of-the-Art SWAT Equipment for Safest Small Town in America

$200,000

Ten years ago, "pork barrel politics at its worst" was how then New York City Mayor Michael Bloomberg described U.S. counterterrorism spending to the 9/11 Commission.[153] Spreading money around might make for good politics, he charged, but would do little to keep the nation safe. A decade later there is evidence little has changed. Two small municipalities around New York received anti-terror grants for SWAT team equipment upgrades, despite being rated among the safest and at least risk of terrorism in the country.

The State of New York awarded two grants worth a total of $200,000 to Ithaca, and the Twin Cities of Tonawanda and North Tonawanda using funds from the Department of Homeland Security's (DHS) State Homeland Security Program.[154] They were distributed as part of the state's "Tactical Team Grant Program."

Ithaca in particular was recently distinguished as the number one "most secure" small town in America by Farmers Insurance Group of Companies.[155] Among other factors, the study looked at "crime statistics, extreme weather, risk of natural disasters, housing depreciation, foreclosures, air quality ... [and] terrorist threats."[156] According to the Ithaca Police Department's website, Ithaca's crime rate is the third lowest in the nation for a metropolitan area of any size.[157] "This grant money is awesome for us," Ithaca police Chief John Barber beamed, explaining that the grant would help purchase night vision goggles, a tactical robot, chemical suits and training among other things.[158]

Farmers Insurance similarly ranked the Buffalo-Niagara Falls metropolitan area, of which both Tonawanda and North Tonawanda are a part, as the sixth safest large metro area in the country.[159] Local police officials said the money would purchase "state-of-the-art equipment."[160]

6. OPM Pays Contractor To "Flush" Security Clearance Investigations "like a dead goldfish"

$124.3 million

What do a goldfish, a leprechaun, and Dick Clark have in common? All were invoked as part of one company's attempt to scam millions of federal dollars, all the while compromising our national security.

Over the past year the government paid $124.3 million to U.S. Investigations Services, Inc. (USIS),[161] the federal contractor hired to conduct security clearance background checks, despite the company's history of security failures and allegations of fraud.[162] Among the firm's most high-profile failures was giving the all-clear to both Edward Snowden, the notorious NSA leaker, and Aaron Alexis, who shot and killed 12 people at the Washington Navy Yard.[163]

While the government uses several contractors to help do background checks, USIS does about half all investigations for federal security clearances.[164] With more than five million government employees and contractors – or 1.6 percent of the entire U.S. population – holding a security clearance, the firm plays a big role in protecting our nation's secrets.[165]

However, this past January, the Department of Justice (DOJ) accused USIS of submitting 665,000 fake background investigations.[166] As a result, hundreds of thousands of people who may not have been eligible for clearances were given access to top secret information.

According to its contract with the Office of Personnel Management (OPM), USIS was paid for each background investigation is completed, along with bonuses for high quality work.[167] In the complaint filed by DOJ, management at USIS "devised and executed a scheme to deliberately circumvent contractually required reviews to increase the company's revenues and profits."[168] The scheme was referred to as "dumping" or "flushing" cases – terms used by the company to send incomplete investigations to OPM when they were trying to hit their performance goals.[169]

An email sent in April 2010 by one employee to the company's Director of National Quality Assurance provided an update on the number of cases dumped that day, commenting, "Shelves are as clean as they could get. Flushed everything like a dead goldfish."[170]

Another email later that year was written in character as a mischievous leprechaun "T'is Flushy McFlushershon at his merry hijinks again!! **leprechaun dance** ...I'm not tired..."[171]

Even the then-ailing Dick Clark's name was invoked during the holiday season: "Scalping tickets for 'Dick Clark's Dumpin' New Year's Eve! Who needs 2? Have a bit of a backlog building, but fortunately, most people are off this week so no one will notice!"[172]

7. Spouses Stab Voodoo Dolls More Often When "Hangry", Study Reveals

$331,000

The feeling of anger caused by hunger is so well-known that pop culture has given the feelings their own name: hanger. Armed with voodoo dolls and chalkboard noises, federally funded researchers wanted to prove a hangry spouse is also an unhappy one.

Over the course of twenty-one consecutive evenings, 107 couples were given a chance to stick up to 51 pins into a voodoo doll representing their spouse.[173] The pin-pushing happened in secret, away from the other partner. Participants then recorded the number of pins they poked into the dolls. Those tests revealed what may already be obvious to many couples: a spouse with low blood sugar was an angrier one, and stuck more pins in the doll (on average).[174]

In a subsequent experiment, partners were allowed to blast loud noises at their partner if they won a game. The winner could play the loud noises – the sound of a smoke alarm, dentist's drill, and fingernails-on-a-chalkboard – for any amount of time they chose.[175]

Again, the results were just as any parent of a toddler might expect. "Hungry people are cranky and aggressive," said the lead researcher.[176] Partners with lower blood glucose levels blasted their spouses with louder and longer noise.[177]

Not all academics believed the results. Two psychologists who reviewed the work suggested, "[I]t might be a big leap to interpret the results with voodoo dolls as indicating risk for actual physical aggression against a spouse."[178]

Funding for the voodoo doll project came in part from National Science Foundation grant worth $331,000.[179]

8. Scientists Hope Gambling Monkeys Unlock Secrets of Free Will

$171,000

It turns out humans are not the only species looking for "Big money, no whammies!" Monkeys also like to play video games and gamble, found an ongoing study supported by the National Science Foundation.

Humans have long been known to have a "hot-hand bias" in which they believe hot or cold streaks exist where there is actually none. Researchers wanted to know if monkeys had the same problem.

"Luckily, monkeys love to gamble," said Tommy Blanchard, a doctoral candidate at the University of Rochester who worked on the study.[180] But scientists "had to create a computerized game that was so captivating monkeys would want to play for hours."[181]

Monkeys were faced with three kinds of games: "two with clear patterns (the correct answer tended to repeat on one side or to alternate from side to side) and a third in which the lucky pick was completely random."[182] They picked up on consistent patterns in the first two games, "but in the random scenarios, the monkeys continued to make choices as if they expected a 'streak.' In other words, even when rewards were random, the monkeys favored one side. The monkeys showed the hot-hand bias consistently over weeks of play."[183] Almost like being stuck in a casino, the three "subjects" played an average of 3,732 games.[184]

Based upon the monkeys' behavior, the researchers concluded monkeys share "our unfounded belief in winning and losing streaks."[185] "Win-stay strategies appear to be more natural for monkeys than win-shift ones," details the study.[186]

The researchers contend the study could "provide nuance to our understanding of free will" or even "inform treatment for gambling addiction."[187] But taxpayers are likely to go totally bananas that NSF is monkeying around with federal research dollars.

The project is being funded as part of a $171,361 continuing grant to be provided by the National Science Foundation from June 2013 to May 2018.[188]

Subsidies for Sports Stadiums Leave Taxpayers Holding the Bill

$146 million

For millions of sports fans, Fall in America means watching the first weeks of football season and catching baseball playoff games from the comfort of their couch. Many of these exciting showdowns are played in spectacular new stadiums largely paid for in part with tax-free financing. Yet, with some tickets costing hundreds of dollars, many taxpayers cannot afford to attend a game or enjoy the stadiums they helped build.

Through the use of municipal bonds, state and local governments are able to finance the building of multi-million dollar sporting arenas to support their favorite local team and wealthy franchise owners. The interest earned by investors on these bonds is not subject to federal income tax, resulting in hundreds of millions of dollars in lost federal revenue.

The only loser in this game is the taxpayer.

This tax preference for the pros costs the government $146 million in lost revenue every year, in tax exemptions on interest from government bonds for sporting facilities, according to a Bloomberg analysis of U.S. Treasury data.[189]

Dallas Cowboy fans may not cheer quite as loud this year considering their unrivaled new stadium was financed by government bonds, resulting in more than $65 million in subsidies to investors over the next 29 years.[190] Despite helping to pay for the stadium, visitors will have to pay up to $27.50 if they even want to tour facility, which boasts a "600-ton, four-screen video" jumbotron, a retractable ceiling, art galleries, and "320 suites with polished marble floors and granite counters" that can cost up to $500,000 to lease per season.[191]

On the East Coast, New York's beloved Yankees are hitting homeruns in the second most expensive baseball stadium ever built,[192] in part thanks to $942 million in tax-free financing, resulting in revenue losses of at least $231 million over 30 years.[193]

These aren't the only teams winning big, even if they lose a game or two in their swanky stadiums. Bloomberg's investigation revealed, "There are 21 NFL owners whose teams play in stadiums built or renovated in the past quarter-century using tax-free public borrowing. Such municipal debt helped build structures used by 64 major-league teams, including baseball, hockey and basketball."[194]

The exclusion of interest from the income tax functions as a federal subsidy through the tax code for state and local government borrowing and for the team owners who do not have to put up as much of their own money. The direct tax subsidy is claimed by the investors who do not pay taxes on the interest earned from these bonds.

The federal tax preference for pro stadiums was not created intentionally, and in fact, Congress specifically attempted to prohibit tax-exempt financing of stadiums. But, Congress left the door open for local governments to use tax-free municipal bonds to help build the stadiums with taxpayer help.[195] Municipal bonds, however, are supposed to be used to finance capital projects such as buildings, utilities, and transportation infrastructure,[196] not subsidize athletic arenas for multi-million dollar sports franchises.

Congress should leave the game playing to the professionals and stop asking taxpayers to take a penalty for the home team.

Tax-free financing for sports stadiums like the Dallas Cowboys' arena, leave taxpayers holding the bill, costing $146 million every year.

10. Teen Zombie Sings, Tries to Get a Date to the Dance

$10,000

While most zombies want to eat your brains, there's one that wants to steal your heart. His story is told in a taxpayer-funded stage production about the ups-and-downs of a lovesick zombie who can't find a date in the land of the living.[197]

The National Endowment for the Arts (NEA) awarded $10,000 to the Oregon Children's Theatre to produce "Zombie in Love,"[198] a musical about Mortimer, a teenage zombie "dying to find true love."[199] He's your typical zombie teenager who, "like[s] having toenails on his pizza, eating brains for lunch, having his intestines for a belt, and hanging out with his best friends, graveyard worms."[200] After a series of unsuccessful dates, Mortimer finally places a personal ad in hopes of meeting his one true love, who he hopes will show up to the school dance.[201]

NEA officials gave taxpayer assistance to the show over other applicants, citing its accessibility for younger audiences – Mortimer "exemplifies anyone who has felt like an outsider"[202] – and recommended it for all audiences aged four and up.[203]

The show is billed as family-friendly, but zombie enthusiasts will be glad to know "[t]here is some brain eating, but it's gentle," noted the theatre's spokesperson.[204]

To accompany the show, the Oregon Children's Theatre produced a "teacher resource guide" to help students learn the show's big lessons, such as, "Even the undead have feelings" and "The right special someone will appreciate your unique, weird, and spooky qualities."[205] Included inside is "vocabulary from the play," with words such as "putrid," "maggots" and "fungus."[206]

This is the fifth consecutive year the Oregon Children's Theatre received an NEA grant, and according to its Managing Director, support for the theatre's productions is "critical," "signal[ing] that [the Oregon Children's Theatre's] work is recognized and respected nationally."[207] After seeing the show at the Oregon Children's Theatre, one mom's assessment of the show noted, "It was like High School Musical, but with Zombies."[208]

While zombies are popular among young adults, parents probably question whether a story about the "undead" eating brains is for children since these aren't the typical subjects of tales by Dr. Seuss or other popular children's fiction over the years. The TV series "The Walking Dead," for example, "carries a rating of TV-MA, which defines the content as a program intended for viewing by people 17 and older."[209] And the recent reanimation of the "Night of the Living of Dead" was rated R, in part, for "bloody horror violence."[210] While "Zombie in Love" is more lighthearted than these with a more upbeat message, the underlying premise still may not be the most age-appropriate story for a children's theater.

11. Watching Grass Grow — $10,000

The federal government is literally paying people to watch grass grow.

While the grass being observed, saltmarsh cordgrass is "a fast-growing plant,"[211] it can reach a length of 6 inches to as high as 7 feet tall.[212]

The Department of Interior's U.S. Fish and Wildlife Service is spending $10,000 on the project being conducted in the Guana-Tolomato-Matanzas preserve by the Florida Department of Environmental Protection (FDEP). The money will "cover the cost to monitor grasses, restore two acres as a demonstration and publish a guide on best practices for cultivating the cordgrass, known formally as Spartina alterniflora"[213]

"Spartina is used a lot now in places that aren't natural, from highway berms and ridges to manicured golf courses," according to the vice president of Beeman's Nursery in New Smyrna Beach.[214]

"About 40,000 plugs of Spartina will be pulled individually" out of salt marsh and observers will "painstakingly document how fast it returns."[215]

"Where plugs of grass are removed, photos are run through computer software to figure the number of plants still standing and how much ground they cover. A chest-high square of PVC-like tubing with strings pulled into a grid makes it easier to track growth and thinning in the grasses."[216]

What lessons might be learned from watching the grass grown back? "Grasses that are thinned differently from one grid to another could end up pointing to lessons in the grass's resilience. If 20 percent of the Spartina is pulled out in one grid and grows back as completely as the grass in an area where only 10 percent was taken," the project's restoration coordinator said "it could mean there's no apparent effect from taking that much more."[217]

While the project may yield some new understandings of how to grow cordgrass, it looks more like just another weed of government waste in the federal budget. There are much more pressing challenges facing our nation that we should focus on than watching grass grow.

12. NIH Asks if Moms Love Dogs as Much as Kids — $371,026

Mothers have the same reaction when looking at photos of their dogs as they do to those of their own kids, according to recent government-funded research published this year.[218]

The unique relationship between man and his pets is nothing new. "Humans began domesticating dogs to serve in a variety of roles, including as human companion or 'pets', 18,000-32,000 years ago," the authors wrote in their study.[219] "Approximately 2/3 of U.S. households have pets, and over $50 billion is spent annually on their care...Many people have a strong emotional attachment to their pets...half of pet owners consider their pet as much a part of the family as any member of the household."[220]

Science has already shown "very similar results for human infants' and dogs' behaviors with their mother or owner have been described under high and low stress conditions."[221] And, bonding has "been implicated in human-human and owner-dog pairs."[222]

But apparently never had mothers' brains been monitored while viewing photos of their kids and dogs. This new study was described by the scientists as "the first report of a comparison of fMRI-related brain activation patterns in women when they viewed images of their child and dog."[223]

Participating moms were solicited "via advertisement in local media, veterinary clinics, dog parks" and a hospital research program.[224] Dogs and children were first "photographed in the participants' home."[225] Mothers were then shown a series of dog and child photos from other participants in the study, as well as photos of their own.[226] As they looked at each, their brains were monitored with an MRI scanner.[227]

"Mothers reported similar emotional ratings for their child and dog, which elicited greater positive emotional responses than unfamiliar children and dogs," and their brains acted in similar ways in viewing both their own kids and dogs.[228]

Two of the scientists performing the study received a combined total of $371,026 from the National Institutes of Health this year, money intended for work in addiction research.[229]

NIH Director Dr. Francis Collins this year claimed that the agency is "throwing away probably half of the innovative, talented research proposal's that the nation's finest biomedical community has produced" due to budget constraints.[231]

Their next step is to include "more people and look at how men and women without children reacted to photos of babies and pets as well."[230]

Taxpayers Help NY Brewery Build Beer Farm

$200,000

"This is the golden age for beer," declared GQ in September 2014, owing largely to the explosion in craft beer throughout the U.S.[232] With nearly 2,800 craft brewers operating around the nation, the ongoing beer renaissance shows no signs of letting up.

Even the White House got in on the act when in 2012 President Obama began brewing his own Honey Brown Ale and Honey Porter. Using honey from the grounds, it was the first time any president has brewed beer right from the White House.[233]

One New York company in particular, Empire Brewing, has been especially successful in growing its business, offering popular beers such as its Chocolate Mint Stout, Blueberry Ale and Empire Strikes Bock.[234] In 2014, the brewer was given $200,000 to expand from one location in Syracuse to a second in Cazenovia, New York, where it plans to open farm and brewpub.[235] Funding was made available through the U.S. Department of Agriculture's Value-Added Producer Grant program.[236]

The second location will be called the Empire Farmstead Brewery, a 22-acre farm with a 28,000 square-foot building to include a brewing facility, restaurant, gift shop and tasting room.[237] Company officials expect it to attract, "the brewing community, farmers, educators, hop historians," and not to be forgotten, "beer geeks."[238]

An artistic rendition of Empire Farmstead Brewery.

Empire Brewing's owner, David Katelski, gushed that the new location was "significant," because, "it allows us to get more beer out there."[239]

Taxpayers might wonder why in a year that the federal deficit will exceed half of a trillion dollars they are subsidizing one beer company's operations. In 2013, the U.S. craft beer market was $14.3 billion, an increase of nearly $2.5 billion over the year prior, according to the Brewers Association.[240]

Senator Chuck Schumer, an advocate for the federal subsidy, acknowledged, "The craft brew industry is booming in Central New York, and Empire is one of the breweries leading the way."[241] With the grant, Empire Brewing will be well on its way to becoming one of the largest brewing operations in the state of New York.[242]

Asked about expanding his operations to include a "brew farm," Katelski noted, "It's going to be a lot of fun."[243]

Sen. Chuck Schumer at a press conference to announce federal funding for the Empire Brewing Company.

Colorado Orchestra Targets Youth with Stoner Symphony

$15,000

"Classically Cannabis: The High Note Series marks a new partnership between the Colorado Symphony and the industry that supports legal cannabis in Colorado."

As fewer Americans regularly attend the symphony, one orchestra in Colorado has an idea to draw in new patrons: smoking dope.

Hoping to raise some funds, the Colorado Symphony Orchestra hosted "Classically Cannabis: The High Note Series," a marijuana-themed musical revue that encourages people not only to show up, but to smoke up.[244] The events featured classical selections from Debussy, Bach, Wagner and Puccini, as well as a "small outdoor area with food trucks and a pair of ice cream and popsicle vendors, where attendees also openly smoked cannabis."[245]

One of the three concerts, called Summer Monsoon, advertised on its website this way, "Smoke up and fill your belly with Manna's spiced pork, Sesame Seed Teriyaki Chicken, & Filipino Empanadas."[246]

Pot dealers were not allowed to sell inside the shows, but people were encouraged to bring their own and smoke just before walking in. For those who wanted to take a drag during the show organizers provided an outdoor patio, which according to spokesperson Laura Bond was needed because marijuana smoke is, "not good for people who play the saxophone."[247]

In 2014, funding for the orchestra in the amount of $15,000 was provided by the National Endowment for the Arts through its "Art Works" program.[248] Art Works grants are for "innovative projects" that offer insights through "unconventional solutions."[249] However, while current federal law prohibits possession or distribution of marijuana, the orchestra will not have to return the NEA grant.[250]

Event organizers emphasized the need to attract Colorado's young people. "The audience has been getting older and smaller," said Colorado Symphony CEO Jerry Kern, adding "It's innovate or die. It's change or die. It's reach new people or die, and we're not going to die."[251]

However, some of the orchestra's older patrons complained, fearing the symphony would follow suit the Florida Orchestra, which tried to draw in a younger crowd with music from popular video games.[252] Bond offered reassurances, though, "We're not bringing in Snoop Dogg as an artist."[253]

Others were thrilled. "I am watching history being made!" a gray-haired woman named Roxanne Prescott told a Slate reporter, "I don't like all those I call punk-ass dead-head stoners. This is more comfortable for me. It feels upper class."[254]

U.S. Coast Guard Party Patrols

$100,000 or more

Faced with budget cuts, the U.S. Coast Guard reduced drug and migrant interdictions while continuing to provide free patrols in the waters along "some of the country's most exclusive real estate" to stop uninvited guests from crashing private parties.

While taxpayers appreciate the crucial role the Coast Guard serves protecting our nation's waterways and rescuing nearly 5,000 people a year,[255] most are probably unaware its crewmen also serve as bouncers to keep the general public and other uninvited guests out of private events on and along yachts, beaches, and estates.

"For some regattas, yacht club parties and even weddings, the maritime agency assigns boats and crews to enforce 'safety zones,'" like "it does for public fireworks displays such as the Macy's Fourth of July celebration in New York City."[256] And "unlike police agencies that provide security support for private events on land, the Coast Guard does not seek reimbursement, leaving the bill to taxpayers."[257]

"While the Coast Guard's efforts are intended to protect other boaters drawn to events, at least in some cases, the hosts of private events that receive safety zones are clear that the intent is not to benefit the public," according to the Associated Press.

In July, "two orange boats carrying nine Coast Guard service members, all clad in body armor and some carrying handguns," were stations in Long Island Sound. Their mission: Keep other boaters away from a "barge launching celebratory fireworks" for a wedding party on Glen Island, "which is connected to the mainland by a drawbridge and taken up mostly by a park that was first developed as a summer resort by a congressman in the 19th century."[258]

"The 15-minute display cost close to $100,000," according to Charlie DeSalvo, executive producer of Fireworks by Grucci.[259] "This is a world-class Grucci choreographed barge," bragged DeSalvo said. "This is not a fireworks show that would normally be produced for the local fire department at their carnival."[260] So while the party hosts could afford $100,000 for just the fireworks display, they did not have to pay a cent for the security of their event, which was provided as an in-kind wedding present from the taxpayers.

The Coast Guard boats arrived around 8 p.m., "when they turned on blue law enforcement lights. Petty Officer 2nd Class Geoffrey Burns sounded a siren as they pulled up to" an uninvited boat. "I need you to go this way," Burns instructed the boater.[261]

"We're not protecting the wedding. We're protecting the people from the wedding," explained a Coast Guard spokesman in New York.[262]

"As fireworks sizzled in the sky and exploded into brilliant colors, Jason Grimm, a chief warrant officer, said the crew had to stay extra vigilant."[263] The Coast Guard boats "remained at the scene for two hours, lingering after the show ended … although there wasn't much boat traffic."[264]

The cost to taxpayers of the party patrol that evening for the two 25-foot boats that are worth $1,500 an hour, totaled $6,000.[265]

The Associated Press found "active-duty Coast Guard crews are involved in security for dozens of privately sponsored events" just in New York and the Long Island Sound, which is 'lined with some of the country's most exclusive real estate."[266] The Coast Guard, however, is unable to estimate the actual cost for patrolling private party safety zones and "the deployment of resources varies for each event." [267] The Associated Press notes, however, that "a manual of Coast Guard reimbursement rates lists small response boats at about $1,500 per hour and medium-size boats at more than $8,000 per hour, in the event they are dispatched for what turns out to be a hoax."[268] [A bogus call for help is the only circumstance in which the Coast Guard charges for dispatching boats.[269]] So the Coast Guard is likely forfeiting $100,000 or more in just the New York area alone this year that could be collected in re-imbursements and put towards drug interdiction efforts elsewhere.

Even last year at the height of sequestration's impact as the Coast Guard reduced "its on-the-water operations around Long Island by as much as 25 percent," it continued "to help with the planning and then be present at larger events such as the Memorial Day weekend air show at Jones Beach State Park."[270] The Coast Guard docked cutters, which USCG Commandant Admiral Bob Papp lamented "was a tremendous, tremendous waste of assets." "We've got good ships and good people out there that want to do their jobs, but putting fuel in ships is one of the most expensive things we do, and during sequestration the only option we had was to cut money out of operations," according to Papp. Faced with $200 million in budget cuts under sequester, Papp claimed "the only place that we could squeeze it a little bit was in drug interdiction and migrant interdiction."[271] He noted "during normal operations there might be six or seven ships deployed in the Caribbean or Eastern Pacific, but at times last year the Coast Guard had only one ship on either side of Central America. The result of that decrease in availability of ships resulted in 30 percent more cocaine made it through the transit zone."[272]

Yet "the New Haven-based Long Island Sound sector of the Coast Guard deployed active-duty vessels, auxiliary Coast Guard boats or both for most of the safety zones involving fireworks displays last year, according to Lt. Ben Duarte, the sector's chief of waterways management. Of 60 safety zones listed in the sector's register last year, the agency said, 21 were sponsored by a city or town. The rest were privately sponsored, including many fireworks displays put on by yacht clubs and beach clubs" and a privately sponsored fireworks display by the owners of the Foxwoods Resort Casino. "In the New York sector, 31 of 43 safety zones last year were supported by active-duty Coast Guard. About half of the events are typically privately sponsored."[273]

The Coast Guard's vital missions should not be compromised by spending limited resources deploying crews to interdict party crashers rather than drugs dealers or others who pose a threat to the security of our nation.

While the Coast Guard reduced drug and migrant interdictions, the maritime agency continued to provide free patrols to interdict potential uninvited guests from crashing exclusive private parties on yachts and beaches, costing thousands of dollars per event.

Chronicling Vermont's Radical Hippie Movement in the 1970's

$117,521

"Nudity, psychedelic drugs and free love" is how one person remembers life at the Tree Frog Farm, a Vermont commune.

It and other Vermont communes will be the focus of new federally funded project to document life among the state's communal hippie radicals during the 1970's.

The Vermont Historical Society is launching a two-year project called "Colleges, Communes and Coops: 1970's Counterculture and Its Lasting Influence on Vermont" to conduce oral interviews and collect artifacts from the time period.[274] Support for the effort is being provided by the Institute for Museum and Library Services in the form of an $117,521 grant.[275]

With the federal money, "Vermont Historical Society (VHS) will undertake a project to research and document the political, social, and cultural changes of the 1970s in Vermont to create a body of primary resources for this period in Vermont's state history."[276]

"In the 1960s and early 1970s," VHS explains, "Vermont acquired a reputation for being a haven for hippies and a hotbed of countercultural communal living."[277]

Peter Simon lived on Tree Frog Farm from 1970 to 1972, recalling, "The highlights were the sense that we were doing something totally unique and different, rebelling against society ... Getting away from city life was one of the ingredients. I always liked walking around barefoot and going around naked."[278]

Life at the Free Farm was similar until it burned to the ground, remembered one-time resident Robert Houriet, noting that they weren't always appreciated by the locals, "'The Free Farm was in plain view of a building where the local Democrats met, and they got offended by all the weeds and the bare-breasted women."[279]

Verandah Porche, a former commune dweller who later became a successful photographer, summed up her experience this way, "In 1968, we were a bunch of ignoramuses ... but the commune became a village."[280]

USDA's "Perfect Poop Pak" Smells Like Government Waste

$50,000

One man's waste may be another man's treasure, but in the case of a $50,000 federal grant, one animal's waste has become its owner's treasure.

Virginia Mary's Alpaca, LLC received a $50,000 Value-Added Producer Grant from the U.S. Department of Agriculture to process, package and market Alpaca manure as plant fertilizer," commercially sold as "Poop Paks."[281]

The company boasts that its product is the "perfect POOP."[282]

"Packaged in colorful, unmistakable green bags," the Alpaca Poop Paks are "hand-tied using rustic hemp twine and recycled paper tags."[283] Twenty Poop Paks retail for $29.95 plus shipping costs.[284]

"The" Mary, for which the company and farm are named, has been winning awards for her alpaca pets for over 15 years.[285] Her 160 acre farm located in The Plains, Virginia, is home to 140 alpacas that she raises and sells (A "roaming" camera will soon be installed to broadcast the movements of the alpacas live on the internet).[286]

Of course, buying and selling Alpaca manure as fertilizer is not new. It is widely available from retailers online and from those who may have pet alpacas. It has become a popular fertilizer, in part, because it doesn't smell as bad as other types of waste, unlike the foul odor of misspent tax dollars.

Virginia Mary's Alpaca received a $50,000 USDA grant to process, package and market alpaca "Poop Paks."[287]

Synchronized Swimming for Sea Monkeys

$307,524

Sea Monkeys have captivated Americans for generations. The novelty pets, which are tiny brine shrimp, have been regular features on toy store shelves and advertisements on the pages of comic books since the 1960s. NASA even launched Sea Monkeys into space with John Glenn in 1998.[288]

Cartoon-style ads for pet Sea-Monkeys promise that you can learn to "make them appear to obey your commands, follow a beam of light, do loop-the-loops and even seem to dance when you play" music.[289] The New York Times says it is "sort of true" that Sea Monkeys can be trained because they do follow light.[290]

With the financial support of three government agencies, researchers put these claims to the test and essentially choreographed a laser guided synchronized swim team of Sea Monkeys as part of a study to measure the swirl created by their collective movements.

Flashing blue and green laser lights lure the aquatic creatures to move in the same direction within an aquarium. "The green laser at the top of the tank provides a bright target" as "a blue laser rising along the side of the tank lights up a path to guide them upward."[291] The spinning of "silver-coated hollow glass spheres" in the water is tracked with "high-speed camera and a red laser" measures how the Sea Monkey's "swimming causes the surrounding water to swirl."[292]

"Coaxing Sea-Monkeys to swim when and where you want them to is even more difficult than it sounds," said John Dabiri, one of the project's researchers and a professor at California Institute of Technology (Caltech).[293]

"It turns out that the collective swimming motion of Sea-Monkeys and other zooplankton—swimming plankton—can generate enough swirling flow to potentially influence the circulation of water in oceans," according to the researchers. They conducted a similar study with jellyfish in 2009 and reached similar conclusions showing "small animals can generate flow in the surrounding water."

"Adding up the effect of all of the zooplankton in the ocean—assuming they have a similar influence—could inject as much as a trillion watts of power into the oceans to drive global circulation, Dabiri says. In comparison,

Sea Monkeys have captivated Americans for generations and now scientists are trying to determine the impact of the swirl created by the synchronized swimming of these tiny sea creatures may have on the flow of the ocean.

Kids around the world are disappointed to learn that the sea monkey family in the advertisements is a little different than the result.

Sea Monkeys are guided to swim in a synchronized direction in this tank to measure the swirl of their collective motion.[305]

the winds and tides contribute a combined two trillion watts."[294]

But "some oceanographers are skeptical of the claim that the movements of organisms contribute significantly to ocean circulation" because "it's a conceptual leap to go from a tankful of Sea-Monkeys to oceans filled with plankton."[295]

Christian Noss, an environmental physicist at the University of Koblenz-Landau in Germany, is "not convinced the effect would scale up from the laboratory to the ocean." He acknowledges "the study was well designed" but notes "unlike water in a small tank, water in the ocean is often stratified, with denser layers lying underneath lighter ones. Noss's work with another tiny crustacean, known as Daphnia, showed that stratified conditions dampened the mixing produced by these animals."[296]

The Sea Monkey researchers are planning more realistic studies, such as using "a tank with increased water density at the bottom, which imitates real-life ocean conditions."[297]

Dabiri also "plans to test the stratification question and hopes to perform the same experiments at a larger scale in the ocean."[298]

Of course, the subjects of this study are not actually monkeys with fins and gills, but rather brine shrimp, which were given the moniker "Sea Monkeys" because their tail resembles a monkey's tail."[299] The tiny animals are about half an inch long with "about 10 small leaf-like fins that flap about."[300]

The Sea Monkey study was funded by the National Science Foundation (NSF) and the Office of Naval Research with support from the U.S.-Israel Binational Science Foundation.[301] The NSF funding is part of a $307,524 collaborate research grant that runs through February 2015.[302]

With kits available online[303] and many toy stores,[304] you can try to train your own team of synchronized swimming Sea Monkeys for as little as $12.

19. Penn State Shame Study Asks How To Boost Morale After Scandal

$41,000

Disgraced in the wake of the revelation that a Penn State assistant football coach had been sexually abusing children for years, and the cover up that ensued, Penn State is turning its public shame into public subsidies.

Former football coaching assistant Jerry Sandusky has been convicted of sexually abusing ten boys and the former school president, vice president and athletic director are awaiting trial for allegedly attempting to cover-up the scandal.[306]

The National Collegiate Athletic Association levied a $60 million penalty against Penn State to fund "programs preventing child sexual abuse or assisting victims."[307]

The school is also sponsoring a study—this one funded by the federal government—to determine how to "protect employee well-being in organizational settings where, too often, there is negative media and scandal."[308] Using the scandal as the basis for the study, a $41,000 grant from the National Science Foundation is paying to examine "how to protect employee well-being" in organizations "when pride becomes shame."[309]

"Employees vary in their organizational identification, the extent they view themselves as personally connected to and part of their work organization," the researchers note. "When the organization is doing well, such identification can benefit self-concept, motivational energy, and health, which is especially beneficial for front-line employees because they actually feel the enthusiasm and pride they need to express to potential clients or donors. Paradoxically, organizational identification can become a liability if the organization becomes associated with scandal or stigma, such that one's pride-by-association turns to feelings of shame and betrayal. In such cases, those who are the most motivated become those who are most threatened; how do such employees respond, and how does this affect their health and performance? To answer these questions, a current real-life event, the scandal at Pennsylvania State University, provides a unique time-sensitive context."[310]

While it is a good thing for everyone to learn from the school's mistakes and to protect students and employees who are not responsible for the inappropriate actions or inactions of others within an organization, taxpayers should not have to subsidize the school's self-reflection in scandal and shame.

20. Promoting U.S. Culture Around the Globe with Nose Flutists, State Department Idol

$90 million

The State Department spent taxpayer dollars to dispel the perceptions of Pakistani journalists that Americans are not all "fat, rude, and cold."[311]

"I thought you would be fat because I have read that Americans are fat," said one of the participating journalists.[312]

In total, the State Department spends $90 million annually on cultural exchange programs. These exchange programs are intended to increase understanding between the U.S. and "the people of other countries by means of educational and cultural exchange that assist in the development of peaceful relations," that are intended to "build cross-cultural bridges across the globe.[313][314]

Here are more examples of how the State Department spends $90 million to bridge the gap between the U.S. and other the rest of the world.

Department Of State Idol - Given the success of music reality shows, the State Department organizes a $1.5 million dollar cultural musical exchange program "including public concerts, interactive performances with local traditional musicians, lecture demonstrations, workshops, jam sessions and media interviews and performances."[315] Many apply for the opportunity to tour the world on the taxpayer dime, and the grant recipient selects ten bands on the basis of "musical talent" and "strong educational programs, aptitude in arranging music from around the world and for their capacity to conduct effective cultural diplomacy programs."[316] The State Department directly participates in the selection of bands and a government official served as a judge for this year's program.[317] The judges went to three live auditions held in New York City, St. Louis and San Francisco all at taxpayer's expense.[318]

One of last year's participants was a nose flutist, or more appropriately, a "snoutist,"[319] This year, a rapper will be touring the world who recently released a song titled "Dem Shawts," which includes the following colorful lyrics: I can't help but stare when you're walking past though/Yo I can't lie—y'all got some ass though/If you don't want me looking, what the hell you wear 'em for?[320] His recent album also features cover art where a woman is aiming a shotgun at the artist's head.[321]

International Band Camp - Through its grant to Bang on a Can, the State Department is spending $1 million on OneBeat, a program that gathers artists from across the world in one location for a month in Florida where they collaborate and create music, after which they travel the country the taxpayer dime to perform and connect with one another.[322]

The website for OneBeat describes the program as "a musical journey like no other."[323] In 2012, the artists formed a flash mob at a Wal-Mart and uploaded a video of it onto YouTube and aptly labeled it "Ruckus."[324] In 2013, the participants had an arts and crafts session and created instruments from straws, balloons and corrugated tubing.[325] Later that year, they toured the country and one of their stops included a Washington, DC venue where a Russian beatboxer, a guy "plucking" his mustache, and a reggaeton artist who performed a song about government being "on leave" and learning "how to represent."[326] The government was shut down at the time.

Not only is much of the cultural exchange funding not the best use of taxpayer funds, the program is poorly run. Often, only a portion of the grant funding is reaching the participants—the money is being spent, in large part, on expenses to run the organizations which include salaries and benefits and that can reach 30% of the amount awarded by agency.[327] Some grant recipients also budgeted or spent a substantial portion of their awards on honoraria costs, at times 15 or 20%, which presumably were paid to artists and other performers.[328]

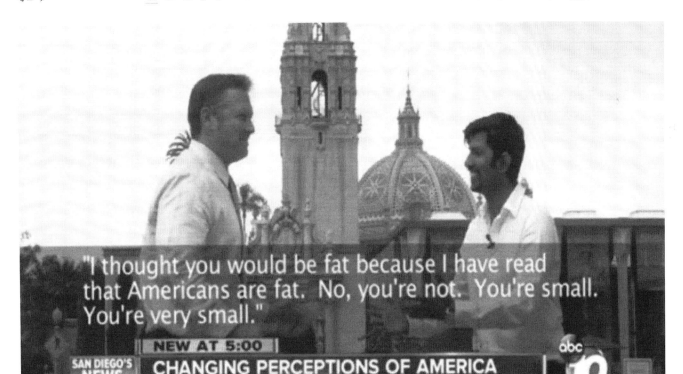

Free "High-End" Gym Memberships for DHS Bureaucrats

$450,000

The Department of Homeland Security (DHS) announced earlier this year that budget cuts "require[ed] difficult choices to align resources to address the greatest needs of the Department."[329]

Apparently one of those greatest needs is 236 memberships to a "state-of-the-art" gym and spa in downtown Washington, D.C. for some of the headquarters employees of Immigration and Customs Enforcement (ICE), a DHS component.[330] The gym, Vida Fitness, describes itself as "more than just a gym," offering an "Aura Spa, Bang Salon, Fuel Bar, Gear Shop, Endless Pools, luxurious locker rooms, and the rooftop Penthouse Pool and Lounge."[331]

Immigration Customs and Enforcement (ICE) employees receive free gym memberships at a state-of-the-art facility courtesy of federal taxpayers

The Transportation Security Administration (TSA) also purchased gym memberships for some of its personnel, spending $52,650 on a contract so workers at Phoenix (Arizona) Sky Harbor International Airport could work out at a private club.[332]

Interestingly, while exercising at a private gym by its employees was important enough for ICE to drop $400,000 on the priority, walking was not: the agency stated in its contract requirements that the gym must be less than 526 feet or one tenth of a mile from its office.[333] Vida Fitness is about 360 feet from ICE's front door.[334]

Golf Club Testing, Elementary School Experiments Aboard the International Space Station

$3 billion

It doesn't take a rocket scientist to design experiments on the International Space Station (ISS). In fact, sixth graders and other elementary student are proposing some of the studies being conducted onboard the space station that is costing billions of dollars a year to operate.

ISS is one of the greatest achievements in manned spaceflight. It is also the "single most expensive object ever created."[335] And some scientists question if the space station's out of this world costs can continue to be justified.

Sold to taxpayers as a one of a kind, orbiting laboratory that would "permit quantum leaps in our research in science, communications, in metals, and in lifesaving medicines,"[336] it has yet to live up to these heavenly expectations, while its costs continue to soar to astronomical heights.

The station's original price tag was $17.4 billion but NASA has spent nearly $75 billion for the space station's development, operations, and transportation by the end of 2013.[337] This year the space agency is spending $3 billion and expects to spend another $20.6 billion before 2020.[338] An independent audit by the NASA Office of Inspector General (OIG) concluded these cost projections were "understated" and "overly optimistic."[339]

The space station, "designed and tested for a 15-year life span," marked 15 years of continuous operations in 2013.[340] In January 2014, the Administration announced the U.S. would extend our participation in ISS "for at least another decade."[341]

While some valuable research is being conducted on the station regarding life in space, the billions being spent to maintain the station could be directed towards much more meaningful studies or projects. The entire NASA budget for Fiscal Year 2014 is $17.7 billion,[342] meaning the space station consumes nearly one-fifth of the agency's resources.

The White House Office of Science and Technology Policy claims the station is necessary and the research conducted onboard has "already resulted in a number of discoveries with significant medical and industrial implications," including potential vaccines.[343] This claim and commitment is quite controversial in the scientific community.

"The station is a marvel," but "it hasn't yet proved it was worth the investment," says John Logsdon, the former director of the Space Policy Institute at George Washington University. "It's an awfully expensive engineering demonstration," according to Logsdon, who notes "if that's all it is, that's a hell of a price to pay."[344]

As far back as 1997, James Van Allen, the pioneering astrophysicist, concluded "the cost of the space station is far beyond any justifiable scientific purpose or any justifiable practical purpose."[345]

The studies conducted onboard the space station "are not remotely comparable to the path-breaking research conducted by NASA's armada of orbiting telescopes and its robotic probes of distant planets," notes the *New York Times*. The newspaper writes "when NASA threatened to abandon the Hubble Space Telescope, astronomers rose in wrath. If the station disappeared tomorrow, the response would most likely be tepid."[346]

And even though Congress "designated the ISS as a national laboratory" in 2005, the Government Accountability Office (GAO) found "research utilization has not been the priority" of the space station.

NASA has most recently averaged about 37.5 hours of research per week on the space station. It cost taxpayers about $1.5 million per hour for the research conducted there at that rate and given the $3 billion per year cost to operate ISS. The total cost of ISS to date has been about $100 billion, and research since 2009 has averaged about 30 hours a week, or 7,800 hours. If all costs to date are included over these 7,800 hours of estimated research, the cost of research is $12.8 million an hour.[347]

One of the experiments currently being conducted aboard the space station "could eventually lead to the design and creation of better golf clubs."[348] A partnership with Cobra Puma Golf developed when some employees from the Center for Advancement of Science and Space, the organization NASA chose to be the sole manager of the International Space Station U.S. National Laboratory,[349] were introduced to members of the Cobra research team at the 2012 PGA Show in Orlando, Florida.[350] The experiment aboard the ISS "will examine a variety of coating and metals used in golf products," according to Mike Yagley, director of research and testing for Cobra Puma Golf. "Cobra Puma hopes the results of the plating experiment -- which may be available as early as December -- will prove beneficial in three areas: function, durability and aesthetics."[351] A Russian cosmonaut tethered to the space station "set a new record for the longest golf drive in history" in November 2006 when he hit a ball NASA estimated traveled a million miles around the Earth.[352]

Some of the other studies being conducted on the space station are designed by elementary and high school students rather than scientists. Fifteen student projects were launched to the space station in July as part of the Student Spaceflight Experiments Program (SSEP). A project that students from California came up with is examining whether tadpole shrimp can be grown in microgravity.[353] High school students in New York are looking at the "effect of microgravity on the growth of mold on white bread."[354] And ninth-graders in Washington "focused their attention on whether radish roots and shoots will grow differently in microgravity."[355]

While encouraging young people to take an interest in science is an important goal, the billions of dollars being borrowed to support space station science fair experiments could make a bigger impact in the lives of these and other children in many other more cost efficient ways.

NASA officials "point to other less tangible benefits of the Station, including maintaining U.S. leadership in space, supporting cooperation with international partners, and inspiring current and future engineers and scientists."[356] But directing so much money into this project over the next decade may actually be compromising our leadership in space by absorbing so many resources that could be better targeted towards other bigger priorities, such as reclaiming our capability to send astronauts on manned missions into space, which is one of the biggest facing NASA.

NASA "faces challenges ... ensuring the station is fully utilized," according to GAO, which "has cautioned for years that NASA should ensure it has a capability to access and utilize the space station following retirement of the space shuttle." GAO notes "NASA's decision to rely on the new commercial vehicles to transport cargo starting in 2012 and to transport crew starting in 2017 is inherently risky because the vehicles are not yet proven and are experiencing delays in development. Further, NASA does not have agreements in place for international partners to provide cargo services to the ISS beyond 2016."[357]

Because NASA retired the Space Shuttle in 2011, the U.S. is paying Russia $1.7 billion over a five years to transport astronauts to and from ISS, for as much as $70 million for a round trip.[358] NASA is spending billions to maintain a space station that it no longer has its own capabilities to reach and is now entirely dependent upon an increasingly hostile Russia to reach the station taxpayers have spent billions of dollars to construct.

There are other questionable expenditures in the ISS budget. NASA may also have paid more than $13 million in bonuses to a contractor that could not be proven to have met the expectations set for financial rewards, according to an OIG audit.[359]

The top NASA official in charge of human spaceflight concedes "we're in the process of proving now whether it's worth it or not."[360]

Because NASA retired the Space Shuttle in 2011, American astronauts must hitch a ride on Russian rockets to reach the International Space Station, costing as much as $70 million for a round trip.[361]

NASA's Tower of Pork Protected by Politician

$44.5 million

From its launch in 1958, the National Aeronautics and Space Administration (NASA) captured the country's imagination and represented the new frontiers America was leading mankind. Today, the agency—almost more than any other—represents the morass and politics of Washington, D.C. The space agency can no longer send astronauts into space and less than half of its budget is even spent on the missions it was created to pursue, aeronautics research and space exploration and operations.[362] NASA has lost its way and Washington politicians are plundering its budget to pay for parochial pork projects rather than redirecting the agency's gaze back to the stars.

The $350 million A-3 rocket testing tower completed this year at Stennis Space Center in Mississippi stands as 300-foot tall monument to NASA's current state of affairs. Now that the tower is completed it has no purpose, but will continue to cost taxpayers.

The tower is "a relic of President George W. Bush's Constellation program," that was intended to send astronauts "back to the moon and beyond" which was canceled by President Obama in 2010[363] That same year, an earmark sponsored by a senator from Mississippi was tucked into a bill passed by Congress, thereby forcing NASA to complete the project even though it was no longer needed.[364] As a result, the useless space tower is being derided as a "Launchpad to Nowhere"[365] and the "Tower of Pork."[366]

"In 2010, I authored an amendment to require the completion of that particular project," admits Senator Roger Wicker unabashedly.[367]

Even with construction completed this year, the tower will cost $840,000 every year to maintain, according to NASA.[368]

The A-3 tower is not the only useless or unneeded facility NASA is wasting money on. The NASA IG has "identified 33 facilities that NASA either wasn't fully using or had no future need for, including six of 36 wind tunnels, 14 of 35 rocket test stands, and two of three airfields," which all cost more than $43 million a year to maintain.[369]

That amounts to $350 million to build a rocket testing tower that will not be used and another $43 million every year to maintain other facilities that are not being used.

NASA officials and Mississippi politicians start digging the hole where NASA buried $350 million for a launch tower that may never be used.

Now what? As soon as the construction of the A-3 Testing Tower was completed, the $350 million project was "mothballed." Maintenance of the site, however, will continue to cost NASA $43 million every year.

24 Congress Blocks Closure of Unneeded "Sheep Station"
$1.98 million

Everyone knows how much Congress loves pork, but perhaps less well-known is its affinity for mutton.

Earlier this year, a congressional committee blocked the U.S. Department of Agriculture (USDA) from closing down a $2 million-a-year sheep research site the agency said was no longer needed.[370]

Known as the U.S. Sheep Experiment Station in Dubois, Idaho, its mission is "increasing production efficiency of sheep and to simultaneously improve the sustainability of rangeland ecosystems."[371] The site is located near the borders of Idaho, Wyoming and Montana and used to graze 3,000 sheep on 28,000 mountainous acres of land.[372]

Secretary of Agriculture Tom Vilsack proposed closing the sheep station saying in June it "no longer has the critical mass of scientists necessary to address high priority research."[373] A spokesperson with USDA said the station was one of several the agency found had "gotten to the point where, from a financial standpoint, they're either marginally viable or they're just not sustainable."[374]

Moreover, the cost of running the station became too expensive after losing $1.5 million fending off lawsuits from environmental groups.[375] The lawsuits stemmed from a dispute over whether grizzly bears or sheep should get priority in a high-altitude pasture, with environmental groups saying both cannot co-exist.[376]

Secretary Vilsack ultimately sided with the bears – believing they needed better access to sites like Yellowstone – and notified Congress in June of plans to close the Sheep Experiment Station in Dubois, Idaho and reallocate its $1,984,000 in annual funding to strengthen higher priority research.[377]

That was the point when Congress stepped in, however, to insist the sheep station remain open. Citing an obscure provision of law giving congressional committees the ability to stop the USDA's plans, members from Idaho, Washington, Montana and Oregon joined forces to insist the closure be halted.[378]

Idaho's governor, Butch Otter, joined in the protest, saying he wanted to protect home-state businesses, "We want to keep it open. The sheep business is big business in Idaho and will continue to be big business in Idaho, we hope."[379]

The decision to keep the sheep station open, however, drew a sharp rebuke from environmental groups, which called the sheep station, "another subsidy to an industry that is already subsidized" with low fees and direct federal funding.[380] "It is ridiculous that Congress will intervene to keep a financially insolvent research station open ..." said John Meyer with the Cottonwood Environmental Law Center.[381]

One Idaho newspaper directly accused Idaho representative Mike Simpson – who intervened to keep the sheep station open – of helping drive up the national debt, saying, "If the sheep industry truly deems this facility's work to be vital, the sheep industry should fund it. Period. This should not fall under the purview of responsible, efficient government."[382]

"We should shut down the Sheep Station," said Phil Knight, resident of Bozeman, Montana, "and stop wasting taxpayer money on outdated science experiments."[383]

25. Spray Parks and "Splashpads" Help Beat The Summer Heat

$3.5 million

Water cannons, lazy rivers and water slides are all part of one federal program's efforts to help overheated kids stay cool during the summer.

Taxpayers have shelled out hundreds of thousands of dollars over the past year to install water playgrounds, known as "splashpads" and "spray parks," all around the country. At least five were constructed in New Jersey, Nebraska, Alabama and Massachusetts with nearly $3.5 million in funding from the Department of Housing and Urban Development's Community Development Block Grant (CDBG) program. CDBG funding is intended to provide "decent housing and a suitable living environment, and by expanding economic opportunities, principally for low- and moderate-income persons."[384]

Outside of Omaha in Nebraska, the Bellevue city council recently approved a splash pad at the cost of nearly $180,000.[385] However, some on the council objected to spending the money this way, noting that the town's five public pools fail to properly accommodate disabled patrons and are leaking water, desperately needing repair.[386]

Omaha Councilman Don Preister responded saying, "Although we didn't specifically promise a splash pad, we promised a nice park, and I think we should finally deliver to a part of the city that is way under-served."[387]

In Gadsden, Alabama, city council members originally decided to spend a $250,000 grant to fix drainage issues at a local park, but decided instead on a splash pad when they realized they needed to spend the money quickly or lose it.[388]

"This is more in line with what the people want," noted Gadsen city councilman Deverick Williams.[389]

Jackson Township, New Jersey mayor Michael Reina helped steer a $150,000 grant to build a 2,700 square-foot spray park in his home town, adding he "could not think of a better addition than a spray park."[390] Likewise, Gloucester, Massachusetts used a $370,000 grant to refurbish Burnham Field to include a spray pad.[391]

In Carbondale, Illinois, a $2.5 million federal grant provided through the Illinois Department of Natural Resources awarded Carbondale will pay for the "Super Splash Park Outdoor Aquatic Center."[392] Proponents of the Carbondale project hail it as an opportunity to "expand recreational and economic opportunities in the region," which will include a $700,000 lap pool, $700,000 for a "leisure pool", $350,000 for water slides and a $1.2 million lazy river.[393]

Kathy Renfro, Carbondale park district executive director, noted, "Everyone I talk to is so excited ... next year we will be to get in the pool. We can all be kicking back on the lazy river and have a good time."[394]

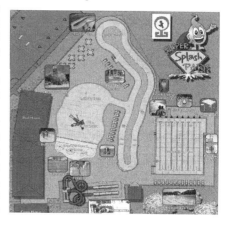

26. Roosevelt and Elvis Make a Hallucinatory Pilgrimage to Graceland

$10,000

Ann is a shy factory worker in Rapid City, South Dakota.[395] She finds that when she channels the boisterous personality of Elvis Presley, it is easier for her to break out of her shell.[396] After a date goes awry with a woman she met online who was obsessed with Teddy Roosevelt, Ann decides to make a pilgrimage from South Dakota all the way to Graceland in Memphis, the renowned estate of the king.[397] As the trip progresses, Ann begins to hallucinate increasingly that she is Elvis, and that Teddy Roosevelt is accompanying her on her journey.[398]

That is the description for the theatrical production RoosevElvis (pronounced "Rose of Elvis"), put on by the company TEAM, an ensemble out of New York described as "Gertrude Stein meets MTV."[399] RoosevElvis ran through November 3, 2013, when it wrapped with a bang after an all-you-can-drink performance.[400]

So what is the role of the federal government in this buddy dramedy about two American icons who lived in different eras? Taxpayers are helping fund the effort to bring RoosevElvis back to the stage, of course.

The National Endowment for the Arts gave $10,000 to TEAM for their next run of RoosevElvis at a still-to-be-determined date before May 2015.[401] In addition to the federal cash, TEAM is receiving $65,000 in non-federal funding.

The play received a generally positive review from the New York Times, which was taken by the play's commentary on gender and masculinity, writing that RoosevElvis "offers a spirited and insightful commentary on two archetypes of American masculinity, while finding teasing ambiguities within both that suggest that machismo is a shaky existential choice."[402]

For example, in one scene, Ann hallucinates that she is Elvis, and that she and Teddy are romping around their hotel room in their underwear, with Teddy eventually riding around on Elvis's back as though he were a bucking bronco.[403]

The review goes on to pan the play's excessive length, finding that after the roadtrip begins, it becomes like a television sitcom that "jumps the shark" time and time again.[404] But it is the National Endowment for the Arts that jumped the shark when sent taxpayer money to support RoosevElvis.

As Arizona Senator Jeff Flake said when he learned that federal funding was going to a play about an Elvis/Roosevelt road trip, "what in San Juan Hill is the federal government doing funding this hunk-a-hunk-a burnin' waste?"[405]

The 26th President and the king of Rock & Roll frolic in their underpants.

27. New Bridge Demolished for Using $3,271 Worth of Canadian Steel

$45,000

A newly reconstructed bridge in the small town of Morrison, Colorado is in fine condition, but it may be ripped down and reconstructed—*again*—and the ramifications could be international.

Earlier this year, the one lane bridge that serves as "the main link across a creek that cuts through" this small town with a population of just 430[406] "got a new coat of paint, new wood planks and new steel to run underneath it."[407] The steel was cast in the U.S., "but rolled into beams across the border in Canada."[408]

The use of steel produced outside of the U.S. "violates the Buy America provisions that mandate federally funded projects use materials made in the United States. The violation could mean a withdrawal of all funding if the steel is not removed."[409] That "means Morrison will either have to pay for the bridge itself – or rip it out and start fresh."[410]

Morrison Mayor Sean Forey "agrees that the foreign steel in question violates the $2,500 minimum allowed by the grant contract" by $771.64.[411]

The project was expected to cost "just over $144,000," with a grant from the Federal Highway Administration "was to cover $52,000."[412] It will "take three months and more than $20,000 to disassemble the bridge, replace the steel and rebuild."[413]

A request by the town to waive the Buy America rule has been rejected by the Federal Highway Administration.[414] "The Buy America provisions are very clearly spelled out and are often not negotiable," says Steve Harelson, who is a project engineer for the Colorado Department of Transportation. "It is involved in every project and it's in the specifications for every project," he notes. "This is the first time I am aware of a project being rejected because of a failure in this."[415]

The town claims "the use of Canadian products was the contractor's mistake," but New Design Construction claimed "it did not receive the mill test reports, which tell buyers where products are made, until after the product was installed."[416]

The bridge is a "lifeline" for many who live in the town and endured its closure for months this year while it underwent "major reconstruction"[417] and now may have to go without its use for another three months.

"It just seems like a waste of everybody's time and money," lamented Kara Zabilansky, Morrison's town administrator.[418]

"Personally, I think it's a big waste of materials and lumber and there's no need to throw away perfectly good materials that are actually working and the community uses them every day," says Carrie Shipley, who lives next to the bridge.[419] "Why didn't they make sure all the materials were from the United States to begin with."[420]

The mess up over this little bridge is making even bigger waves. Steel makers and some municipalities are pushing for retaliatory actions.

"The kind of situation happening in Colorado should be a wake-up call for the Canadian government," said Jayson Myers, the chief executive officer the Canadian Manufacturers and Exporters (CME), which want the Canadian government to impose similar restrictions on "infrastructure projects, such as the $5-billion (Canadian) replacement of Montreal's Champlain Bridge."[421]

Marcy Grossman, Canada's consul general based in Denver, asked "does it really make sense that $800 worth of American steel rolled in Canada may cost the Colorado taxpayer an additional $20,000?"[422]

Kara Zabilansky, Morrison's town administrator, "is dismayed that her bridge is at the center of a cross-border backlash."[423] She acknowledges ""It's pretty much a real big mess."[424]

The lesson is even when building a small bridge, you must read the fine print or else there can be big consequences, especially for taxpayers who get stuck paying the bill—in this case maybe twice.

The newly reconstructed bridge in Morrison, Colorado is in fine condition, but it is going to be ripped down and reconstructed—again—and the ramifications may be international.

28. Exploding Claims of "Sleep Apnea" Threaten to Bankrupt VA Disability Program

$1.2 billion

Military personnel diagnosed with sleep apnea are given a 50 percent rating – and some believe it's causing an explosion of abuse in the VA's disability program.

The number of active and retired service members getting sleep apnea-related payments has surged in recent years. Today, more than 143,000 service members are getting them, at a cost to taxpayers of $1.2 billion every year.[425] By comparison, the number getting the same payments in 2001 was fewer than 1,000.[426]

Sleep apnea affects as many as 18 million Americans[427], and is diagnosed through a combination of a physical exam and a sleep study.[428] While it can be a serious condition, for most people it is easily treatable with "lifestyle changes, mouthpieces, surgery, and breathing devices."[429]

When a service member claims a disability, the Department of Veterans Affairs (VA) determines the severity of the condition using a "rating" system.[430] Current VA policy rates someone with sleep apnea to have a rating of 50 percent, meaning fifty percent disabled. By contrast, Representative Tammy Duckworth, who served in the Army as a helicopter pilot, lost both of her legs in combat and had her right arm blown off.[431] After the arm was reattached, her disability rating by the VA was 20 percent.[432]

One attorney, Michael Webster, represented a number of veterans seeking disability payments for what he believed to be questionable sleep apnea claims, and came to Congress demanding an investigation. "Virtually every single family law case which I have handled involving military members during the past three years has had the military retiree receiving a VA 'disability' based upon sleep apnea," he told Congress, adding "A recently retired colonel told me that military members approaching retirement are actually briefed that if they claim VA disability based on sleep apnea, then they receive an automatic 50 percent disability rating ..."[433]

The VA itself has acknowledged the surge in sleep apnea claims, and taken steps to study the situation, but denies that there is any abuse in the system and defends the 50 percent rating.[434] But critics allege the increase is nothing more than a scam on the VA disability system that takes resources away from veterans who are truly disabled. Even the Philadelphia VA Medical Center's chief of sleep medicine has said the "majority" of "people who have sleep apnea and are on treatment are not disabled."[435]

Some veterans have begun speaking out in letters to the editor, including one retired colonel with a Purple Heart who has had sleep apnea for 15 years, "I would never think of asking VA for a disability rating based on sleep apnea," calling the payments "a travesty."[436]

Jeff Gottlob, a veterans service officer in Texas, agreed, "In my opinion, the automatic 50 percent rating for sleep apnea is excessive and being abused."[437]

Retired staff sergeant, Frank Manno, was even more direct, "As a retired soldier I am extremely disappointed that Congress and the VA can't see how the sleep apnea issue is crossing the line of fraud and waste ... Did the military make us obese or overweight?"[438]

29. Pentagon to Spend $1 Billion to Destroy $16 Billion in Unneeded Ammunition

$1 billion

The Pentagon is spending a billion dollars to destroy $16 billion in over purchases of military-grade ammunition. The amount of surplus ammunition is now so large that the cost of destroying it will equal the full years' salary for over 54,000 Army privates.[439]

How the military came to purchase so much ammunition it didn't need was uncovered in a 2014 Government Accountability Office (GAO) investigation.[440] Certain kinds of ammunition became "obsolete, unusable or their use is banned by international treaty," according to Pentagon officials.[441] However, GAO found that record-keeping for ammunition was also poor, and that accurate records were hard to come by for the nation's $70 billion ammunition arsenal.[442]

Over time, the amount of ammunition deemed no longer necessary has grown to nearly 40 percent of the Army's total inventory: "According to an Army financial statement in June 2013, the Army had about 39 percent of its total inventory (valued at about $16 billion) in a storage category for ammunition items that were excess to all the services' requirements."[443]

However, the Pentagon may be throwing away ammunition that could still be used. According to GAO, some of the material set for destruction has at times been found usable.[444]

30. NASA Wonders How Humans Will React to Meeting Space Aliens

$392,000

Encountering aliens may one day pose a communications problem, read one official NASA document published this year.

By using our experience with anthropology "we can be much better prepared for contact with an extraterrestrial civilization, should that day ever come,"[445] says the editor of the NASA eBook titled, "Archaeology, Anthropology, and Interstellar Communication."[446] The publication was put on NASA's website in May and was edited and officially published through the Office of Communications.[447]

Learning from history itself is difficult. "Communicating with intelligent terrestrial beings removed from us in time is deeply problematic," concludes the work.[448] If humans find aliens, they may have to confront these issues in new ways, finds the author: "[T]he constraints that humans now contend with will be refined, removed, or simply accepted as [communication with extraterrestrial intelligence] is engaged." [449]

In publishing a review of the book, NASA's Chief Historian said the title may sound like an odd one for the space agency's history program," but nonetheless the book is "an enjoyable and thought-provoking read."[450] It wistfully recounts the days when the federal government actually funded a program called the "Search for Extraterrestrial Intelligence" (SETI). Unfortunately, yearning for the days of yore and producing books on communicating with E.T. cannot change the fact NASA cannot even get its own astronauts into space. Perhaps the agency could shoot for the stars and make better use of the history program's $392,000 budget for 2014.[451]

31. Bruce Lee Dance Play Panned As Promoting Racial Stereotypes

$70,000

A taxpayer-funded play about the iconic martial arts figure Bruce Lee has been broadly panned as suffering from a mediocre plot, with some critics going as far as to say that it evokes a racial stereotype.[452]

It is unclear why the federal governmental supported this flop. But, perhaps the National Endowment of the Arts (NEA) decided to spend $70,000 for the play "Kung Fu," which features a dozen fight scenes,[453] because it exemplified the NEA's mission to "fund and promote artistic excellence, creativity, and innovation for the benefit of individuals and communities."[454]

Others did not find such artistic excellence, creativity, or benefit.

Variety Magazine panned it as "lack[ing] a cohesive narrative structure" with "no dramatic objective."[455] The New York Times slammed the play's clunky dialogue and corny jokes.[456] Even worse, the paper suggested the "mangled English" of Bruce Lee's speech throughout the play may actually perpetuate the prejudicial stereotype of the "Oriental sidekick."[457]

On its website, the Signature Theatre in New York City credits support for "Kung Fu" from individuals, foundations, corporations, and government agencies for its continued success as a non-profit organization.[458]

Since the play received $1,127,370 in non-federal funding, taxpayers are left wondering why the NEA didn't give a karate chop to the theatre's grant request.[459]

The dialogue and plot of "Kung Fu," according to the New York Times, never reaches the "fluid grace" of its action sequences

If they build it, will they come? City hopes that $16 million dollar will revitalize "ghost mall."

32. Road through "Ghost Mall" Hopes to Scare Up Business

$16 million

Fulton Mall in downtown Fresno, California – built in 1960's as the nation's second pedestrian mall – was once hailed as a landmark in landscape architecture. Today, years of neglect have left it in disrepair with broken fountains, crumbling sculptures, overgrown shrubbery and vacant buildings. The City of Fresno is hoping a new influx of $16 million from the U.S. Department of Transportation will bring revitalization by helping build a road through the mall, reopening it to vehicle traffic.[460]

After opening to significant fanfare in 1964, the mall quickly became an economic engine that started to sputter. By 1970, Montgomery Ward's, one of the mall's retail anchors, closed its doors and moved to a different part of the city.[461] Nearly every store present when the mall first opened would follow suit, including in 2013 an iconic bridal store left after 72 years.[462]

As retailers fled, the city government neglected to maintain the property and it deteriorated. A report commissioned by the city found:

The high design character of the Mall is in stark contrast with its state of advanced physical deterioration. Partly because of its age, and partly because of poor maintenance over several decades, most of its design features are beginning to fail. The Mall's pavement is cracked throughout and in many locations is heaving due to interference by tree roots. ... The state of disrepair is so extreme, that it is difficult for the casual observer to appreciate the design value of the Fulton Mall. ... The state of buildings along the Mall projects a similarly forbidding image.[463]

As the mall's buildings degraded, the vacancy rates skyrocketed to nearly three-quarters of the space in the mall's historic buildings sat empty.

In particular, most of the seven buildings along the Mall listed on the Local Register of Historic Places suffer from disinvestment, vacancy and disrepair. In 2010 the City of Fresno estimated that the seven large historic office buildings on the Fulton Mall, representing nearly 745,000 square feet of office space, are 71 percent vacant.[464]

The mall as a whole does not fare much better, which is over half empty, "The mall's 45 buildings have a 56% vacancy rate."[465]

For years, local officials debated what to do about the mall, including whether to tear it down.[466] Complicating matters, however, was a dark cloud of corruption stemming from a decades-long bribery scheme in which a developer paid off city government officials.

Fresno's long history of corrupt city planning efforts was documented in a 1999 *San Francisco Chronicle* story highlighting what it called the city's "ghost malls," including Fulton Mall: "It has endless strip malls that make the town appear to be one huge franchise, a kind of Anywhere USA. The malls, some critics say, are like cannibals -- new malls devour the older malls. At one end of town is the huge new River Park shopping center, which is booming; at the other is the East Gate mall, which is boarded up. Other regions have ghost towns: Fresno has ghost malls."[467]

Many wanted to build a road through the middle of the mall. However, a study commissioned by the City of Fresno found the road would have no discernible impact on transportation – the purpose of the specific Department of Transportation funding. The 2007 report found: "Fulton Street is not a critical component of the traffic and transit circulation network in downtown; therefore, transportation should not drive decisions on the future of the Mall. Economic development opportunities and cultural factors should be the principal determinants along the Mall."[468]

Yet, when the $15.9 million in grant funding was announced, political leaders said the opposite, declaring it a major transportation initiative. "These TIGER projects are the best argument you can make for investment in our transportation infrastructure," said Secretary U.S. Transportation Secretary, Anthony Foxx, "The Fulton Mall reconstruction project will revitalize Fresno's downtown business district, increase local economic activity and improve transportation options for residents."[469]

Perhaps the most notable aspect of the project, though, is not its multi-million dollar price tag, but the fact that the City of Fresno itself will not be spending its own money on something it has deemed an essential priority. In describing the importance of the road, city council president Steve Brandau called the mall, "an economic Berlin Wall – the economy stops there."[470] But when they announced the $16 million grant, the same leaders struck a different note, announcing proudly, "No City of Fresno General Fund money will be used for the project."[471]

> **Another example of a government program gone wrong, the initial purpose was to improve service and remove bottlenecks, but it has evolved into a subsidized freight service that ships Coke, Mountain Dew, Gatorade, frozen honey wings, and Clorox wipes**

33 Postal Service Pays Thousands to Ship Soda to Alaska for Hundreds

$77 million

The Postal Service is responsible for shipping consumer items to remote villages in Alaska under a program called "Alaska Bypass" started in 1972. [472] Over three decades, moving this freight has cost the agency $2.5 billion, including $77 million per year in recent years.[473]

Another example of a government program gone wrong, the initial purpose was to improve service and remove bottlenecks, but it has evolved into a subsidized freight service that ships Coke, Mountain Dew, Gatorade, frozen honey wings, and Clorox wipes, for example, on 1,000-pound pallets. In a Washington Post report, a 1366-pound pallet caused the Postal Service to pay $3,167 to the airlines (the fare is regulated by the Department of Transportation, and competition among carriers is limited[474]), and the revenue received was $485, for a loss of more than $260,0.[475]

The Postal Service has an obligation to deliver mail to every part of the country --- but this isn't mail. Ordinary pieces of mail can weigh up to 70 pounds, but these pallets often weigh well over 1,000 pounds, yet the postage is calculated based on Standard Post prices, per pound.

One can be sympathetic to the states that lack infrastructure to serve the needs of remote residents, but whether the financially-strapped Postal Service (and perhaps the taxpayers eventually) should bear the cost is questionable. Also questionable is whether this subsidy actually helps those remote residents, or merely improves the profit of the middlemen providing the service. These airlines make a profit of about 15.5%, whereas the typical airline struggles to make a 3% profit margin.[476] In any event, the subsidized transportation reduces the incentive to make delivery more efficient. If the taxpayer is paying for it, why reduce the cost?

Taxpayers Sing the Blues for the Grammy's Museum

$1.25 million

The Grammy's have no reason to sing the blues, but taxpayers do.

Despite collecting tens of millions of dollars tax free every year, the music industry organization is paying nothing for the construction of its new museum while taxpayers have been committed to spending millions by state and federal governments.

The 20,000-plus square-foot museum, which will be located in Cleveland, Mississippi, will cost $18 million and "is planned to be the most technologically advanced music-themed museum in the world." It is expected to open in summer 2015 and will be "the only official Grammy Museum location outside of Los Angeles."[477]

The Grammy Museum Mississippi "will help the rest of the world recognize Mississippi's contribution to American music culture," according to Bob Santelli, Executive Director of the Grammy Museum at L.A. Live.[478] The museum will be just 25 miles from another museum that also focuses on the musical heritage of the Mississippi Delta—the recently opened B.B. King Museum and Delta Interpretive Center in Indianola.[479]

"Federal, state and local government funds, as well as private donations, are paying for it" and Cleveland Music Foundation President Lucy Janoush notes "organizers have been planning on the federal money as part of the $18 million budget."[480]

"The Grammy Museum in Los Angeles will control curatorial and public program decisions as well as the hiring," however, "neither the museum, the Recording Academy or AEG, which owns the Grammy Museum property, will invest in the Mississippi site."[481] Meanwhile, the U.S. Commerce Department's Economic Development Administration provided $1.25 million to the city of Cleveland "to build an access road and upgrade infrastructure on the Delta State University campus," where the museum will be located.[482] The state of Mississippi is also providing $6 million to support the project.[483]

There is no question the museum will generate interest and attract visitors and that the Grammy's and its associated organizations have more than enough resources, which is exactly why the museum does not need financial handouts from taxpayers. And since the Grammy's and its associated organizations do not pay any taxes, it seems unfair to make those who do pay taxes to pick up the bill.

Consider, the Grammy's licensing fee to broadcast the awards exceeds $20 million annually, which it doesn't even have to pay taxes on because The Recording Academy – GRAMMY.org is "classed as a type of non-profit."[484] There are also millions of dollars collected in private donations and membership fees. "Call it the Academy, the Recording Academy, the National Academy of Recording Arts and Sciences or NARAS, it is made up of 22,000 members paying $125 a year." The Academy collects "donations and corporate sponsorships" for its charity MusiCares, which spends millions "to help struggling musicians" as well as other activities like "music research, the preservation and archiving of recordings" and lobbying politicians.[485] The Academy also runs the Latin Grammys and The Grammy Museum."[486] The Grammy Foundation "offers scholarships, grants and opportunities for music education."[487]

To provide some perspective, the $1.25 million federal grant for the Grammy Museum is just *less* than the annual salary of the Academy's current President, which is reportedly $1.5 million.[488] Now that is something to sing about!

The big winner this year at the Grammy's may have been Daft Punk, but the big losers were taxpayers since the organization—which pays no taxes—is taking millions of dollars from state and locals governments to support its new museum.

> It is the **FIRST TIME** humanity can **HEAR ▶ THE FUTURE**

Voicemails From the Future Warn of Post Apocalyptic World

$5.2 million

A disruption in the time-space continuum has somehow caused voicemails from the future to fall from the sky, warning everyone who hears them about the disastrous effects of global warming: Zombies on the loose, airports underwater and bananas nearly impossible to find. So sets the stage for a game called *FutureCoast*, which attempts to teach people about what the future might hold if climate change makes the seas rise.[489]

It's all funded by the National Science Foundation using a portion of a $5.2 million grant to Columbia University given, in part, to develop an interactive game to spur climate change activism.[490] *FutureCoast* is a "collaborative game" set in an alternative world where fictional voicemails have been transported back in time – cased in pieces of circular plastic called "chronofacts" – allowing people to listen in on what earthlings from the future say about the climate.[491]

Participants play along by discovering the location of chronofacts, which are stashed around the country in different locations – all tagged with GPS coordinates. Every so often, the game's organizers will release the coordinates of one or two over Twitter, allowing players to go out and search for them. Once found, players load information from the chronofacts online and a new voicemail is made available on the *FutureCoast* website.[492]

One message describes sunny 75 degree weather in Antarctica compared to a chilly -2 degrees in Arizona with expected hailstorms.[493] In another message, someone talks about how Washington, D.C. was hit with ten feet of snow.[494] A different character leaves a voicemail about rioting over food shortages and rationing across the country.[495] One caller claims "neo-luddites" are out to kill anyone with scientific knowledge,[496] and another paints a cryptic image of a zombie apocalypse saying that "when you see them, you will know what to do."[497]

The game's creator, Ken Eklund, calls his work "authentic fiction" and insists he "create[s] the attractive narrative vacuum that people fill up with their stories – playfully, yet with intention."[498] In designing the game, he tried to create a world "that has this ring of authenticity to it, even though it might be wildly fictional."[499] According to him, "[t]he fiction part is kind of a term for a playful world that you're creating together, and a playful process."[500]

The game's producer, Sara Thacher, believes the game allows people from different viewpoints to discuss climate change using their voicemail messages.[501] Eklund agrees, but adds that the game is more than that, "We're looking for black swans. We're looking for people who have an insight about the future."[502]

"I think that there are a lot of people who want to have an invitation to say something about climate change," Eklund continued, "And I think this is the opportunity. It is this sort of creative challenge – you say it, but you say it in your future voice."[503]

In the end, the goal of the game was modest, according to its designers. Stephanie Pfirman, a professor affiliated with the project noted that the goal of the game wasn't necessarily to educate people on climate research, but rather to get people able to address the issue to simply think about it.[504]

In one voicemail from the future, a little girl asks grandma to see the last living lobster.

36. The Funny Ways Government Wastes Your Money: Laughing Classes

$47,000

Taxpayers' funny bones may not be tickled by the federal government's laughing classes for college students.

The University of California, Los Angeles is offering an undergraduate course exploring "the nature of human laughter and humor" with the support of $25,000 from the National Endowment for the Humanities (NEH).[505]

Another comedy class is being developed by Butler University in Indianapolis with the support of nearly $22,000 from NEH.[506] The seminar, called "Why Is It Funny" will "examine issues such as how laughter plays with our perceptions, the appeal of subversive humor, whether comedy is 'a guy thing,' the role of laughter in civic discourse, and whether we can laugh at war."[507] In addition to readings from Aristotle, Shakespeare, and Oscar Wilde, students will watch classic films and episodes of M*A*S*H.[508] "As a final project, students will develop either a stand-up routine or a, "comedy piece using the tools of digital storytelling."[509]

This ROFL (internet slang for rolling on the floor inducing laughter) curriculum may offer students a comedy break from the not so funny STEM[510] courses, but our nation's $17 trillion in debt is nothing to laugh at.

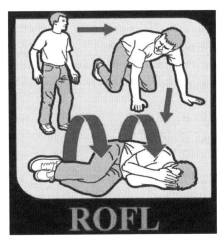

The federal government is spending nearly $50,000 on laughing classes for college students

37. FAA Upgrades Low-Traffic Airport Serving High-End Ski Resort

$18 million

The airport for "Sun Valley ski resort that is a magnet for the rich and famous"[511] is getting a multi-million dollar facelift courtesy of taxpayers.

The Federal Aviation Administration (FAA) awarded $18 million as part of a series of federal grants to cover the majority of the $34 million construction project for Friedman Memorial Airport.[512] The federal requirements that supposedly warrant the project includes a waiting lounge for arriving passengers that "will have comfortable chairs and a fireplace."[513]

As the home of some of the best resort golf courses in the country, Sun Valley is also very popular summer destination for the well-heeled.[514] For example, "Media stalwarts, CEOs, and technology luminaries" come to the area "for the 30th annual conference – known as 'summer camp' for moguls." The multi-billion decision by Comcast to purchase NBC Universal supposedly occurred there.[515]

Some of the celebrities that frequent or have second homes in Sun Valley include Tom Hanks, Bruce Willis, Ashton Kutcher and Arnold Schwarzenegger.[516]

In 1936, the Resort was built to mirror the "luxury" of Swiss ski resorts.[517] It was the home of "the first chairlift in the world" and almost immediately, became "the place to ski and be seen for the top start, Garry Cooper, Clark Gable, Lucille Ball, Marilyn Monroe" among others.[518] The two main hotels foyers are "jammed with pictures of celebrities spanning three quarters of a century."[519]

There are only four daily commercial departures on average.[520] Of those flights, about eighty percent of the airport users are visiting the area or are part-time residents.[521]

Even the airport manager, Rick Baird, is surprised at the multi-million dollar grant: "Airports of our size don't normally get grants of this size."[522]

38. FEMA Overlooks Flood Victims, Rebuilds Golf Course Instead

$202,291

The federal government rebuffed pleas for assistance from Austin, Texas homeowners that were directly impacted by what some called the storm of the century,[523] but paid hundreds of thousands of dollars to rebuild local golf courses.

Last Halloween, central Texas, including the city of Austin, experienced a historic storm. Five people were killed during the flooding, and more than 500 homes were damaged.[524] Texas Governor Rick Perry requested a disaster declaration noting that the floods had left a "devastating financial burden on our local communities."[525] Although Federal Emergency Management Agency (FEMA) denied the state's request to provide funds to individuals directly affected by the storm, it approved the state's request for funds to rebuild damaged infrastructure.[526]

The city's publicly-owned golf courses suffered in the flooding too.[527]

The Roy Kizer public course, characterized by a "links style layout spread out over 200 acres," with "ample fairways and the choice of five sets of tees" for every golfer, had two greens under water for a few hours, and lost a section of cart path, according to the City's Golf Division.[528] The Lions and Morris Williams courses were described as having minimal damage, but the City secured $37,663 in FEMA grants.[529] The Jimmy Clay course suffered the worst damage, with "several greens submerged in up to 6 feet of water," "three fairways with standing water," and worst of all, the need to replace the sand in bunkers on holes 4 and 11.[530] The course was closed for nine days following the storm.[531]

Although FEMA grant funds are only supposed to be used to pay for damage specifically caused by the disaster, the same greens damaged in the flood were also suffering from the ill effects of a nematode infestation, an insect referred to as the "Hidden Enemy" of golf courses.[532]

Natural disasters can wreak havoc on American cities and towns. FEMA oversees a number of programs that are intended to provide taxpayer funds to individuals, and state and local governments to help pay for repairs to critical publicly-owned infrastructure, like community hospitals, and schools after severe disasters. Since 1999, FEMA has spent more than $18 million rebuilding public golf courses damaged during disasters.[533]

39. Disney Polynesian Resort Gets Makeover
$1,437,966 in guarantees

The "happiest place on earth" got a little happier in 2014 as taxpayers helped Walt Disney World renovate its Polynesian Resort.

When the Polynesian Village resort opened in 1971, it was "one of the first on-site hotels at the Walt Disney World Resort."[535] Today, it is undergoing a massive renovation to bring the resort up to date, all with a little help from the Small Business Administration.

The Small Business Administration provided a total of $1.4 million in surety bond guarantees to two firms hired by Disney, meaning if they fail to perform the taxpayer will step into make sure Disney is made whole. The first was $455,684 for a construction company working to install a "Complete Skylight System at the Grand Ceremonial House in Disney's Polynesian Resort,"[536] and $982,282 guarantees for other rehab work at the resort.[537]

One of the biggest companies in the world, the Walt Disney Company ranked 61st in the Fortune 100 rankings for 2014 – and may not seem like an obvious candidate to benefit from small business assistance.[538] It operates nine of the world's ten most popular amusement parks, which together bring in more than $2 billion in annual profit.[539]

However, with backing from the taxpayer, the renovation will help the Polynesian resort get a new deck, a children's play area at the Nanea Volcano pool, 20 new bungalows and "a hot tub with expansive views of the Seven Seas Lagoon."[540] In the Great Ceremonial House, Trader Sam's Grotto "will feature a highly themed lounge area, with handcrafted tiki cocktails served in souvenir mugs that will complement Polynesian-themed small plates."

"Tiki bars to me are a classic experience, so if you take that and then you put Disney magic over the top of it, it doesn't get any better than that," said Disney executive vice president, Debbie Petersen.[541]

Disney's Polynesian Resort is one of Walt Disney World's most luxurious resorts, with rooms starting at $429. Touted as an "oasis of tropical palms, lush vegetation, koi ponds and white-sand beaches," the resort is a short ride from the Magic Kingdom.8 Guests can enjoy the Spirit of Aloha Dinner Show, with hula dancing, fire dancing, and an all-you-can-eat tropical feast.[542]

"In size and scope, the renovation of Disney's Polynesian Village Resort is a significant investment in the guest experience," said senior vice president Tom Wolber, adding, "Once completed, the iconic resort hotel will be re-imagined with a level of detail as only Disney can deliver."[543]

Walt Disney World's Polynesian Resort.[534]

The Great Ceremonial House at Disney's Polynesian Resort will benefit from federal bond guarantees.

Space Agency Hunts for the Lost Tomb of Genghis Khan

$15,000

With NASA's manned space missions grounded indefinitely, NASA is now searching for signs of ancient civilization right here on Earth.

The space agency sponsored a $15,000 challenge[545] to locate the lost tomb of Genghis Khan, the Mongol leader "responsible for the deaths of as many as 40 million people" and conquering more territory "than any individual in history."[546]

According to legend, Khan died in 1227 and his final resting place was kept a secret. His tomb is most likely on or around a Mongolian mountain called Burkhan, "but to this day its precise location is unknown."[547]

The NASA Tournament Lab at Harvard University, which received $1,761,065 from NASA in 2014,[548] offered the $15,000 prize through the crowd-sourcing platform TopCoder, Inc., to help find the tomb.[549] The project hopes that "TopCoder community members from around the world to study select satellite imagery of the region of the lost tomb of Genghis Khan and then develop an algorithm that will recognize human built, and potentially historically significant, structures found in those images."[550]

Officially known as the Collaborative Minds and Machine Learning Exploration Challenge, the project is a "first of its kind" mash-up of "Crowd-sourcing, Open Innovation, human exploration, space exploration, and machine learning algorithms."[551]

The project employed "state-of-the-art technologies to conduct a noninvasive survey of Genghis Khan's homeland" with an "online crowd of explorers" using satellite imagery to spot human-built structures.[552]

"The quest to find Genghis Khan's tomb has mystified scientists for hundreds of years," notes TopCoder President and COO Rob Hughes.[553]

Alas, while the concept for the challenge was ambitious and innovative, even with the assistance of NASA's space imagery, the participants—like many who tried before them—failed to find the lost tomb of Genghis Khan.

A video presentation shows how the TopCoder community can help study NASA satellite imagery and develop algorithms that could uncover the lost tomb of Genghis Khan

Abandoned Pennsylvania Mall Wants to be the East Coast Hollywood

$15 million

Norristown, Pennsylvania, a beleaguered manufacturing hub, appears to have been swindled into the idea of transforming an old shuttered Sears department store into a sort of East Coast incarnation of Hollywood.[554]

The Sears store sits in a half-abandoned 1950s-era mall about two miles north of downtown Norristown called Logan Square. It is probably safe to say that most folks would greet any proposal claiming to be able to transform a hollowed-out old Philly mall like Logan Square into the next MGM with a raised eyebrow or roll of the eyes.[555]

But in 2008, a real estate developer named Charles Gallub bought up the old Logan Square property. In a masterful display of salesmanship, Gallub came before the county government with an astonishing plan. Pointing to tax credits that Governor Ed Rendell was then backing to promote filmmaking in the state, Gallub stated that he could "create one of the best film studios on the East Coast of the United States."[556] His brainchild, named "Studio Centre," would have a "multiplier effect on the local economy," he said, projecting 1,300 new jobs with an appealing average annual salary of $60,000.[557]

All that Gallub needed to transform Norristown into the next silver screen mecca was a little money. Well, a lot of money. In addition to the $18.3 million he had already sunk into the property, Gallub would eventually obtain an additional $24.5 million from the county.[558] Some county officials wondered whether they should get a financial guarantee from Gallub should the project fail.[559] No guarantee was ever signed.

Today, one of Logan Square's primary tenants is a thrift store. It shares the remains of the mall with a deli, pharmacy, Social Security Administration Office, and a political office for a state legislator.

42 Wineries Get Help Selling Beer, Chile-Infused Wine

$50,000

There is chile-flavored ice cream, chile-flavored soda, chile-flavored beer – and now with some help from the taxpayer, chile-flavored wine.

Every year, wineries around the world produce an estimated 36 billion bottles of wine[560] – with nearly 8,000 wineries in the U.S. alone.[561] One New Mexico winery hopes to add a few more bottles to that number with a federal subsidy to help distribute its brand of "chile-infused" wines.

New Mexico Wineries, also known for operating the St. Clair Winery & Bistro, has created "Hatch Red Chile Wine" and "Hatch Green Chile Wine" using locally grown chiles.[562] To help market and distribute their wine, USDA provided the winery with a $50,000 grant through the Value-Added Producer program.

It's a program that offloads some of the burden for producing and marketing locally-grown products, and places it on the backs of taxpayers. This fiscal year, the USDA provided $4.5 million in grants to 28 recipients in 20 states, and footed the bill for all kinds of operating costs that are normally born by the businesses.[563]

While the USDA says grants are awarded on a "competitive basis,"[564] it seems that politics may also have contributed. Senator Tom Udall of New Mexico boasted that his position on the powerful Senate Appropriations Committee was instrumental in sending money back home to the winery, raising questions about the hatch chile wine's competitive edge.[565]

The vineyard describes both of its chile wines as "bringing to life the flavor of the Southwest with [their] unique New Mexican flair."[566]

However, wine critic Jen Van Tieghem, gave the wine a less than glowing review, finding, "I expected the chiles to pack a crisp punch, but, in the end, the spicy tones also fell short of the vibrancy I was hoping for."[567]

After taking the chile wine to a party, she described the crowd's reaction this way, "after the initial taste test, no one asked for a second sample but, rather, started thinking of other ways to use it—in cooking or to make sangria, perhaps?[568]

Others received funding as well, including Harvest Ridge Winery in Delaware, which received funds to "expand the winery's reach and draw visitors through agro-tourism,"[569] while the Wine Barn in Kansas is using grant money to develop "a billboard campaign and [strategically place] rack cards in hotels and corporate offices."[570]

Other farmers are raising their glasses of craft beer and cider in celebration of the grant program. Three breweries received money to develop a line of craft brews and nine farms received more grant money to build or expand their production of hard cider.[571] And just for good measure, a company in Hawaii even received taxpayer funds to produce mead from tropical fruit.[572]

Roaches, Mice, and Feces in Public Housing Funded by Uncle Sam, Slumlord

$27 million

"I just got tired of the poop falling on me," complained Everett Dennis Lewis, resident of The Hacienda, an apartment building run by the Richmond Housing Authority in California.

The Hacienda is one of five low-income housing facilities run by the Richmond Housing Authority with deplorable living conditions. Known by residents as the "Haci-hellhole," an investigation by the Center for Investigative Reporting found the facility to be riddled with "handfuls of half-dead mice," "drug dealers," and "blue and green mold."[573]

Across the country, hundreds of public housing authorities are overseen and funded by the U.S. Department of Housing and Urban Development (HUD). In 2014, HUD provided the Richmond Housing Authority with over $27 million, despite longstanding reports that its residents have been living in squalor.[574]

One paralyzed veteran became trapped in the building when the elevator broke for several days,[575] leaving firefighters to rescue him through a third-story window.[576] Resident Janae Fletcher complained of bedbugs in her apartment, but was told they were her fault.[577] "I was scratching so hard that I had holes in my skin," Fletcher said, "and housing told me, 'Maybe it's the company you keep.'"[578]

Residents at the Hacienda filed dozens of complaints, most that went unheeded. "This building should be bulldozed," finally conceded city councilman Jael Myrick, adding that the primitive living conditions "should not have been allowed to persist for this long."[579]

However, HUD knew for a long time about the problems with the facility, even as it sent it tens of millions of dollars a year – a situation the failed to produce change. "Federal inspectors in 2009 and then again in 2011 also warned of severe problems with the roof. In 2009, an entire electrical closet's walls were 'saturated with water mold and mildew,'" reported a major investigation of the authority's failures.[580] Major gaps have existed in between the foundation and walls for at least five years.[581]

In 2011, the Senate fell one vote short of changing HUD policy to punish slumlords who take taxpayer money. An amendment offered by Sen. Tom Coburn would have revoked funding from any slumlord who persisted in leaving life-threatening conditions in place without remedy.[582] It lost by a vote of 59 in favor and 40 against, or one less than required to overcome a filibuster led by Sen. Patty Murray.[583]

Some of the people appointed to serve the Hacienda seemed to hardly stand being near it, instead spending tens of thousands to travel the country. Between 2008-2011, members of the Richmond Housing Advisory Commission, which oversees the authority's work, spent nearly $80,000 for travel to "conferences in places such as Nashville, Washington, D.C., and Palm Springs."[584] Their travel budget exceeded that for the members of the City Council.[585]

HUD eventually found that the travel was not "an eligible us of operating funds," adding, "Whether it was a wise use of money (by the housing authority) is not a determination we will make."[586]

All the while, residents of the building were afraid for their health and safety. "I'm afraid that the building's going to come down on me," said Rhonda Marshall.[587]

Another resident concluded, "Not one single human being should be living here. This is an uninhabitable building."[588]

DHS Buys Too Many Cars and Let's Them Sit Underused

$35 million

With the second largest vehicle fleet in the federal government, the Department of Homeland Security (DHS) could save tens of millions in taxpayer dollars by reducing underused vehicles.

The DHS vehicle fleet is comprised of 56,000 vehicles costing $485 million to operate annually. Three DHS components, Customs and Border Protection (CBP), U.S. Immigration and Customs Enforcement (ICE), and the National Protection and Programs Directorate (NPPD), maintain approximately 42,000 vehicles, or 75% of fleet.[589]

DHS Office of Inspector General (OIG) audited the vehicle fleet, by inspecting the use of hundreds of DHS vehicles across several DHS components.

Of the vehicles inspected, about two-thirds were underused[590]. With the average operating cost per vehicle at $988, $2,914, and $8,329 for CBP, ICE, and NPPD vehicles respectively this adds up quite quickly. The Inspector General estimated that the total amount wasted on underused vehicles to be between $35.3 and $48.6 million.[591]

The IG's conclusion was that DHS does not "adequately manage" the 56,000 vehicles because "each DHS component manages its own vehicle fleet" which makes it tough "to provide adequate oversight and ensure compliance with Federal laws."[592]

45. Costs Skyrocket for "Birds In Space" Replica

$410,000

Can a taxpayer-funded sculpture fly? Chicago-based artist Iñigo Manglano-Ovalle tried to figure this out by "fabricating a life-size steel-and-aluminium replica"[593] of Constantin Brancusi's iconic Birds in Space sculpture that sold in 2005 for a whopping $27.4 million.[594]

The artist placed the replica sculpture, "in a hypervelocity wind tunnel at Mach 10, or ten times the speed of sound."[595] The *Bird in Space* replica "had unexpectedly good aerodynamic efficiency at hypersonic speeds, a goal not achieved by engineering for decades."[596]

This replica was purchased for the building that houses the Food and Drug Administration's Center for Biologics Evaluation and Research. The artist thought the Bird in Space knock-off "would raise awareness for the FDA employees to the existence of the U.S. Air Force mission that shares their campus."[597]

The sculpture was purchased as part of the General Services Administration Art in Architecture Program, where a percentage of construction costs are "reserved for art in each government building."[598]

The taxpayer cost of the replica was $410,000, which because of modifications doubled in price.[599]

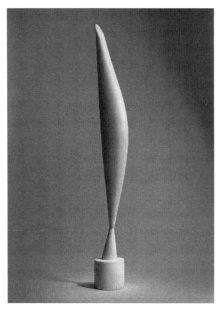

Life-size replica of the "Birds in Space" sculpture (seen on the right) cost taxpayers $410,000

46. DOD Tries To Build Real-Life "Iron Man" Suit

$80 million

Government contractors have built a suit of military super-armor to withstand bullets and carry hundreds of pounds, all powered by futuristic energy source. No, that's not the plot of Hollywood's blockbuster movie series, *Iron Man*, but the hope of Pentagon officials to bring science fiction to the battlefield.

The Department of Defense has set aside millions to try and create what it's calling a Tactical Assault Light Operator Suit (TALOS). "We sometimes refer to it as the Iron Man suit, frankly, to attract the attention, imagination and excitement of industry and academia," said Michael Fieldson, heading up the TALOS program.[600]

In addition to dozens of defense contractors and experts, the Pentagon is also collaborating with the big time Hollywood costume designers from movies such as Terminator, RoboCop, Captain America, and Iron Man.[601]

"When you're doing something for a movie, it is all make-believe," said a founder of the Hollywood company that designed the Iron Man suit.[602] Crediting computer-generated special effects for the fictional technologies of the Iron Man suit, she explained that "for the military, that's not really going to be the case."[603]

TALOS has an estimated budget of $80 million over the next four years,[604] but one industry official of a large defense firm has predicted that the TALOS program will "need about a billion dollars" for a successful prototype.[605]

Like most things in Washington, the cost of producing even the simplest of things often cost many times what it would elsewhere, as one observer unwittingly noted. "To do it right, they need about a billion dollars," said one industry official, adding, "Twenty million dollars a year in an R&D budget -- you couldn't even develop a pencil on that."[606]

That sentiment perfectly describes the problem with the military industrial complex—they really honestly probably could not develop a pencil for DOD for only $20 million.

The Iron-Man suit would protect U.S. soldiers with body armor made of an agile exoskeleton, which could also carry hundreds of pounds of gear.[607]

However, not everyone in the defense industry thinks this is a good idea. A 2013 study funded by the Department of Defense and the National Academy of Sciences found that soldiers' combat loads are far already too excessive, and that "the approach of acquiring and fielding every 'new' technology is both impractical and unaffordable.[608]

And while a promotional video for the TALOS program shows bullets ricocheting off a cartoon soldier dressed in the suit,[609] field tests have so far found soldiers struggling to run, dive, and shoot when using the real thing.[610]

Part of the problem is the final suit is projected to weigh up to 400 pounds,[611] mostly just to carry its 365 pounds of batteries to power the suit.[612] One researcher noted that Hollywood special effects made the Iron Man suit "impossibly thin, impossibly light, impossibly agile, and impossibly energy efficient."[613]

Drug Enforcement Administration Celebrates Itself With Own Museum

$95,000

Alongside fighting drug dealers and narco-traffickers, the Drug Enforcement Administration (DEA) has another, lesser-important mission: operating a museum.

Since 1999, the "DEA Museum" has been housed in the foyer of a non-descript Virginia DEA headquarters office complex.[614] Some have raised the pertinent question of why taxpayer money is being spent to detail its history of fighting drugs rather than the usual federal entities that fund museums[615]

In 2014, taxpayers spent $95,000 to the operation and promotion of the museum. The largest portion of those funds – $65,000 – helped support one of its traveling exhibits, *Target America*, which was displayed at the Maryland Science Center.[616] An additional $25,000 paid for one of the museum's staff members[617] and $5,000 purchased an advertisement at a nearby subway station.[618]

Whether the money has been effective in drawing people in is highly suspect. Attendance at the museum has been light over the years, with the average number of weekly visitors at a little less than 225.[619] A report from 2007 noted that most of the museum's visitors were "middle and high school students on class trips."[620]

When the Drug Enforcement Administration (DEA) opened a museum in 1999 about the agency's fight against illegal drugs, it hoped the exhibits would prompt parents and teachers to talk with kids.[621] However, the museum's website cautions that exhibits may not be appropriate for kids under ten years old.[622] In addition to the replica 1970's head shop, the exhibits are filled with stacks of drug paraphernalia, a Santa Muerte occultist statue and "a grisly photo of a junkie killed by an overdose."[623]

Despite the gruesome exhibits, museum officials are still hoping that kids will show up. In 2013, the museum rolled out its DEA Junior Special Agent program for third-graders as young as eight years old that show up and explore the museum.[624] When they're done with that, the gift shop also caters to little ones, offering DEA-themed "onesies," rubber duckies with gestapo-style hats or miniature plush German Shepherds.[625]

The museum was given $349,000 from Congress when it first opened its doors in 1999, but today it is run by the DEA Educational Foundation.[626] In 2013, the museum closed its doors for renovation, which included expanding the gift shop and incorporating iPads into the exhibits.[627]

DEA agents seized this Santa Muerte statue from drug dealers in Mexico.

Items on display at the DEA Museum gift shop

Missile Defense Misses the Target
$998 million

By the time it is completed, the Defense Department will have spent more than $41 billion on a missile defense system that with a 30% success rate at stopping missiles.[628] Our Ballistic Missile Defense System (BMDS) consists of both ground- and sea-based radar and interceptor missiles that provide a "layered" defense against a nuclear strike on our homeland.[629] Developed to intercept intermediate and intercontinental ballistic missiles (ICBM), the Ground-based Midcourse Defense (GMD) system is the backbone of our ground-based missile defense system.

It is built around the hit-to-kill Exoatmospheric Kill Vehicle (EKV) warhead, which in theory intercepts and destroys an incoming ICBM in our upper atmosphere. The U.S. currently has 30 GMD Ground-Based Interceptors (GBIs) deployed in Alaska and California, and plans to deploy an additional 14 by 2017, even though the system's performance has been marred by failure and final testing of the system's capabilities and limitations won't be completed until 2022.[630]

A successor to the Reagan era "Star Wars" Strategic Defense Initiative (SDI) program, development of GMD was fast tracked in 2002 with a Bush administration plan to deploy an "initial set of missile defense capabilities" by 2005.[631] To meet the timeline, GMD was rushed into a high-risk, concurrent development, production, and fielding process known as "concurrency." In 2012, the Government Accountability Office (GAO) reported that the program's "highly concurrent development, production, and fielding strategy" had resulted in "disrupted production, increased costs, and delayed fielding" of the system.[632]

Critics of the program remain skeptical that the system will ever be able to intercept an operational ICBM as intended. The Defense Department's Operational Test and Evaluation (DOT&E), the final authority on weapon system performance, has long warned the system falls short.[633] Its former director, Philip Coyle, said recently, "The GMD system still has no demonstrated effectiveness to defend the U.S. ...against enemy attack under realistic operational conditions."[634] That's because the tests on the GMD system are conducted at lower velocity than what the system would encounter against an actual operational ICBM, making them a poor approximation of the conditions of a real attack.[635]

And even at the lower velocity, the test results don't inspire confidence. Of the 17 highly scripted tests performed on the GMD system to date, only 9 (53 percent) have successfully intercepted their target, and the last test in June of this year was the first successful test of the improved EKV, the Capability Enhancement (CE-II) model. Two previous tests of the CE-II failed in 2010,[636] prompting Congress to impose a delay on further production until successful tests could be demonstrated.[637] The MDA's official release following the system's June test hailed it as the fourth intercept of "the GMD... operationally configured interceptor since 2006,"[638] even though GAO has reported that the first test of the operationally configured interceptor in 2006 would not have resulted in a kill of the incoming missile.[639]

The DOD Inspector General (IG) attributes three of the test failures directly to the EKV, which it says suffers from quality control issues resulting from a culture driven by "schedule and cost priorities" that created "a manufacturing challenge" for the EKV.[640] The National Research Council (NRC) was less kind in its 2012 assessment of the program, noting that the GMD system exemplified the MDA's ""hobby shop" approach, with many false starts on poorly analyzed concepts."[641] Because of the number of design changes the EKV has undergone over the years, costly retrofits will have to be made to the 30 GBIs that are already deployed. GAO has reported a cost increase from $236 million to $1.309 billion to "demonstrate as well as fix, the already produced CE-IIs."[642]

Even if the issues with the EKV can be resolved, the GMD system is designed to repel only a limited ICBM attack and would be easily overwhelmed by the simple countermeasures that would be deployed in a real attack, such as "decoys" designed to confuse the system, or "structured attacks involving simultaneous launches and/or attacks on key components of the defense, notably its sensors."[643]

But the MDA and its supporters in Congress continue to proclaim the system's success and fund the program, in spite of the fact the GAO found MDA was purposely obscuring the program's cost growth in an effort to make oversight of the program more difficult.[644] By the time all 44 GBIs are deployed in 2017 the GMD program will have cost taxpayers $41 billion, at least "30 to 50 percent more" than it should have cost as compared to "successful programs with missiles of comparable complexity."[645]

Despite obvious flaws, the MDA and Congress are moving forward with a $1 billion decision based on a 30% success rate in tests that fail to replicate a real world scenario. Almost immediately after the June test results were announced, production of the EKV was resumed and the MDA announced it was moving forward with its plan to deploy the additional 14 missiles. Even more concerning, Congress is moving to expand the program to develop an East Coast missile defense site, at a potential cost of billions more for taxpayers—the House's version of the fiscal year 2015 National Defense Authorization Act (NDAA) included $20M for construction costs, and the MDA is already conducting an Environmental Impact Study at four possible locations for the new site.

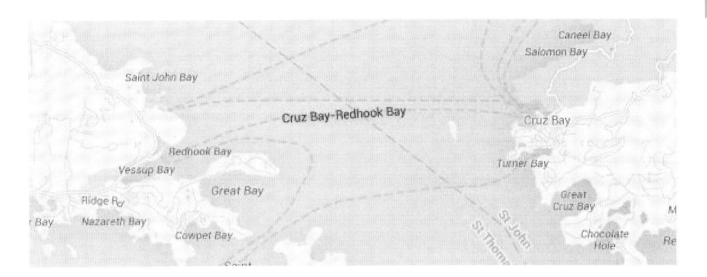

Virgin Island Ferries Sit Unused for Nearly a Year

$7.6 million

For residents and visitors of the Virgin Islands (V.I.), reliable ferries that travel from island to island are a necessity. Yet, after spending millions for two ferries to transport passengers between two islands, the vessels have sat largely unused in 2014.

Purchasing the new ships was part of a plan by Virgin Islands government officials to upgrade the aging ferries that make the two-mile trip back and forth each day between the islands of St. Thomas and St. John.[646] With $7.6 million in federal funding, they were able in 2014 to purchase two new vessels to upgrade the existing fleet – the Cruz Bay 1 and the Red Hook 1.[647]

When the plan was first announced, local officials on the Virgin Islands estimated they could buy two "300-passenger ferry boats [that] cost between $2 million to $2.5 million each."[648] To help fund the purchases, the federal government awarded several federal grants and earmarks since 2007 to make the upgrades, including the biggest portion – $3 million – from the 2009 stimulus legislation.[649]

The federal stimulus award was not without controversy, however. Elected officials in Washington State questioned why their state, with the largest ferry network in the nation, was shut out from an early round of stimulus funding while millions went to the Virgin Islands.[650] Federal officials responded by stating the urgency of the need – a point which the island government seems to have missed.

From the start, the plan to purchase the ferries was itself beset by problems. First, cost overruns for the project saw expenses soar and the final purchase price was $3.25 million each for vessels that could carry around 200 people – nearly 100 fewer than originally estimated.[651] Next, though the ferries were acquired in November 2013, nearly a year has passed without the ships being put into permanent use.

The ships were supposed to be operational by the end of 2013, but insurance problems prevented that from happening.[652] Then in January, V.I. Public Works Commissioner Darryl Smalls said the ferries should be ready to go by the end of February.[653] However, delays in scheduling Coast Guard inspections pushed back the date they would be ready. The inspections were not completed until June and the ferries were finally launched in early July.[654]

After only a month in operation, however, the ferries were once again taken out of service and docked in Cruz Bay since early August.[655] Commissioner Smalls explained in early September that legal issues with contractors were to blame and that the vessels would be back up and running "within the next few days."[656] As the photos below demonstrate, though, the ferries remained docked nearly two weeks later.

While the ships are in good working order, according to Smalls, there is no telling when they'll be reinstated.[657]

Top: Vessels docked in Cruz Bay on September 3, 2014
Bottom: Vessels remain unmoved October 10, 2014

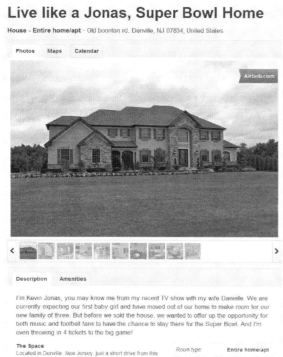

Jonas Bonus: Rich and Famous Rent Out Their Pads Tax Free

$10 million

One provision in the tax code allows the rich and famous to rent out their property for short periods of time without reporting the revenue on their tax returns. This may seem inconsequential, but the celebs that rent out their digs for thousands per day sure appreciate it.

Under IRS rules, income received for short-term rentals total less than 15 days per year is tax-free. Even a second home or a vacation property can be rented out, as long as the total stay per year is less than 15 days.[658] There is no limit on the total income that can be excluded, nor is there any prohibition against high earners.

The result is a potential bonanza for rentals around major sporting events, and about $10 million in federal revenue is lost each year to the loophole.[659]

At Super Bowl XLVIII, held in East Rutherford, New Jersey earlier this year, asking rates for studios, apartments, and houses frequently ran into thousands of dollars per night. Just a few weeks before football's greatest game of the year, the average rental close to the stadium cost $1,600 a night, though many went for much more.[660]

One three bedroom home advertised for $5,000 per night, boasting, "You won't find a more perfect location for your New York Superbowl trip than this handsomely decorated 3 bedroom home in Secaucus."[661] And these landlords won't find a better deal, making several thousand dollars tax free.

One young enterprising football fan, rented three of his bedrooms for $2,000 per night, more than enough to cover his $5,600 rent and utilities bill that month. "There's no need to stay there if we can make up a month's rent," he told a local reporter.[662]

During last year's Super Bowl, one superstar scored a touchdown renting his property, avoiding tax penalties. Kevin Jonas rented his mansion out for $20,000 per night for 12 nights (just under the limit).[663] Complete with "a walk-out basement, a billiard room, and home theater complete with stadium seating and a 3-D projector…a 6,500-bottle wine cellar and the property's in-ground saltwater pool," the rental scheme could have brought in $240,000 tax-free, adding to his estimated net worth of $18 million.[664,665]

Kevin Jonas was not the only celebrity to benefit from the IRS's generosity. An NFL player even put his two-bedroom apartment up for rent on Craigslist.[666] He was asking $9,000 for the week to supplement his $450,000 salary.[667,668]

Jonas' home was also not the only one in the $100,000-plus club either. Another home advertised for $119,500 for "Super Bowl Week Only."[669]

Major events that homeowners take advantage of are not limited just to the Super Bowl. PGA Tour tournaments, the South by Southwest music festival in Austin, Texas, and NCAA college basketball games have all been magnets for these types of tax-free loopholes.[670]

51. State Department Tweets @ Terrorists

$3 million

The State Department's Center for Strategic Counterterrorism Communications (CSCC) is responsible for crafting the official online presence of the U.S. government on social media sites like Facebook and Twitter with the mission to counter the sophisticated propaganda machines of terrorist groups around the globe. This year, a portion of the $3 million[671] taxpayers entrusted to CSCC was used to create the Think Again Turn Away Twitter account, which currently counts more than 2,000 tweets and 7,654 followers.[672]

According to the State Department, the theory behind Think Again Turn Away is that it provides a counter to the tweets of "extremists [who] were previously able to spread their bile without fear of pushback."[673] Each tweet sent out by the CSCC's Digital Outreach Team is crafted to "redirect the conversation" and put the extremists "on the defensive" to make them "aware that when they try to spread their message, they will encounter resistance."[674]

There are of course no hard metrics on the campaign's impact on jihadist recruiting numbers. As evidence the campaign is having effect—"unnerving the adversary" in the parlance of this digital battlefield—the State Department cites the more than 80,000 views of a video titled "ISIS Kills Muslims," which it says "debunked [the Islamic State of Iraq and Syria (ISIS)]'s role as self-proclaimed defender of Sunni Muslims," and the "extreme indignation" of "affiliated media units and avowed supporters of the group" who are targeted by the campaign.[675]

The campaign falls short on even these rather squishy objectives. Dubbed "trolling for terrorists," critics have questioned the utility of such a campaign that is "less set on converting would-be terrorists than simply preventing these accounts from running uninterrupted and unchallenged feeds."[676] A recent commentator in Time Magazine put it more bluntly, saying, "this outreach by the U.S. government is not only ineffective, but also provides jihadists with a stage to voice their arguments..."[677]

It's hard to disagree with the characterization of Think Again Turn Away as a "gaffe machine."[678] Despite the State Department's efforts to put lipstick on the program, its latest video cited called "Welcome to ISIS Land" was widely panned as a taxpayer funded ISIS recruitment video. And it's unclear how some of the tweets are actually countering the ISIS propaganda. This mildly worded tweet and its accompanying picture of an ISIS victory parade in Syria could be mistaken for blatant ISIS propaganda if tweeted under another hashtag:

Other tweets read more like bad one-liners than witty quips dispelling ISIS ideology, such as this zinger referencing the Syrian refugee crisis:

And though someone probably scored points with the boss, radicalized 18-25 year olds are unlikely to be swayed by this tweet of Secretary Kerry's monotone plea about ISIS's treatment of women during a recent Congressional hearing:

Rita Katz, the author of the Time Magazine article, who has made a career out of studying terrorists, offered that "had the people behind Think Again Turn Away understood jihadists' mindsets and reasons for their behavior, they would have known that their project of counter messaging would not only be a waste of taxpayer money, but ultimately be counterproductive."[679]

Even those who hope Think Again Turn Away could one day be the tweeting near peer to ISIS acknowledge social media's limitations as an effective tool in the war of ideas we find ourselves in today. "The government may one day become brilliant at hashtag diplomacy, capable of beating IS[IS] to the punch. But that would seem unlikely given the structural advantages the medium gives to sensationalism and attack on established positions."[680]

The extremist message that resonates with a would-be ISIS jihadist is born of the want and disaffection that comes from the lack of better opportunities. What the State Department fails to realize with its taxpayer-funded social media experiment is that efforts like this will always fail because they attempt to address the war of ideas at its downstream effect as opposed to its root cause. Instead of sending one more State Department tweet, we should reinvest these funds in activities that improve basic education and develop the free market in places that remain disconnected from the global economy. We can yield better results for our scarce taxpayer dollars than extreme indignation.

Border Patrol Builds Over-Priced Houses for Temporary Workers

$4.6 million

Quartz countertops, plantation shutters, spacious open kitchens, three bedrooms and the latest in stainless steel appliances. No, that's not a real estate ad from the nice part of town, but a description of ritzy housing units for Border Patrol agents in Ajo, Arizona.

The homes were purchased by Customs and Border Patrol (CBP) for agents reporting temporarily to Ajo, where few border agents live. However, a report by the Department of Homeland Security's (DHS) inspector general found the agency "vastly overpaid" for homes and built them far bigger than they should have.[681]

Customs and Border Patrol (CBP) – a component of DHS – devised a plan in 2008 to acquire housing units in several remote areas along the southwest border, and paid the General Services Administration $1.4 million to manage the project.[682] The project was badly mismanaged, though, leading to the inspector general accusing CBP of wasting $4.6 million.

To start, the agency paid "nearly $1 million for 12 acres of land," but the inspector general determined the price was "almost triple the amount it may have actually needed to pay" based on the local market.[683]

Next, CBP designed and built housing that exceeded employee needs. A 2009 CBP study to determine the housing needs for border agents stationed in Ajo found they would best be served by one-bedroom apartment-style housing for use during the workweek.[684] Rather than build apartments, however, CBP built 21 two- and three-bedroom single family homes.[685]

These were no average homes, though, but instead cost nearly $700,000 apiece – or nearly six times the going rate for home in Ajo, Arizona.[686] In the same year the homes were built, the average cost of housing in Ajo was $86,500.[687]

"You could buy any house in town for $100,000," said Tina West, a member of the Western Pima County Community Council, "It's just another multimillion-dollar waste."[688]

In part, prices were driven up because they equipped each house with expensive upgrades, such as quartz countertops, stainless steel appliances, free-standing additional freezers, wireless ceiling fans, plantation shutters, and walk-in pantries.[689] The new homes range from 1,276 to 1,570 square feet.

According to the DHS Office of Inspector General, since the completion of the Ajo project, the houses have not been fully occupied, citing the rental rates as the likely cause. The price to rent the two- and three-bedroom houses ranged from $1,075 to $1,314 for a single tenant.

The agency installed expensive wireless fans to avoid having to replace the pull strings on standard ceiling fans.[690] When asked why they spent so much money on these things, CBP said "if they spent more up front, they would save money in the end."[691]

CBP added attached garages large enough to accommodate three cars, measuring 748 square feet, citing most agents and officers assigned Ajo stations have two cars.[692]

CBP also paid more than $2.4 million to buy 20 park-model trailer homes and lease land on which to park them to satisfy the same purpose as the single family homes. Between October 2013 and March 2014, 18 of the 20 mobile homes were vacant.

CBP has built half of a complex in Ajo, Arizona and intends to build the same type of housing in five other locations once funding becomes available.

NASA Goes to Comic-Con, Explores the Marvel Universe

At least $10,000

With its manned space program grounded, NASA boldly voyaged to an extraterrestrial world of another kind this year— the Marvel Universe.

With appearances at Comic-Con International in San Diego, California and a Marvel Comic's exhibit in New York's Time Square, NASA launched missions into the worlds of science fiction and comic book superheroes.

Marvel's Avengers S.T.A.T.I.O.N. (Scientific Training and Tactical Intelligence Operative Network) at the Discovery Center in Times Square brings "to life the science behind Marvel Super Heroes" and explores "the history and scientific origins of Marvel's The Avengers, including Iron Man, The Hulk, Captain America, Thor, and others."[693] The exhibit opened May 30, 2014 and will run through January 5, 2015. Tickets prices are $27 for adults and $19.50 for children.[694]

Avengers S.T.A.T.I.O.N. includes "authentic props from the Marvel movies — including Thor's hammer, Captain America's star-spangled shield and Black Widow's form-fitting costume," as well as "a life-sized, three-dimensional hologram of the Hulk, who punches the wall making the whole building shake."[695] And "visitors will map out the stars to find Asgard," Thor's fictional world.[696]

NASA provided content to "enhance the authenticity of the experience and pique visitors' interest in real-world science and technology. The exhibit's NASA-supplied material -- written content, images and videos -- focuses on topics such as the electromagnetic spectrum, black holes as powerful energy sources, and aerospace materials used in creating Iron Man's armor. Deeper connections to NASA content are planned for the exhibit's online companion website. NASA's Eyes on Exoplanets interactive is featured prominently in the S.T.A.T.I.O.N. exhibit, helping to place otherworldly content related to The Avengers' Thor into the context of real exoplanets – planets beyond our solar system -- that NASA is studying."[697]

"The thrill of exploring other worlds is not limited to the silver screen, and we're pleased to help bring some real NASA excitement to the project," said NASA's liaison for film and TV collaborations.[698]

This is not NASA's first voyage into the Marvel

The Associate Administrator for the Science Mission Directorate at NASA Headquarters explores the Marvel Universe at the Opening Night of the Avengers S.T.A.T.I.O.N. Exhibition in New York City's Times Square on May 29, 2014.[713]

universe. NASA also helped out with the 2012 Avengers movie,[699] which raised over $2 billion in ticket and home movie sales.[700] By comparison, the total budget for NASA's Mars Mission in 2014 added up to $3.1 billion.

So why is NASA participating in the promotion of a movie that brought in enough revenue to rival the annual budget of its premier manned space mission of the future?

"The thrill of exploring other worlds is not limited to the silver screen, and we're pleased to help bring some real NASA excitement to the project," explained Bert Ulrich, liaison for film and TV collaborations at NASA Headquarters in Washington, D.C.[701]

Another reason may be because NASA was one of the agencies that fared well in the budget deal approved by Congress this year. Sequestration was set to trim the agency's budget from $16.9 billion to "as little as $16 billion," but instead NASA got a boost to $17.65 billion.[702]

The extra money in the budget may also explain why NASA—which a year ago was warning "its goals of future space travel may be put on hold" by budget concerns[703]—sent a manned mission to Comic-Con, which is an annual comic book convention "dedicated to creating awareness of, and appreciation for, comics and related popular artforms," and celebrating "the historic and ongoing contribution of comics to art and culture."[704]

While Comic-Con typically features comic book artists, illustrators, writers, and authors, this year the convention hosted NASA scientists and astronauts. The panel entitled "NASA's Next Giant Leap," was moderated by actor Seth Green, and included legendary astronaut Buzz Aldrin, NASA Planetary Science Division Director Jim Green, NASA astronaut Mike Fincke, and Jet Propulsion Laboratory systems engineer Bobak Ferdowsi.[705] The group discussed the Orion spacecraft and the Space Launch System rocket, which the agency hopes will return Americans to space sometime in the next decade.[706]

While this "marks the first time that NASA has officially participated in Comic-Con,"[707] the space agency has been star struck with pop culture for some time. "NASA also takes an active role in generating science-based fiction. They frequently partner with entertainment producers to help bring authenticity and accuracy to movies and television."[708]

NASA points to comic books readers' lack of exposure to reality to justify its attendance at Comic Con. "Participation in these types of events not only reaches audiences who are not normally exposed to the realities of America's space exploration initiatives but directly meets the mandate outlined in the National Aeronautics and Space Act of 1958 (P.L. 85-568) to "...provide for the widest practicable and appropriate dissemination of information concerning its activities and the results thereof," according to a NASA official.[709]

"To support this event, six NASA employees and three NASA contractor employees were in attendance and the total travel expenses for the nine participants amounted to $9,554. All NASA employees were participating at the conference on official business within a public outreach capacity similar to NASA's public outreach participation at school and museum events," according to NASA.[710]

NASA issued guidance earlier in the year to contractors that attendance at domestic conferences for "the remainder of FY 14 (through 9/30/2014)" was limited to meetings "essential and/or necessary" and "there are no alternative methods of participating."[711] Clearly, NASA did not apply these standards to its own staff and probably won't be next year either. Jim Green said "We'd love to come back" to Comic Con.[712]

Perhaps, NASA should be more focused on returning astronauts to exploration in the real universe rather than the imaginary worlds of the Marvel Universe and Comic Con.

54. Army Corps Buildings in Afghanistan Keep Burning to the Ground

$21.3 million

The Army Corps of Engineers spent millions of dollars on fire-prone buildings caused by shoddy contractors, despite government watchdogs reports showing that these projects were dangerous and not in compliance with international building standards.

In 2012, the Special Inspector General for Afghanistan Reconstruction (SIGAR), uncovered that three buildings constructed by the Army Corps for the Afghans caught fire.[714] The Army Corps found that two of the fires resulted in a total of $788,000 in damages, and were caused by foam installation and thermal barrier systems installed by contractors that did not comply with International Building Code standards.[715]

There were 1002 buildings in various stages of construction in Afghanistan in 2013, with 704 in various stages using the fire hazard-causing foam and thermal barriers, and 298 that had nothing.[716] Instead of fixing the fire risk problem, the Army Corps decided that to have its contractors keep using the hazardous materials that had already been approved, and advised the local personnel to only put up fire safety cards, and implement a "fire-watch during rest hours."[717]

Despite assuring government watchdogs that the problem was fixed, Army Corps officials decided to continue turning hazardous buildings over to Afghan interests.[719] According to a senior Army Corps official, turning the buildings over was fine because, "the typical occupant populations for these facilities are young, fit Afghan soldiers and recruits who have the physical ability to make a hasty retreat during a developing situation."[720] In other words, although they might be tired after a long day fighting, Afghan soldiers are fit enough to escape the burning buildings we provided them. [721]

This was also not the first time the Army Corps was cited for overseeing the construction of major fire hazards: in 2013, the same problem was found in a school in Afghanistan paid for by the Army Corps that was found to expose students and teachers to potential electrocution, fire hazards, and poisoning from a well placed too close to the sewer system.[722]

Although only $21.3 million was added to contracts for these facilities during 2014, SIGAR noted the total cost of the program, which was started in 2010, at $1.57 billion.[723]

Flame retardent fills warehouse[718]

Army Corps building burns in Afghanistan

Airport Tree-Trimming Project Turns into 27-Hole Golf Course Renovation

$5 million

With a serendipitous change of heart from the Federal Aviation Administration (FAA), a city golf course was able to turn a slight fencing realignment at an adjacent airport into a $5 million renovation of a 27-hole course – compliments of the American taxpayers.

In December 2010, Sioux Falls Regional Airport Authority determined that the Sioux Falls Regional Airport needed to remove objects from the Runway Safety Area (RSA) and the Object Free Area (OFA) in order to comply with FAA safety regulations. This project included relocating the perimeter road and fencing that abuts the adjacent Elmwood Golf Course about 150-250 feet, impacting the two golf holes nearest to the airport. Due to the location of the new fence line, one hole would have to be straightened, "reducing its 'dogleg' characteristic."[724] Another hole would have to relocate the tee boxes, shortening it from a par-five to a par-four. With the fortunate reversal of an FAA decision and some persuading by a golf course architect, these modest impacts of two golf holes would eventually transform into a full scale 27-hole renovation.

In 2011, a golf course architect hired by the city to examine the impact the fence realignment would have on the golf course issued an analysis that justified the need to realign several more holes and relocate the 6-hole junior golf course to another area at a cost estimate of between $900 thousand and $1.73 million.[725] According to the architect's analysis, the additional taxpayer funded course modifications were needed to prevent the course from changing from a par 72 to a par 71 and to increase the landing area of one hole because "most people are right handed and tend to slice the ball (to the right)."[726] Because Elmwood Golf Club is a city-owned course, it is protected under Section 4(f) of the Department of Transportation Act of 1966, and up to 90 percent of the costs to the golf course related to the airport safety project are reimbursable by the FAA.[727]

Perhaps recognizing the lucrative 4(f) reimbursement provision, the city conducted a survey in 2011 to identify trees on the Elmwood Golf Course that could be intruding into the airport's airspace in violation of federal regulations. In September 2012, the city submitted the tree survey to FAA for an Obstruction Evaluation/Airport Airspace analysis. The FAA circulated its findings for public comment on November 28th and, after receiving no comments, issued a "Determination of No Hazard to Air Navigation" notice on January 18th, 2013.[728] According to the analysis of 135 trees on the Elmwood Golf Course, FAA only identified two trees that they recommended be removed or topped, but stated that a notice to airmen and safety lights would suffice. The FAA analysis concluded that "the existing tree line would not have a substantial adverse effect on the safe and efficient utilization of the navigable airspace by aircraft or on any air navigation facility and would not be a hazard to air navigation."[729]

On January 31st, 2013, not even two weeks after the FAA's "Determination of No Hazard to Air Navigation" report was released, the FAA issued a one-page Letter of Correction stating that multiple trees penetrate the runway's airspace, and that a plan to mitigate the penetrations should be submitted by August, 2013.[730] This reversal of the FAA's original decision, based on a single one-day inspection, would have tremendous ramifications on the golf course's renovation plans – and the cost implications to the American taxpayers backing the golf course overhaul.

On February 21st, 2013, only three weeks after the reversal, the golf course architect that the city hired in 2011 released a new, comprehensive $5 million proposal to renovate the entire 27 hole golf course along with constructing a new 6 hole junior course. The justification for the change from the original $900,000 renovation to a full scale, three year renovation project was due to the fact that "the results of the tree survey in 2011 far exceeded what anyone had anticipated."[731] The tree line that the FAA determined was not a safety hazard but was quickly overturned not even two weeks later was the basis for a $5 million taxpayer backed full scale course makeover. These suspiciously short timelines suggest the renovation plans may have already been completed under the assumption that the trees would need to be removed.

Even with the questionable set of events that led to the need for the trees to be re-

Workers build a new sand bunker to ensure safety of air space[734]

moved to meet FAA safety standards, only 14 of the 27 regulation holes needed to be redesigned due the impacts of the tree removal and fence adjustment. However, the golf course architect's proposal argued that the remaining 13 golf holes should be renovated to provide the golf course with consistent playing conditions and character.

[T]he required reconstruction of such a large percentage of holes raises concern about the resulting mix of new and old holes. Visually, the individual holes will appear different because of the loss of trees. More importantly, the new holes will play differently as a result of different turf conditions, drainage conditions, irrigation coverage, soil compaction and soil mixes. Most obvious to the golfer will be the difference in the way which the golf ball will react on the greens.[732]

Thus, what began as a two hole change transformed into a 27 hole project. The three year golf course renovation is taking place in three phases of nine holes each, so that at least 18 holes will be playable during the entire project. The first phase was recently completed and the golf course is expected to complete phase two of the project next summer. The president of Dakota Golf Management lauded the benefit the taxpayer funded renovation will have on the course, stating "golf courses, you know, they have life spans and this is going to regenerate and rejuvenate Elmwood well into the future."[733]

In a possibly incriminating admission of how this project came to fruition, the President of Dakota Golf Management, Inc. said that "obviously we wouldn't be doing it if we didn't think it's going to be a significant improvement."[735] Perhaps, the driving force behind the renovation and the opportune FAA reversal was not about air safety after all.

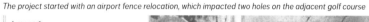
The project started with an airport fence relocation, which impacted two holes on the adjacent golf course

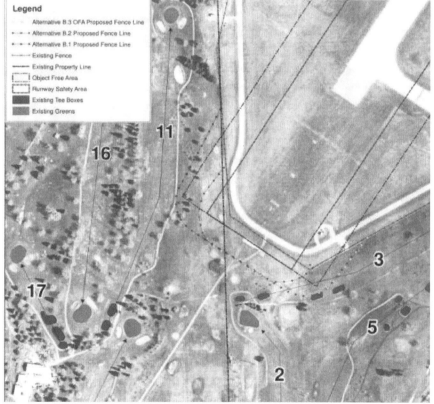

Suspicious Timing

- **September 2012:**
  City submits tree study for Obstruction Evaluation/ Airport Airspace analysis

- **January 18th, 2013:**
  FAA issues "Determination of No Hazard to Air Navigation" for Elmwood tree study

- **January 31st, 2013:**
  FAA reverses the decision with one-page Letter of Correction

- **February 21st, 2013:**
  Golf Course architect releases $5 million full course renovation proposal using required tree removal as key

Earmark-Funded High-Speed Ferry Sinks Alaska Community

$12.3 million

An "experimental" high speed federal-funded ferry, which was supposed to turn a "2 ½ hour drive into a 15-minute trip"[736] has turned into a titanic sinkhole for taxpayers and one Alaskan community.

The Mat-Su borough, where Port MacKenzie and the ferry is currently located, inherited the $78 million ferry when the community pledged "to use it for ferry runs between Anchorage and Port MacKenzie."[737]

The ferry has "been lauded for its sleek look and powerful capabilities, but criticized as less-than-desirable for transporting Alaskans."[738]

"It's a unique boat and its one-of-a-kind," said one local Mat-Su official, "but when you're putting it (into) operation that's where we're getting the biggest concern: It's so unique; how do we make it work?"[739] That concern became a reality when the project was mothballed when "work on an Anchorage landing (for the ferry) fizzled."[740]

In August, the federal government had asked the borough to pay back $12.3 million that has been spent to get the ferry line operational. In total, the Federal Transportation Administration had allocated $21.2 million for this purpose.[741] Monthly costs have been in the "several hundred thousand per month," which includes dock fees, insurance and general upkeep. Money owed to the federal government also includes $3.6 million used to build a ferry terminal in Port MacKenzie.[742]

The ferry has become so much trouble that Mat-Su officials sent a letter last year to the national Passenger Vessel Association attempting to offload the controversial ferry to another government entity "free of charge."[743]

The borough has also tried to sell it privately. Over the years there has been many prospective buyers for the ferry. Most recently the Philippine Navy has been most interested.[744]

The actual ferry project was funded by at least $70 million in federal earmarks between 2002-2007. At the time, the Office of Naval Research has stated that it never requested the funds.[745] $12 million in federal transportation funds were used "for extra design work and outfitting to make the twin-hulled military craft into a ferry."[746]

The final cost to taxpayers is significantly more expensive than the initial cost estimates of the ferry of about $30 million.[747]

Some local officials have raised the concern that what was promised for a passenger ferry was never delivered. Steve Colligan, a local Mat-Su Borough assembly member stated "what was envisioned…is not what was delivered to us. It was a research project we could have benefited from. But when the Navy delivered a vessel half the size and half the capacity, there's not much we can do with that."[748]

The Selling of an Airport to Nowhere

$1.2 million+

An airfield in upper New York state that sees more deer than planes is for sale.[749] But, despite paying for the land, runaway and other amenities, federal taxpayers are not likely to recoup any of these costs when the property is sold.

Between 2004-2009, the Syracuse Suburban Airport received five grants from the Federal Aviation Administration (FAA) totaling $2,973,621 "to be used for planning and development" at the proposed airport.[750] The purpose of the spending was to provide the region a reliever airport, but was found to have, "little, if any, measurable economic benefit to air traffic this area serves and could potentially cause economic damage to other local airports."[751]

In fact, when first proposed, there was concern that the proposed airport would duplicate services of other regional airports. Hancock International Airport is just 11 miles away and running well under capacity.[752]

Now the airport is an overgrown field that was abandoned several years ago when, "the owner got into a dispute with the town," partly because the nearby communities "did not want a large airport."[753]

David Pizio, one of the former owners of the airport, is awaiting federal sentencing for bank fraud related to the misuse of $2.9 million in federal grant funds. Pizio is scheduled to be sentenced in December 2014, and could face up to the "statutory maximum of 30 years."[754] Before securing millions in federal aviation funding, Pizio's previous experience was as a manager of a local comedy club.[755]

Local officials have been authorized by the county to attempt to auction off the properties to collect property taxes connected to the airport.[756]

Thus far the FAA has not place a lien on the property, so the local county will be the only benefit from the revenue of the sale, while the federal government loses millions to this ill-conceived project.

58. NASA Study Predicts the Collapse of Human Civilization
$30,000

When the results of a provocative scientific research paper study hit the newsstands this past spring, a media firestorm erupted over a mathematician's claim that human civilization may be on the verge of collapse. The study, officially titled "Human and Nature Dynamics (HANDY): Modeling Inequality and Use of Resources in the Collapse or Sustainability of Societies," (hereinafter referred to as "the HANDY study") was authored by University of Maryland researchers Safa Motesharrei and Eugenia Kalnay and University of Minnesota contributor Jorge Rivas. [757]

The paper posits the collapse of a modern and advanced civilization – such as our own – may be more prevalent that one might think. Specifically, it contends that historical data reveals the interchange of two social factors – the exploitation of resources and the unequal distribution of wealth – have often led to civilizational collapse. [758] As these factors become more prominent in present day society, a global collapse of the world as we know it "is not inevitable," according to the study. [759]

A grant from NASA financed the questionable study, fueling many to express reservations regarding how NASA distributes its taxpayer-funded grant money. The study was funded in-part by a five-year cooperative agreement between NASA's Goddard Space Flight Center and the University of Maryland Earth System Science Interdisciplinary Center (EESIC). [760] The study examined "the impacts of Earth's connected systems on global and regional environment, weather and climate . . . after a thorough technical review and determination of the high scientific merit of the areas of research proposed." [761]

According to the NASA procurement database, the total five-year budget estimate for the grant is $36,334,811. [762] This money will be available to approved individual research projects through 2017. [763] This amount was allocated to numerous research projects and studies, so it is unclear exactly how much of the money was used to fund the HANDY study. However, in a summary of the cooperative grant agreement, NASA said the money used to fund the HANDY study was "less than $30K." [764]

The controversy that ensued should not have been surprising, given the audacity of the claim the researchers were making. Warnings of global collapse are often seen as far-flung; thus, it is interesting NASA was involved in funding such a radical study.

The debate following the study's release was heated enough that NASA felt the need to issue a public statement in an attempt to distance the federal agency from it. [765] NASA stated the paper suggesting that social inequality and unsustainability could prompt the downfall of modern human civilization "was not solicited, directed or reviewed by NASA. It is an independent study by the university researchers utilizing research tools developed for a separate NASA activity. As is the case with all independent research, the views and conclusions in the paper are those of the authors alone. NASA does not endorse the paper or its conclusions." [766]

Although NASA distanced itself from the paper's findings, the scientific space agency must do more to ensure its grant programs that are based in science fact instead of science fiction. Given that the HANDY study was labeled a "thought experiment" with admittedly "largely theoretical" contentions, NASA's money could have likely been better spent elsewhere—or not spent at all. [767]

59. Facebook for Fossil Enthusiasts
$1.97 million

They may as well call it Fossil Facebook. A team of University of Florida (UF) researchers this year won a $1.97 million grant from the National Science Foundation (NSF) to create a new communication network for fossil enthusiasts and professionals. [768]

Fossil clubs exist nationwide but are stuck in the Stone Age in how they interact with one another, according to the grantees. They typically "function independently and do not communicate with each other or professionals as most science-hobbyist groups do." [769] The project goal is to create a "web-based education community that connects people with a shared interested in paleontology" where users will be able to input data and request information from one other. [770]

Ironically, the grantees have been using Facebook to get the word out about their new project. [771] As of September 2014, the page had 655 likes. [772] Competition for followers on social media may be as fierce as dinosaurs. Similar clubs have already staked their claims on Facebook, including "Fossils: A forum to share your experiences of all things fossil" [773] and the "Fossil Forum," which credits itself as the "largest and fastest growing online community on the topic of paleontology with over 400,000 posted messages and 11,000 registered members." [774]

The data collection efforts may also duplicate those already underway with NSF funding, such as the Paleobiology Database for collecting fossil data. That project received a $693,931 grant in 2010. [775]

Gamers Tune In to Radio Show About Video Game Music

$47,000

The challenge for video games today is "manufacturers want to avoid repetitive music" [776] like the "various bloops, bleeps, and simplistic-yet-catchy background music"[777] in titles like Frogger and Donkey Kong. One federally funded podcast wants to take listeners beyond these computer beeps of yesteryear's video games.

"Top Score" is a podcast on Minnesota Public Radio that "brings music nerds and gamer nerds together," according to one fan.[778] In each show, the host is featured interviewing "composers about their experiences writing for video games." [779] The mission statement is simple: "Spreading the love for game music, one episode at a time."[780] Featured game soundtracks have included those from blockbuster first-person shooters like Assassin's Creed and Call of Duty: Black Ops as well as those known by tamer crowds playing Angry Birds and Rayman.

This year, the podcast received $47,000 in federal funding from the National Endowment for the Arts.[781] Episodes generally run about 4 minutes, and the show has produced about four hours of content so far this year.[782]

Two Dozen Teachers Travel to Germany for Classes on Bach, Baroque Dancing Lessons

$180,000

Lance Eagen, art teacher at Churchill High School in Oregon, speaks for many teachers who see music education as always the first to go when budgets are tight. "Art always, always falls afterwards," he complained after learning of new cuts at his school, "It's always scheduled after 'the real classes' are scheduled."[783]

He might be surprised to learn, then, that there was enough federal money lying around to send 25 teachers on an all-expense paid trip to Germany for several weeks over the summer to tour Europe and learn about Johann Sebastian Bach.

It was made possible by an $180,000 grant from the National Endowment for the Humanities to Moravian College in Pennsylvania, which held a four-week workshop in Germany called "Johann Sebastian Bach: Music of the Baroque and Enlightenment."[784] Teachers from around the U.S. were selected to participate, which involved traveling to cities where Bach was born and worked, including Eisenach, Liepzig and Potsdam.[785] The entire course lasted from July 6 through August 1, and each participant received a $3,300 stipend to help cover their living expenses, in addition to free airfare and housing.

The 2014 trip was the fifth time the National Endowment for the Humanities funded Moravian College to host the program.[786]

Once in Germany, most days featured morning lectures from Bach historians, but the teachers also enjoyed Baroque dancing lessons, which Moravian College claimed were absolutely "essential to understanding much of Bach's music."[787]

While its purpose was to prepare K-12 teachers to incorporate Bach into their classroom curriculums, the teachers were also able to do their fair share of sightseeing.[788]

One teacher recorded the group's adventures throughout Europe in an online diary, noting stops in Berlin, Munich, Paris, Prague, Warsaw and Krakow.[789] And because the trip overlapped with the World Cup, the group was eager the join the locals in watching as many games as they could. During Germany's match against Brazil, the teacher narrated, "We finally found [a bar] that was great – big screen, lots of Germans who loved to shout, and beer (well actually, the beer was not hard to find ...)."[790]

The group was sure to join the locals once more for the World Cup Final, which the teacher remarked, "integrates Germany's two favorite sports: Soccer and Public Drinking. (The latter is rapidly followed by public urination, but I won't elaborate)."[791]

"It is just great for them. It's rejuvenating for them," said Moravian's music department chair and head of the Bach workshop, "They get together with other teachers and it is great for their professional development."[792]

Teachers enjoy a little downtime between lessons on Bach.

62. Funding to Reduce Road Crashes Used to Restore Non-Working Lighthouse – $160,000

In 2012, there were more than 33,500 fatalities resulting from crashes on U.S. roadways, according to the U.S. Department of Transportation, representing the first increase after a six-year decline. Federal transportation officials, however, used a portion of the money set aside to reduce crashes instead to restore a lighthouse that stopped working over 130 years ago.

Cape Henry Lighthouse was awarded a $160,000 grant from the U.S. Department of Transportation under its Moving Ahead for Progress in the 21st Century (MAP-21) program. Far from being intended to restore old lighthouses, though, the program is intended to "reduce crashes, injuries and fatalities involving large trucks and buses," according to the department.[793]

Located at the entrance of the Chesapeake Bay in Virginia Beach, Virginia, it was the first lighthouse funded by Congress in 1789, and it is said George Washington himself helped select its first keeper. The lighthouse operated for nearly 90 years until it was deemed unsafe and a replacement was built 350 feet away. The original was left standing, and today the two lighthouses remain.

Cape Henry Lighthouse today is privately owned and operated by Preservation Virginia, a non-profit organization that focuses on historical preservation.

The 2014 grant, however, was the third given to the lighthouse restoration project. In total, taxpayers have contributed $515,000 in federal transportation funding to restore the Cape Henry Lighthouse since 2002.[794]

Costs for the project have increased steadily through the years, however. Early estimates expected the restoration to cost $200,000, and would be shared by public and private sources. A second grant was given in 2011, and at that time the total project cost was $444,000. Today, it is estimated that the total cost of restoring the lighthouse will be $644,000.

According to the Virginia Department of Motor Vehicles, however, there were more vehicle crashes in 2013 than in the three years prior. During that period from 2010 to 2013, vehicle re-

63. "Gateway to Blues" Museum Funded Over Deteriorating Bridges – $200,000

The Mississippi Department of Transportation (MDOT) received grant money to help build a "Gateway to the Blues" Museum expected to open late this year.[794] The museum is expected to be a "must-see" attraction and will showcase the role the town in which the museum sits played in developing the genre.[795]

It is not entirely clear what will be exhibited in the museum. Although reported back in 2011 that the museum will house the collection from a nearby casino,[796] the current description of what will be displayed is vague. All we know is that the museum "will tell the remarkable story of how The Blues was born" and there no longer is any reference to what collection will be displayed.[797]

In a time when the aging infrastructure is a looming national concern,[798] the Department of Transportation (DOT) chose to allocate money to build a museum rather than repair roads and bridges. Mississippi, in fact, is among the largest in the nation for having a substantial percentage of bridges deemed "structurally deficient." There are 2,274 such state-operated bridges.[799] Perhaps Mississippi believes the decrepit state of the roads will add to the charm of getting to museum to be built alongside the pictured visitor center.

Study Shows How Buddhism Explains the Science of Meditation

$533,376

Not happy with its current budget, the director of the National Institute of Health (NIH) has lamented that a grant application for biomedical research now has less than a one in six change of being successful."[800] The director argued that the NIH's declining budget "has the potential to inflict profound, long-term damage to U.S. scientific momentum and morale."[801] But while the NIH was blaming Congress for low morale among U.S. scientists, it was overlooking the fact that the NIH chose to deny these scientists funding in lieu of grants for studies lacking in scientific basis.

Despite concerns about the availability of federal funding to study cures to the major diseases of the 21st Century, NIH shelled out a total of $533,376[802], to investigate the effects of meditation not from scientific analysis, but from reading Buddhist texts.[803] [804] Undermining the NIH's demands for more funding, both of these studies, published in January 2014, have concluded that Buddhist literature, not science, is key to understanding meditation experiences.[805] [806] Taxpayers spent over half a million dollars incorporating Buddhist literature to "scientifically" analyze if meditation causes sleepiness or wakefulness[807], as well as to explain if and why some people see lights while meditating.[808]

For the U.S. taxpayers who funded this research, as well as the five out of six rejected scientists seeking NIH funding, this unenlightened spending on non-scientific research definitely does not provide a moment of Zen.

"Get Fruved:" Social Media Campaign Featuring Students Dressed as Fruits and Vegetables

$5 million

At the University of Tennessee, students are dressing in their favorite fruit and vegetable costumes as they peruse campus, telling peers and others in earshot to "fruve themselves." This is not Halloween, but a federal funded campaign to promote healthy eating choices campaign.[809]

Students created the term "fruved" to describe "the process of eating **FRU**its and **VE**getables."[810] The campaign is to be developed by a collaboration of college students from different states to "lead a creative, exciting, and interactive social marketing campaign."[811] The students are divided into five teams – amusingly labeled Spinach, Carrot, Banana, Grapes, and Tomato – which are led by costumed mascots.[812]

Instilling healthy habits in our nation's children is important. The government's decision to take the initiative to promote sustainable lifestyles by eating well, exercising, and managing stress is commendable.

However, spending close to $5 million dollars to a program without any clear guidelines and one where tangible results are not the best way to achieve these goals. Negative public sentiments towards the "Get Fruved" campaign are not surprising – in a time of higher insurance premiums, pay freezes and cuts, and other government spending reductions, many are not happy taxpayer money is being spent to craft a campaign that "creepy" fruit and vegetable costumes for college students.[813] [814]

Further, the Fruved.com website, which is supposed to be the initiative's main platform, is largely undeveloped. Other than a background of the project, none of the fruit and vegetable teams have tweeted or posted any updates on social media.

Other than some kids running around dressed up like bananas, it remains a mystery how they are spending taxpayer dollars.

66. USDA Holds Contest to Build Wooden Skyscraper

$2 million

The Big Bad Wolf can huff and puff all he wants, but he'll never blow this wooden building down. So hopes the U.S. Department of Agriculture (USDA), which is sponsoring a contest to design wooden skyscrapers – known as "plyscrapers" – in an effort to boost the timber industry.

The administration will spend $2 million on a campaign to convince architects, engineers and developers that building high-rises with wood can be just as effective as steel.[815]

The first million will go to WoodWorks, a non-profit funded by the lumber industry, while the second million will fund a contest "to demonstrate the architectural and commercial viability of using sustainable wood products in high-rise construction."[816]

While the USDA hopes spending millions will spur economic growth here at home, it may unintentionally be stimulating the European economy. With the exception of SmartLam, a manufacturer of cross-laminated timber in Montana,[817] "there are no U.S. manufacturers of this type of super-strong timber, so it would have to be imported from Europe," notes one architectural publication.[818]

But as the one and only U.S. manufacturer that stands to benefit from this taxpayer subsidy for timber, SmartLam came out strong to support the new $2 million timber investment. Casey Mahlmquist, the company's general manager, participated in a White House-sponsored event where he declared, "the future is wood and the future is good."[819] Moreover, it might be a long time before high-rise wood construction projects become a staple of American construction. Local ordinances and city codes restrict construction of wooden structures to no more than five or six stories, dampening opportunities for business.[820]

Perhaps the stiffest resistance to using wood for constructing high-rise buildings comes from the engineers and developers within the industry. However, supporters are hoping that taxpayer funding for the industry will help move the dial.

"Architects and engineers can start out as skeptics," said Pete McCrone of Innovative Timber Solutions, another would-be manufacturer, adding, "In a very short space of time they get it, because it's simple — its large panels held together with large screws."[821]

67. Social Security IT Project Wastes Hundreds of Millions

$288 million

The Social Security Administration's (SSA) project to update their system for tracking disability claims is "two years from completion."[822] That's what SSA said 6 years ago in 2008.[823] What is their update on the project?

SSA's current plan in 2014 to update their system is still two to two-and-a-half years away from completion, and that's after spending almost $300 million.[824]

The program was supposed to streamline and track various disability claims while simultaneously lowering administrative costs and enhancing quality.[825] Instead, it is adding to the nation's ever increasing debt and plaguing the already strained disability program, set to run out of money in 2016.

An analysis revealed that nearly $300 million has been wasted on this project that is permanently being tested to no avail. Each year "for the past five years, Release 1.0 is consistently projected to be 24-32 months away."[826] Thus far, DCPS has produced "limited functionality, and faced schedule delays as well as increasing stakeholder concerns."[827] The project has made no progress and is costing more and more each year to "fix."

According to the House Oversight and Government Reform Committee, the stagnation may be attributed to a failure of leadership.[828] There is no single person in charge of the completion of the project and the resulting "IT Boondoggle" has cost taxpayers $288 million over six years and delivered nothing.[829] SSA officials have decided to "reset" the project in order to complete the initiative, but without clear direction from a single leader responsible for overseeing the project it will remain "adrift, [with] the scope of the project ambiguous."[830]

Today, the project is still being tested and cannot process any new claims or track existing ones.[831] It is sure to cost the federal government more in the future to fix the current system or develop a new one. Every dollar thrown away on this project is a dollar that could have been spent on developing a new system or at least fixing the present one.[832]

"Agency officials routinely testify that the agency needs more funding from Congress," after already wasting $288 million and five years' time developing a system that doesn't work and even by their own estimates is not projected to work for at least another two to three years.[833]

Feds Waste Millions Trying to Convince Afghans to Grow Soybeans They Won't Eat

$34 million

Afghans don't like soybeans or soy-based products. What's more, the crop's growing cycle and water needs make it a poor choice for their country, as a British report concluded in 2008.

None of that stopped the U.S. Department of Agriculture in 2009 from committing to a years-long effort to encourage Afghans to cultivate, process and consume the crop. USDA staff who made the decision reportedly weren't even aware of the research, and they did no feasibility study of their own before green-lighting the soy project.[834]

Five years and $34 million later, the project was singled out as a flop by the Special Inspector General for Afghan Reconstruction (SIGAR), John Sopko. "I'm concerned about the viability of the project and the apparent lack of analysis and planning performed prior to the project's initiation," Sopko wrote USDA Secretary Tom Vilsack in June.[835]

Experts in Afghanistan told Sopko there was no "significant demand for soybean products" there, despite five years of USDA efforts. Soy crops planted by farmers under USDA direction and funding failed, and Afghan consumers shunned products made with soy flour produced through the USDA program.[836]

"What is troubling about this particular project is that it appears that many of these problems could have been foreseen and, therefore, possibly avoided," Sopko wrote.[837]

There were other problems too. Security concerns – including farmers who sometimes "responded with guns in hand" when project staff tried to verify seeds had been received and planted – hampered the U.S. soy effort.[838]

Corporate Welfare for Mega Farmers

$8,536,052

While taxpayers were voicing concern about corporate bailouts for Wall Street bankers, titans of industry located closer to home have been steadily receiving government grants. The Department of Agriculture (USDA) operates two programs designed to grow agricultural business and stimulate the introduction of products into markets. Under the Value-Added Producer Grants program, the USDA makes money available for people wishing to capitalize on recent food trends and developing new businesses.[839] Specifically, the USDA "help[s] agricultural producers enter into value-added activities," which the program broadly defines as anything that generates new products and transforms what naturally exists (i.e. milk to yogurt, pork to sausage), or is simply marketed or sold in a way that enhances its value (i.e. free-range, organic, etc.).[840] Applicants can receive money either for a "planning grant," which would fund a study to assess the viability of a proposed venture, or a "working capital grant," which would provide money for operating costs that relate to the processing or marketing of the value-added product.[841]

Big Agra has jumped at the opportunity. Ocean Spray, one of the largest cranberry cooperatives in the world with net sales at over $1.6 billion for the 2013 fiscal year,[842] received $200,000 to produce what it already does so well—a cranberry beverage.[843] Blue Diamond, which boasts that it is "the world's largest almond processing and marketing company,"[844] also received $200,000 to introduce a product into the international market "to ensure [the] venture's success"[845] although it failed to mention the help when it wrote that the cooperative "build[s] markets and create[s] new products, new uses, and new opportunities for global consumers."[846] Sunsweet, a marketing cooperative that "boasts enviable brand recognition of 85 percent in American households," and leads by holding thirty percent of the worldwide prune market,[847] also received the same amount to pay for costs of processing and marketing a prune juice. Each of these cooperatives has gotten capital injections entirely at the cost of taxpayers.

The USDA continues to operate another grant program, the Market Access Program (MAP), which subsidizes the "costs of overseas marketing and promotional activities" for many more large businesses.[848] We recently exposed this program that shifts the costs of advertising for large companies and trade associations to the taxpayer,[849] but remarkably, Congress has turned a blind eye to this spending. Household names like Sunkist and Welch Foods continue to receive in excess of $3 million this fiscal year alone when it is more important than ever to spend responsibly.[850] Moreover, Blue Diamond receives an additional $4.7 million in taxpayer support for what it essentially received under the Value-Added Producer Grants program.[851] Congress quickly needs to end taxpayer support for these profitable industry leaders.

70. Snowmobile Race Part of NSF Zero Emissions Challenge

$45,900

Snowmobiles are trying not to blow smoke with Uncle Sam's dollars.

This year, Michigan Technological University used a $45,900 grant from the National Science Foundation (NSF) to support the annual Clean Snowmobile Challenge.[852] It's an annual competition hosted by the school to determine which college students can make the quietest, lowest emission snow mobile.[853]

NSF is hardly the only contributor to the event, which has a number of major sponsors, including the Society of Automotive Engineers, SolidWorks, Coca-Cola, and Chrysler.[854]

Funds from the grant were used to subsidize travel to teams participating in the "zero emissions" category, which NSF boasted includes "University Teams from across the US and Canada."[855] In this category, teams build and race electric snowmobiles.

During this year's competition four teams entered, but only one "was able to pass inspection and get out on the snow."

"The internal combustion teams were more competitive than ever," noted Jay Meldrum, the event's coordinator, adding, "There were problems with the zero emissions sleds ..."[856]

71. Unwanted, Unneeded and Unused Ice House

$965,000

A Louisiana community is wasting more than $1.2 million for an ice house that is unwanted, unneeded, and probably will never be used.

In 2011, St. Bernard Parish spent $289,000 of HUD Community Development Block Grant (CDBG) funds to purchase the Amigo Ice House property with the intent of providing ice to fishermen.[857] "A subsequent engineering review revealed some bad news: the previous plan to refurbish the old icehouse and put it back into commerce was not economically feasible.[858] A new parish president elected in 2011 also questioned the need for the project because it would be "taking profits from businesses that already sell ice to fishers."[859]

The parish found itself in a conundrum, either refund the federal government or spend another $965,000 of federal funds to complete the unwanted, unnecessary, and most likely unused ice house project.

Local officials opted to waste more money, which they tapped out of CDBG disaster recovery funds.[860]

There is no hiding the fact that the only reason another $1 million is being spent on the project is to avoid having to repay the original amount. St. Bernard Parish officials "freely admit they don't think it's needed" and they are simply spending a larger sum of federal money to get off the hook from repaying the original federal grant.[861]

Parish President Dave Peralta says "the parish's hands are tied because if it doesn't move forward the parish would have to repay nearly $300,000, 'which we don't have,'" to the federal government."[862] Peralta conceded the amount is "an exorbitant price for that thing."[863]

"Basically, we were too far into it to turn around," admits Councilman Monty Montelongo, noting "I don't think we will ever need it. I can see much better uses for that money."[864]

"We're about $1 million into it and right now all we have is a vacant piece of land with an old battered icehouse sitting on it" lamented parish Chief Administrative Officer Jerry Graves.[865] Soon that "crumbling eyesore"[866] will be replaced with a new 30'x60' building that will have just as little use as the current structure.[867]

The ice house is unnecessary because there are "private ice operations that sell to fishers," who don't see a need for a government run ice house.[868]

"I don't see where the parish should have gotten into an icehouse. At all. It makes no sense," said shrimper Nicky Mones. "It was a bad purchase. Economically, it was a terrible purchase."[869]

"I guess it's what you would call a catastrophic screw-up on the parish's part," fisherman F.J. Campo said. "We spent a lot of money and we got nothing for it. Nothing."[870]

The parish president, who was recently indicted on charges unrelated to wasting tax payer dollars[871], says "the ice house will be strictly for emergencies," such as "hurricane recovery scenarios when no other ice is available."[872] However, "based on recent history, that would mean ice would be made once every few years. And it might not be needed even during a hurricane. After Hurricane Isaac, which hit the area hard, the National Guard provided all the ice that was needed," noted a local newspaper urging "HUD and St. Bernard to put the project on ice."[873]

But instead of freezing spending on the project, the parish is now wasting three times the original amount to demolish the old ice house and the reconstruct a new ice house.

Ground was broken in August[874] and construction "is scheduled for completion in April."[875] The facility "will be equipped a 'flaked-ice' machine capable of producing 25 tons of ice daily" and "provide storage for 300,000 pounds of flaked ice."[876]

The icehouse boondoggle "wasn't the parish's only misadventure in the ice business. "After Katrina, Shell Oil Company donated two industrial ice machines to the parish" which were "leased to two local seafood dock owners at no cost, but the machines were never hooked up and never used." Both were destroyed during Hurricane Isaac in 2012. "Isaac comes along and they wind up in the marsh somewhere," Campo said. "They're gone, basically gone. Destroyed. And we still have no ice."[877]

72. Virtual Food Fight Smartphone Game
$804,254

A federally funded video game wants to give parents the edge over their children who continue to wage war over veggies. The app's main character -- a fussy eater named Kiddio -- will give mom and dad a chance to test out new negotiation styles.

"Kiddio: Food Fight" will consist of 24 episodes in which parents will select a vegetable to offer Kiddio and then select a tactic for influencing Kiddio to eat the veggie.[878] Parents can also tailor Kiddio's mood so it mimics that of the parent's child. "Kiddio's responses to these options – whether to take a bit or say something like 'Yuk!' – are based on what we've learned so far about kids' reactions to these parental tactics," according to one of the creators.[879]

The hope for the game is "to give [parents] a safe, low-risk, nonthreatening way to sharpen their parenting skills," according to one of the scientists behind "Kiddio: Food Fight."[880]

The developers hope to turn a profit off the smartphone video game by selling it on app stores. "Though over 300 parenting iPhone and iPad apps have been identified in the Apple iTunes App Store, none train in food parenting practices. The investigators believe national and international markets exist for mobile video games that both train and entertain," they wrote in their grant application to the National Institutes of Health.[881]

For now, they'll continue using up their grant from the National Institutes of Health, from which they have received a total of $804,254 this year.[882] Taxpayers should teach Washington bureaucrats not to waste tax dollars on corny smartphone apps that no one is going to play by sending them to their room without dessert.

73. Prescription for Higher Medicare Bills
$5 billion

The method the federal government uses to place some low-income Medicare beneficiaries in prescription drug plans causes both taxpayers and patients to overpay by at least $5 billion annually.[883]

Every year, HHS randomly assigns a Part D plan to some low-income subsidy recipients who had been previously been enrolled in the program but did not indicate a plan preference.[884] Even though HHS bureaucrats have a mountain of data they could use to automatically find the best-suited plan for each beneficiary, they have resorted to random assignment for years. But the plans do not cover drugs equally and have major variations in copays and requirements. Some patients end up paying more out-of-pocket for their drugs if the newly assigned plan covers less of the cost or the premiums are higher.[885] Because the government subsidizes most of this beneficiaries' care, the Medicare program also picks up much of the slack when insurance copays and premiums go up.

Researchers found a better practice would be for recipients to be assigned to plans that provide better coverage based on individual prescription patterns.[886] Doing so would drop copays for both patients and the government by an average of $738 per beneficiary. Total estimated savings could be over $5 billion annually.[887] Some of the savings would go to the beneficiaries themselves, which is significant because many are already struggling to get by.

Implementing "intelligent reassignment" itself should be fairly inexpensive, the researchers concluded.[888]

> Taxpayers should teach Washington bureaucrats not to waste tax dollars on corny smartphone apps that no one is going to play by sending them to their room without dessert.

74. Boutique Hotel Offers Luxury Spa Services, Afternoon Tea, and Upscale Nightcaps

$1.4 million

The Department of Housing and Urban Development (HUD) is providing $1.4 million in federal assistance to the town of Cary, North Carolina, to finance a boutique hotel intended to employ lower income residents and pamper guests with luxury services.[889]

The aid for the Mayton Inn is being provided under HUD's Section 108 loan program. In a strange arrangement, if the loan is not repaid by the hotel owners, taxpayers get stuck footing the bill. The HUD loan would be "repaid" with HUD Community Development Block Grants (CDBG). "The specific loan received by Cary typically goes toward projects that could help bolster impoverished areas. The Mayton Inn qualified for the money because" the owners "plan to create 40 jobs targeted toward people from low- to moderate-income families."[890] Additional support for the hotel is provided by the Small Business Administration loan.[891]

"Even though the building will be new, it will be designed with the '20s in mind," what one of the owners "says many people today think of as luxury."[892]

The posh hotel's amenities will include afternoon tea ("Choose from a wide variety of gourmet teas."), spa services ("you can enjoy delicious teas while unwinding in your robe before a fabulous massage, facial, or reflexology," and you can even "enjoy massage and reflexology services in the comfort of your room."), "evening spirits"[893] at an "upscale cocktail bar"[894] ("With your choice of nightcap from a variety of top shelf spirits."), an "outdoor pergola for cocktailing,"[895] and "turndown service" ("Enjoy a complimentary aperitif of tawny port and signature hand-made chocolate truffles.").[896]

"The project is part of Cary's urban renewal program, which is designed to encourage growth and activity in the heart of" the town.[897] Regardless, a number of local residents oppose the effort for a number of reasons including doubts the hotel would spur economic development, "concerns construction of the hotel might harm a nearby stream," and concerns "the town is unfairly supporting a specific business interest" and "entering a contract without going through a bidding process."[898]

The government aid is giving a financial advantage to the owners of the Mayton Inn to compete with other lodging establishments already operating in the area. At least ten hotels are within ten minutes of downtown Carry, including the Umstead Hotel and Spa, a Hyatt, a Best Western, and a Red Roof Inn.[899] Drive another five minutes and the number of lodging options includes nearly 50 hotels and inns.[900]

The Mayton Inn is expected to be opened to guests in summer 2015.[901]

The Mayton Inn is receiving more than $1.4 million in federal assistance to create jobs for lower income residents and pamper guests with luxuries including spa services, afternoon tea, and swanky martini night caps.

Transportation Dollars Fund Media Campaign to Raise Austin Taxes

$157,000

An extensive, and expensive, rail project for the City of Austin, Texas, is getting some fiscal assistance from Washington. Project Connect, the program management group spearheading transit for the Central Corridor Advisory Group in central Texas, has spent $157,000 on an ad campaign to prop up public support to approve floating a billion dollar bond to help pay for the rail line.[902]

The catch? Approximately 80% of the ad campaign is being financed with federal grant money, essentially using taxpayer money to encourage taxpayers to pay more taxes. Critics have voiced concerns over the media campaign's funding sources and questioned want to know how it can be considered appropriate when "Taxpayers are paying money to the federal government, which is then turning around and lobbying Austinites to support more taxpayer spending."[903] The advertisements ended just before being subjected to provisions on election laws regarding ballot measures.[904]

In addition to questions about how public funds have been used to shape public opinion, Project Connect changed the line route, invalidating public comments collected regarding the original plan. The change in route and need for a new round of public comments is required for Project Connect to seek additional funds from the Federal Transit Administration to finance the rail line.

Project Connect also spent time and money canvassing Austin with flyers that local groups claim provide misleading propaganda regarding the actual route and benefits of the line.[905] Instead, they claim, the fliers are intended to gauge locals knowledge of Project Connect and encourage people to attend their open houses.[906]

The potential bond could put Austinites on the hook for over $500 million.[907]

76. NASA Loses Hundreds of Electronic Devices Each Month

$1.1 million

Houston, we have a problem...even in the midst of a budget crunch, NASA has been issuing smartphones, tablets, and AirCards (which provide roaming access to the Internet from mobile computers) without keeping track of who has them or even if they are being used at all. Both federal employees and contractors have received devices, under the guise of allowing to the "access [Agency] networks from anywhere at any time."[908]

Over 2,000 devices – 14 percent of the total owned by the agency– went unused for at least 7 months from 2013-2014, found a report by the NASA Inspector General.[909] The estimated cost of the unused and lost devices is at least $97,000 every month. [910]

On top of that, "NASA does not have a complete and accurate inventory of Agency-issued smartphones, tablets, cell phones, and AirCards."[911] Top officials were even not sure the agency's contractor – HP – "could accurately account for the full inventory of mobile devices it provides to the Agency."[912] With NASA in the dark about what it should be paying for, it has no way to verify the accuracy of its payments to HP.[913]

Cell phones are not the only equipment NASA has had trouble keeping track of in recent years. On the agency's list of hard-to-track items seem to be laptops, [914] video tapes,[915] and moon rocks.[916]

77. Huge EPA Warehouse for Paper Reports Thwarts Recycling Efforts

$1.5 million

People sometimes think of hoarding as a problem that needs to be helped, and it seems an intervention is overdue for the Environmental Protection Agency (EPA). Somewhat ironically, an agency that encourages "green" behavior by others needs to take some of its own advice.

In its investigation into personal property being stored at sites used by the agency, the Inspector General discovered a warehouse the size of an average Walmart needing immediate attention.[917] Inspectors explored a space "filled . . . with a considerable amount of printed material, including many years' worth of agency publications."[918] As it turns out, the EPA was storing 18.5 million publications and other materials. Considerable is an understatement—shipping at an average of 3 million units per year, the EPA had an inventory of over six years' worth of material.[919]

Hoarders sometimes try to change behavior when they are first alerted to it, but they rarely succeed without strong support. In this instance, the Inspector General discussed their findings with the EPA and the agency took steps to recycle 2 million items.[920] We applaud the EPA for setting an example by recycling, but it has a long road to recovery. The agency is still storing around 5.5 years' worth of material. Given that the recycled items weighed in at 140 tons,[921] perhaps the EPA just needs help discarding the rest of its waste.

The EPA is spending $1.2 million a year for storing and maintaining the excess materials and another $359,000 for leasing the space.[922]

According to inspectors, the above is "an inside view of the EPA warehouse . . . in Blue Ash, Ohio. The image shows rows of boxed publications."

78. Food Stamps Get Traded for Cash and Drugs, Go to People Who Hide Their Income

$3 billion

"Improper payment" is the bureaucratic term for a government payment in the wrong amount, to the wrong person, or used by the recipient inappropriately.[923] These types of federal payment top $100 billion annually.[924] While the food stamp program has been on a downward trend, from a 5% improper payment rate in 2009 to a 3.4% improper payment 2013, the government is actually projecting an increase in 2014 to 3.8%.[925] While that may seem insignificant, in a massive federal program like food stamps, that slight shift amounts to a $400 million increase, bringing the total up to $3 billion just this year.[926] Below are just a few examples of how the program is abused.

Tennessee

A Tennessee food stamp eligibility counselor created fake accounts that she exchanged for cash and drugs.

Earlier this year, officials at the state Department of Human Services (DHS) became suspicious fraudulent Supplemental Nutrition Assistance Program (SNAP) accounts were being "created and sold for profit out of its Lebanon office." An eligibility counselor there "apparently tampered with government records to create the accounts" and produce Electronic Benefit Transfer (EBT) cards "in exchange for cash and drugs."

Investigators "identified more than 40 false accounts with more than $150,000 in benefits distributed fraudulently." The case remains "open, and more charges and suspects may be forthcoming."

The eligibility counselor has been fired.

In July, a Tennessee law also took effect requiring drug testing for those seeking welfare benefits. The law does not apply to eligibility counselors however.

Louisiana

In Louisiana, 11 were convicted this year for food stamp fraud. Nine of those convicted simply lied about their income to receive the benefits.[927] One woman deliberately hid the fact that she was married and hid her spouse's income, taking in $17,755 in food stamps. Another woman stole the identity of another person to get their benefits.

Rhode Island

In Providence, Rhode Island, 11 more were convicted after scamming the system for $3.6 million.[928] In this more elaborate scheme, seedy store owners gave out cash in exchange for the food stamps instead of food. Under the rules of the program, only food items are supposed to be purchased. With cash in hand, the food stamp recipients are free to purchase whatever they please.

Pennsylvania

Pennsylvania investigators took down another 23 food stamp scammers, almost all for lying about their income.[929] What is remarkable about the food stamp program is that the fraudsters are not always barred from receiving future food stamps. In the Pennsylvania cases, the sentences for some of the individuals included 6 or 12 month bans from the program.

79. DOD Pays 16 Times the Going Price for Helicopter Parts

$9 million

The Department of Defense (DOD) spent more than $8,000 on helicopter gears that cost under $500.

Bell Helicopter of Textron Inc. received more than $9 million in excess payments from the military for 33 of 35 replacement spare parts reviewed.[930] The gears and other spare parts were purchased under a sole-source, noncompetitive contract worth $128 million.[931] The DOD inspector general recommended that the military attempt to recoup the excess payments.[932]

The maker of the gears, Bell Helicopters, disagreed with the findings, avowing that they had fully complied with regulations and terms of the contract and "ensures that the U.S. Government consistently receives the best price on commercial items acquired for its use."[933] In addition, department officials maintain that prices are fair simply because federal and defense acquisition regulations had been followed, despite the significant differences in price.[934]

However, the IG report blames the acquisition workforce for performing inadequate price comparisons, particularly with regards to a noncompetitive contract.[935] According to the Bloomberg news report, the Defense Logistics Agency calculated other prices discrepancies from the Bell contract, including a round inner cap at $297.08 but sold for $2,355.85, a pin at $51.67 but sold for $492.17 and a one-inch bushing at $25.72 but sold for $295.57.[936]

80. Injured ICE Employees Cleared to Work, Stay on Workers Comp Instead

$1 million

Despite being cleared to work, some Immigrations Customs and Enforcement (ICE) employees received hundreds of thousands in workers compensation payments.

While the number of employees who have filed for workers compensation has steadily risen since 2009, the Department of Homeland Security's own Office of Inspector General ("OIG") – thinks ICE has wholly failed to manage the costs of the program.

Most of problems involve ignoring requirements that the situation that caused the injury be a covered activity that justifies a federal payment. In almost 20 percent of the claims reviewed by OIG, ICE failed to include the necessary evidence to make that decision,[937] and in another 71 percent of the cases reviewed involving an accident in a government-owned vehicle, there was no evidence at all the employee was doing an on-duty activity eligible for pay.[938]

One federal worker received $43,225 in taxpayer funds without a single medical document justifying the workers compensation pay. In all, 31% of cases reviewed by OIG lacked any medical evidence or other documentation to support an award.

Even federal employees who are able to work are reaping the benefits of this poorly-run problem.

The OIG report found that five ICE employees continued received approximately $1 million in workers' compensation payments even though they had already been cleared to return to work.[939]

81. DOD Sends 16 Planes to the Scrap Heap for $32,000

$468 million

After spending over $468 million on a fleet of 20 planes that were supposed to be the backbone of the Afghan Air Force's (AAF) air transport mission, the Department of Defense (DOD) has scrapped 16 of the planes for a mere $.06 per pound, recouping only $32,000 for its multi-million dollar investment.[940]

The refurbished planes were purchased from Italian manufacturer Alenia Aermacchi North America in 2008 to provide the AAF with the capability to transport troops and conduct air evacuation missions. However, by January 2013, the DOD Inspector General (DOD IG) was reporting that not only had the NATO Training Mission and program management officials not "effectively manage[d] the G222 program," the planes did "not meet operational requirements, may be cost prohibitive to fly, and … several critical spare parts to sustain the G222 are unavailable."[941] The planes flew only 234 hours before they were permanently parked in Afghanistan and Germany and the contract cancelled.[942]

Though the Special Inspector General for Afghanistan Reconstruction (SIGAR) is still conducting its investigation to determine "why DOD purchased aircraft that apparently could not be sustained" and what options exist for disposing or selling the planes,[943] DOD destroyed the planes this summer "to minimize impact on drawdown of U.S. forces in Afghanistan"[944] after no buyers could be found because "nobody was interested in trying to maintain an airplane that was no longer sustainable."[945] Nobody, that is, except the Pentagon acquisition officials and Congressional appropriators who thought the planes were a good investment for American tax dollars.

Unbuilt Eisenhower Memorial Burning Through Cash

$1 million

Behind schedule, over-priced, tone-deaf, controversial and ugly. No, that's not a description of last year's federal budget – it's how some are describing the effort to build a memorial for President Dwight Eisenhower. While construction was supposed to be completed seven years ago, it has yet to begin – and taxpayers have already spent $65 million.[946]

In 1999, Congress first approved construction on the National Mall of a memorial to President Eisenhower,[947] with plans for it to be open by 2007.[948] However, after 15 years, even the design for the memorial has yet to be approved, with construction possibly several more years away.[949]

Some have said questionable decisions by the Eisenhower Memorial Commission – set up to build the memorial – lie at the heart of the delays and serious cost overruns. The biggest of which has been picking a high-profile fight with the Eisenhower family over the memorial's design.

John Eisenhower, son of the late president, advocated for something simple, saying, "taxpayers and donors alike will be better served with an Eisenhower Square that is a green space with a simple statue."[950] Instead, the commission pursued a design from well-known architect, Frank Gehry, which many supporters inside and out of the family have strongly opposed for failing to capture Eisenhower's legacy.

According to an investigation by the House Committee on Natural Resources, multiple designs were submitted by competitors, including Gehry, all of which were called "mediocre" by the design jury, which concluded, "[none] of the visions expressed the whole essence of Eisenhower."[951] Nonetheless, Gehry's was selected, leading one art critic to compare it with, "a scene from 'Planet of the Apes."[952]

One commission member, Bruce Cole, was even harsher, dismissing the design as "a blizzard of tapestries" and "a memorial to Gehry's ego rather than to Ike's accomplishments."[953] Harvard urban designer, Alex Krieger, was equally brutal, saying that even as a "traditional first-semester architecture exercise," Gehry's design "would fail."[954]

The cost of the design left some scratching their heads. For his efforts, the commission paid Gehry's architecture firm $16.4 million, not counting an additional $13.3 million "to the multiple parties responsible for managing the design process and providing administrative support."[955] All of this accounted for a significant part of the nearly $65 million Congress has awarded thus far to help build the memorial.

Generating private financial support has also been slow-going. In 2012, the commission "paid a private fundraising consultant more than $1.2 million … but had received $448,000 in donations through March [2014]."[956]

However, the cost is sure to go higher as the commission requested an additional $50 million this year to continue moving ahead.[957] Because of the complications, Congress only provided $1 million in 2014, intended simply to keep the lights on.[958]

The first major hurdle for the plan has been securing approval for the controversial design. Federal and District of Columbia rules required multiple rounds of approval, but in April 2014 the National Planning Commission for D.C. rejected the Gehry proposal.[959]

In the end, the question on everyone's mind is that uttered by Justin Shubow, president of the National Civic Art Society, when he asked, "Everyone wants to know, where is the money going?"[960]

Butterfly Farm Flies Away with federal Funds

$500,000

The U.S. Department of Agriculture is spending half-a-million dollars this year to subsidize the farming of... butterflies.

Unlike cows and pigs, these livestock don't live in the barn, but in their own butterfly castles.[961] When they mature, the butterflies are sold, often to be "released at weddings or funerals."[962] A single butterfly can cost 75 cents or as much as $7, "depending on the time of year and species."[963] And butterflies only live for a couple weeks with some species lasting "only a few days—so the window to raise and ship them for a specific event is small."[964]

This $500,000 grant will pay for "free" starting materials including castles and eggs for farmers and a vehicle to transport the butterflies.[965] The project will also support a butterfly visitor center where people would be charged an admission fee to see butterflies.[966]

The Rural Business Enterprise Grant program of the U.S. Department of Agriculture (USDA) provided the grant, which is "the largest awarded this year by the program."[967] USDA "recognized the potential for jobs in the industry and awarded" the "grant to the Thlopthlocco Tribal Town in Oklahoma."[968]

"What attracted the most attention was the amount of jobs this could create," said the business and energy program director at the USDA's Oklahoma Rural Development office.[969]

"To get one person really rocking and rolling, it's about $150," said David Bohlken, one of the owners of the Euchee Butterfly Farm, who came up with the idea.[970] With 845 members of the Thlopthlocco Tribal Town,[971] every member of the tribe could be provide their own start kit for a total cost of $127,000, not $500,000 as provided by USDA. But so far, only "about 50 people are signed up for the program."[972]

Butterfly farming generates annual profits of $64 million,[973] but "the money in butterfly farming certainly isn't equivalent to a full time job at first."[974] Those who sign up "can expect make between $400 and $500 a month from about March through October," according Jane Breckinridge,[975] who has been in the butterfly business for two decades.[976]

While the goals of the initiative are worthy and the Euchee Butterfly Farm is a great example of how ingenuity matched with hard work can produce success, this is not a project that needs federal assistance, especially when matched up against our nation's much larger economic and fiscal challenges.

So how is it that a federal government $17 trillion in debt ends up subsidizing butterfly farming?

Millie Wind, the environmental specialist for the Thlopthlocco Tribal Town who "brought the idea back to the tribe council," said "some tribal members were skeptical about the project originally, but the grant helped eliminate that."[977] This might be referred to as the "butterfly effect" of government waste—when the availability of "free" government money causes a ripple effect resulting in waves of unnecessary frivolous spending.

Transit Security Grant for "Feel Good" Ads That Promote Local Tax Increase

$181,000

The Pinellas Suncoast Transit Authority (PSTA) in Florida received two Department of Homeland Security (DHS) grants for security and emergency awareness marketing, which consisted of two phases.

- Phase I ($96,000) – To develop a public awareness/education program that will incorporate the basics of the Federal Transit Administration's (FTA's) existing "Transit Watch Program" which encourages transit patrons to alert authorities if they see anything suspicious. Approximately $12,000 of the grant is programmed for PSTA printing and material preparation costs and the remaining $84,000 is for consultant costs.

- Phase II ($439,500) – This phase develops and implements a mass media campaign to further promote public awareness of security issues related to public transportation and to enhance coordination with safety and security partners within the community.[978]

The Phase II money was used by PSTA to pay for puff piece commercials that have nothing to do with promoting public safety when using transit. For example:

"Eva is a college student with an internship at an office downtown. She takes the bus from home, to school to her job. With such a busy schedule, Eva's time is valuable; she knows that PSTA cares about her time and her security. Eva can use a computer or her phone check real time bus information (shot of a Eva scanning QR code at bus stop) to see exactly where her PSTA bus is and when it will arrive (shot of friendly bus driver). And PSTA is working to make it easier to get around the county. To learn more, visit Greenlight Pinellas. com or PSTA.net (Shot of Greenlight logo, PSTA CARES logo and disclaimer indicating the ad was paid for by a grant from the Department of Homeland Security)."[979]

The end of each ad directs viewers to the Greenlight Pinellas website to learn more. The Greenlight Pinellas Plan consists of "transformational bus improvements and future passenger rail that will significantly enhance public transportation in Pinellas County. If the proposed 1% sales tax referendum passes in November 2014, PSTA would implement the Greenlight Pinellas Plan."[980]

Aside from mentioning the word "security" once, these ads are simply promoting transit and the PSTA's Greenlight Pinellas plan. These commercials are not informing viewers how to protect against a terrorist attack or other disaster or even how to protect themselves when using transit infrastructure. It's to encourage voters to vote for Greenlight in November and for a sales tax increase that will benefit them.

After media scrutiny of the campaign, PSTA repaid a portion of the grants--$385,500 went back, but the taxpayer is still on the hook.

Identity Thieves Steal Billions Each Year With Bogus Tax Returns

At least $4.2 billion

Identity thieves are making out like bandits when it comes to stealing tax refunds from unsuspecting taxpayers.

Described as a "tsunami of fraud" by a United States attorney, every year the Internal Revenue Service (IRS) pays out billions of dollars in fraudulent refunds to clever criminals filing fake tax returns. Some identify thieves have even thrown "filing parties," where they teach their friends how to file fraudulent returns, in exchange for a cut of the refund. [981]

Just last year, the tax enforcement agency issued $5.2 billion in refunds based on more than three million phony federal tax returns.[982] The Treasury Inspector General predicts this number will only continue to grow, estimating the IRS "could issue approximately $21 billion in fraudulent tax refunds resulting from identity theft" over five years, an average of $4.2 billion each year.[983]

Little more than a stolen Social Security number, a date of birth, and an electronic device to file a federal tax return because significant gaps exist in the IRS' ability to verify taxpayer information and prevent fraudulent payouts. Online tax filers are not required to provide a paper copy of their W-2 to the IRS. Most electronic filers submit their taxes in February, several months before the IRS is able to verify their accuracy because of several month delay in receiving employer-provided W-2s.[984]

Criminals often receive their refund from the IRS within a couple weeks because federal law requires the IRS to pay interest on any refund distributed more than 45 days after the return's due date.[985] This encourages the agency to turn around refunds as quickly as possible. In many cases, identity thieves submit the fake tax return and receive a refund before the victim has even filed their tax return.[986]

While the IRS is increasing efforts to address identity theft and stolen refunds, much remains to be accomplished. In one case detailed by CBS's 60 minutes, at least 25 refunds were mailed to the same address.[987] In a review of the IRS' ability to prevent stolen refunds through identity theft, the Government Accountability Office found the IRS has failed to identify any cost-effective solutions for updating their electronic technology processes that detect overlap or refund mismatches.[988]

The IRS' identity crisis should not affect taxpayers awaiting their tax refund. These individuals send billions of dollars to the Treasury every year, and deserve to receive their tax refund without wondering if the IRS mailed it to an identity thief instead.

Feds Study Science Festival Attendance

$1,523,133

The federal government is spending a million and a half dollars to monitor your festival attendance. Science festivals, that is.

Each year states and private groups host hundreds of science festivals all over the country. Apparently, though, the hosts don't do a very good job of communicating with one another and getting data from their participants, so they have a hard time figuring out if their efforts are helping the cause of science.

These aren't your grandparent's science fairs, either. A sampling of festivals include: "Nerd Nite" at Sea on an aircraft carrier in San Francisco; "E=MC Beered," sponsored by the Philadelphia Science Festival and Yards Brewing Company; and "Science Ink," hosted by a body artist to discuss "science-y tattoos."[989] The NC Science Festival is soliciting ideas for other fun festivals, suggesting Rocket Science serving Rocket Science IPA, a video game tournament, and even a robot zoo: "the wackier, the better."[990]

Researchers at University of California at San Francisco and University of North Carolina at Chapel Hill are using the National Science Foundation grant money to help figure out whether all these festivals are actually making Americans love science. They are also developing a database for "the festival community" to use to share information about their participants.[991]

In addition, the federal government is funding a three-year project (concluding in 2015) to support the development of more of these festivals and provide resources for mentoring and travel costs with the goal of creating a network of scientists and festival organizers.[992][993]

On what one would think would be an unrelated note, the funding will also "develop some new evaluation tools such as secret shopper observational protocols."[994]

87 Five Decades of Controversy for Beleaguered Government Program

$1.7 billion

On its 50th anniversary, the $1.7 billion federal Job Corps program – the centers where American youth often go for their first job -- is been plagued by questions of ineffectiveness, violence and drug use at many of its job centers.

One Job Corps center in McKinney, Texas is under federal investigation for violent crime and drug use. An official said the center has "an atrocious drug problem" and others shared information about violent assaults resulting in students being taken to the hospital.[995]

Job Corps has a supposed zero tolerance policy for drugs and violence. However, a Safety and Security Manager at the north Texas center has said that he was told the center had an amnesty policy in which a student caught with drugs or weapons is allowed to stay at the center.[996] That manager was told not to contact the local police department about the violence and drug use.[997]

Teachers at the McKinney center have also filed complaints that charge they were made to give students a "diploma by any means necessary," through "extensive fraud and cheating."[998] In one example, a student at the center began his freshman year of high school on February 21, 2014, he was advanced to a sophomore two months later, and graduated two weeks after that.[999] When questioned how the student was able to complete his junior and senior year in one week and the teacher said it was "not possible."[1000] Another teacher resigned due to immense pressure to graduate students even "if someone else has to sit with that mouse and click A, click B, click C, click D. It does not matter who does it."[1001]

An article in the Washington Post recently highlighted one of the worst performing Job Corps centers in the country: Treasure Lake Job Corps in Indiahoma, Oklahoma. One student said the center "reminded her of a homeless shelter, full of people hustling and fighting," while another student posted on Facebook it "reminded me of bein bk in jail lol."[1002] After years of poor performance and criticism, the Jobs Corps announced in August that it was closing the troubled center.[1003]

Students are allowed to leave whenever they want. In fact, "Over the decades, auditors found that many students quit before they graduated — homesick, bored, or tired of conflicts with other students. Today, about 59 percent complete all of their training. The rest leave early, with no penalty or requirement to pay money back."[1004]

Despite the poor education the students receive, Job Corps costs taxpayers about $45,000 per student per year – more than four years of tuition at the University of Texas.[1005]

One of the few studies of the program found that while there were positive short term effects in students' earnings, after four years, there was no virtually no difference between those who had attended Job Corps and those who had applied but not attended.[1006]

Yet, given anecdotes of past success stories – not to mention the fact that Job Corps centers can employ hundreds of staff in politicians' own districts – the program's massive cost is rarely questioned.

"'What you find is that the program — from society's perspective — does not pay for itself... But it is a good deal for the enrollees themselves.' In Washington today, that much good is good enough."[1007]

Congress recently passed the Workforce Innovation and Opportunity Act, which authorizes nearly $13 billion in funding for the Job Corps program through fiscal year 2020.

> "I believe the Job Corps got lazy. I believe they stopped trying to help people and started going through the motions."
> – former Job Corps student

> "[Treasure Lake graduate Austin] Brown — who watched his roommates make prison-style hooch — did get his training in culinary skills, and afterward he did get a job in his field. He is now a cook at Burger King."

Navy Sends Hundreds of Magazines to Congress to Promote Green Initiatives

$72,000

Currents magazine is the Navy's flagship, quarterly publication showcasing its commitment to environmental stewardship and progress toward meeting its energy goals. According to the Navy, the magazine's publication enables it to "share best practices/lessons learned and increase awareness regarding environmental compliance and energy efficiency for ships and commands in their daily work."[1008]

Articles published this year have included a story on the Navy's updated *Buy It Green* guide, a "compilation of products that are classified as sustainable by the Defense Logistics Agency (DLA) and/or the General Services Administration (GSA)" that Navy procurement officials can use to ensure the Navy reaches the goal of having "95 percent of all procurements and contracts incorporate sustainable products and services,"[1009] and a feature on winners of the Chief of Naval Operations' award for exceptional environmental stewardship.[1010]

Yet for all its efforts to showcase itself as the "Great Green Fleet,"[1011] the Navy still mails out 9,500 hard copies of the magazine every quarter, including 535 to each member of Congress, at a cost of an additional $72,000 a year over the $260,000 it takes the staff of four contractors and federal employees to develop the content.[1012]

The issues going as far back as 2010 are accessible online, which begs the question why the Navy thinks continued distribution of hard copies is necessary? The Navy maintains that each issue contains a notice "requesting that recipients...confirm that they still want to receive the magazine,"[1013] but if the magazine really serves a purpose beyond self-aggrandizing propaganda

NSF Studies Why Wikipedia is Sexist

$202,000

In September 2013, the National Science Foundation awarded federal grants to Yale and New York University researchers to study perceived gender bias on Wikipedia.[1014]

The National Science Foundation awarded $132,000 to Yale Sociology Professor Julia Adams and $70,000 to Hannah Brückner, NYU Abu Dhabi Associate Dean of Social Sciences, to study "how and why ... Wikipedia suffers from systemic gender bias."[1015]

The study follows accusations of sexism in content and among contributors at Wikipedia.[1016] For example, a 2013 opinion piece in the New York Times, argued Wikipedia contributors were biased because they had characterized some female novelists as "American Female Novelists" on Wikipedia, rather than "American Novelists."[1017]

Others disagree that Wikipedia is biased or argue it's not a real problem. For example, an opinion article in Slate concluded "Wikipedia's gender imbalance is a non-problem in search of a misguided solution," arguing that it "would do a lot less damage to equality to acknowledge that men and women are not identical in their interests than to suggest that 'freedom, openness, [and] egalitarian ideas' are inconsistent with female self-realization."[1018]

Wikipedia is a free online encyclopedia where the content is created and edited by anyone with Internet access.

The study is expected to be completed by August 2015.[1019]

Maine Town Rebuilds 38 "Speed Humps" to Slow Traffic Through Neighborhood

$335,00

According to a national study found Maine to have the ninth-worst track record in the nation for repairing deficient bridges, nearly one million people drive on Maine's crumbling bridges every day.[1020] But instead of fixing the Pine Tree State's crumbling bridges and roads, federal funds will help install "speed humps" to slow traffic in two Portland neighborhoods.[1021]

Local officials grew concerned over time that roads in the Libbytown and Rosemont neighborhoods were "frequently used by motorists as a cut through."[1022] To slow these drivers down while they cut through, the city built "mini traffic circles and islands," as well as 38 "speed humps."[1023]

In all, the project is slated to cost $335,000, using a portion of a $1.5 million grant from the U.S. Department of Commerce Economic Development Administration (EDA) and $90,000 from the U.S. Department of Transportation.[1024] According to the EDA, the $1.5 million grant was part of a broader effort to redevelop Thompson's Point as a "mixed-use center that will include a convention center, sports complex and office space."[1025]

However, several neighborhood residents sounded a note of skepticism that using several hundred thousand dollars for traffic calming was a good idea. "I'm not sure people who speed are going to be deterred," commented Bernie Cohen.[1026] Fellow neighbor, Norm Reef, added that drivers may still speed, "When they get to the speed bump, they slow down. As soon as they get over the bump, bingo, they take off again. ... I question how much good it's going to do for the investment they're going to make."[1027] To be sure, while the measures were intended to reduce speed, Portland officials were also quick to point out they were designed to "not force drivers to significantly adjust their travel speed."[1028]

Mike Bobinsky, Portland's public services director, said the speed humps would not be as "severe" as others used in the city.[1029] Added Bobinsky, "We are trying to create friction that causes greater awareness by drivers to be conscious it is a neighborhood with children, walkers and bicyclists."[1030]

91. DOJ Buys Premium LinkedIn Account to Promote Jobs During Hiring Freeze

$544,338

Following in the footsteps of the State Department's purchase of Facebook likes,[1031] the Department of Justice's (DOJ) Criminal Division has forked over $544,338 of taxpayers' dollars to have "an enhanced company profile" on LinkedIn.com, a professional networking website, so that it can "increase brand awareness beyond job advertisements" and determine which job applicants are qualified candidates based on self-reported user profiles.[1032]

The DOJ described the LinkedIn services as "freeing up staff time and workload that would otherwise be spent reviewing applications and inquiries of unqualified candidates."[1033] But when this contract for LinkedIn services was awarded, the DOJ was scarcely posting job advertisements, because it was almost three years into a hiring freeze[1034]

But since the Attorney General lifted the DOJ's hiring freeze in February 2014, taxpayer dollars are no longer being wasted advertising for limited job openings for federal agents, prosecutors, and analysts.[1035] Instead, the DOJ still wasted taxpayer money by turning to LinkedIn to find qualified job applicants while the unemployment rate was at 6.6%[1036], and the unemployment rate of recent law school graduates, a hiring pool for future prosecutors, is 12.8%.[1037] One news outlet noted that, "[i]n a stagnant economy with high unemployment, Americans are clamoring for jobs...You'd think recruiting expenses would be cut back, not stepped up."[1038] When it comes to jobs, it's a sellers' market, yet taxpayers continue paying to promote the only seller of federal law enforcement jobs.

The DOJ stated that using LinkedIn will free up time and resources in the hiring process.[1039] How will the DOJ's enhanced online presence on LinkedIn achieve this? The LinkedIn services will assist the DOJ in "serving job advertisements to the most relevant, targeted audiences, generating the most qualified leads."[1040]

Taxpayers would be alarmed to know the next generation of federal criminal law enforcement is being selected by a social media website on their dime. Even more, taxpayers can only hope that these LinkedIn services will be able to weed out the thousands of fake profiles on LinkedIn as effectively as the DOJ expects LinkedIn to weed out unqualified candidates for employment.[1041]

92. Taxpayers Charged to Promote Hillary Clinton's $14 Million Book in Europe

$55,000

Like other former First Ladies, Hillary Clinton will receive Secret Service protection for life. That does not explain why the State Department and Department of Homeland Security spent more than $55,000 for the former Secretary of State's European book tour this year, especially since she "was not traveling on official government business."[1042]

Clinton retired as Secretary of State in February 2013, yet the State Department "paid for nearly $50,000 of the costs" of her European excursion to promote her book "Hard Choices" in July 2014.[1043] This is not a perk typically extended to former Cabinet secretaries, "making it curious the State Department's Paris Embassy was on the hook" for her costs.[1044] A Department spokeswoman could not answer whether or not "her agency had paid for Clinton's private travel on other non-government trips."[1045]

DHS spent $5,100 to rent three Mercedes-Benz "executive limousine vans" for a single day in Berlin, Germany.[1046]

According to documents obtained by the Daily Mail, the federal government paid more than "$55,000 on travel expenses related to her book tour" in July alone.[1047]

The expenses for Clinton Tour de France included $3,668 charge for "a single night's lodging in a suite at the posh Four Seasons George V hotel in Paris. That rate corresponds to the cost of a suite with a 'large and superbly appointed marble bathroom,' a 'deep soaking tub,' 'sparkling chandeliers' and 'elegant period furniture, according to the Four Seasons website," notes the Daily Mail.[1048]

The Secret Service spent $11,291 to rent vehicles for agents in Paris. "The government spent another $35,183 on lodging there, but the purchase order doesn't say where Clinton's personal protection detail stayed," reported the Daily Mail.[1049]

Mrs. Clinton reportedly received a $14 million advance for her book "Hard Choices."[1050] Her speaking fees have ranged from $225,000 to $300,000 for a single appearance.[1051]

FAA Spending to Study What to Do With a FAA-Violating Municipal

$520,000

For many business owners, failure to comply with federal regulations can result in steep fines or orders to close up shop. But for the Burley Municipal Airport in Burley, Idaho, failure to adhere to Federal Aviation Administration (FAA) standards results in a $520,000 taxpayer-funded feasibility study just to decide if this problematic airport should be fixed, moved, or closed.[1052]

A failed compliance review in March 2014 presented the city of Burley with an ultimatum: fix or move the airport or lose any FAA funding.[1053] Burley has been studying places for relocating the airport since 1995.[1054] So far, not including the newest study, the FAA has funded $624,082 worth of studies for possible airport sites for Burley.[1055] Burley attempted to move the airport in 1997, 2008, and 2011, but all of these attempts were thwarted by land-use disputes.[1056] While one intuitive Burley City Councilman stated that the FAA has funded these studies because it thinks the Burley airport needs to be moved, apparently the ultimate decision between two proposed relocation sites or improvements to the current site cannot be reached without an additional half a million dollars of taxpayers' money.[1057]

Early reporting on the newest FAA study is already taking an ominous direction for the Burley Municipal Airport and for the U.S. taxpayers funding the study. One decision from the study will be how much money the FAA wants to invest in an airport that is only used by local pilots.[1058] At the meeting to approve the city's application for the FAA study, one city councilman suggested that the airport should just be closed instead of moved.[1059] Lengthening one of the runways to meet FAA standards for safety zones could come with an estimated price tag of over $100 million, some of which would also be paid by U.S. taxpayers.[1060] This would leave one runway being a published length of 2,500 feet, which is prohibited by many insurers of corporate planes.[1061] In addition, non-local pilots would be unaware that the runway is actually longer than 2,500 feet, causing them to bypass the Burley airport for another airport with a longer published runway length.[1062] One proposed relocation site only has one runway to accommodate the area's prevailing wind, causing landing problems for arriving pilots.[1063] This site also does not have readily available interstate access, making it not time-effective to travel to the airport.[1064] The proposed sites also fail to address security concerns, as their rural locations have little protections against theft of the $200,000 small airplanes that use the Burley airport.[1065]

The Burley Airport Users Association has already voiced its opposition to the proposed relocation sites, with the group of local pilots' president stating that "[i]f they put the airport at either of the sites, I'll just start going to Twin Falls because the [Burley] airport will be so difficult to access."[1066] However, the executive director of the Southern Idaho Economic Development Organization predicted that relocating the Burley airport is not "a deal-maker nor –breaker," because major corporations are satisfied using an airport that is 25 minutes away.[1067]

So while the FAA is spending $520,000 of taxpayers' money on a study to assess the fate of the Burley Municipal Airport, the Magic Valley Regional Airport operates less than an hour's drive away in Twin Falls, Idaho.[1068] One Burley businessman posed "[i]f the [Burley] airport doesn't meet FAA standards, how in good conscience can we keep it open?"[1069] The question U.S. taxpayers should be asking is: if the Burley airport is only fifty miles away from a perfectly functioning airport, how in good conscience can the FAA spend taxpayer dollars to study keeping this crumbling rural airport afloat?

Texting Drunks Asking Them Not to Drink

$194,090

"Btw, don't have 2 much 2 drink." Researchers have received $194,090 this year to determine if text messages can encourage heavy drinkers to put down that cocktail.[1070]

Researchers have acknowledged that other internet-based interventions have "proven mildly effective but have limited ability to help individuals maintain changes."[1071] They are hoping that tapping into a drinker's cell phone will be more effective in reaching the drinker before problem drinking occurs.[1072] For example, some study subjects will get a daily 3 P.M. text message reminding them of the consequences of heavy drinking.[1073]

Not just any ordinary drinker qualifies for the study. The focus is on women and men who drink more than 15 and 24 drinks in an average week, respectively.[1074] Up to 300 participants will receive up to 115 text messages a month over the course of four months.[1075] They will be measured by the reduction in the number of drinks consumed each day, the number of days of heavy drinking, and the average number of drinks per week.[1076] Any drinkers who "express a desire or intent to obtain additional substance abuse treatment" during the study are excluded from participating.[1077]

95. We All Scream for Federally Funded Ice Cream

$1,253,309

Some in the dairy industry are milking the federal government. While some grants are being used to develop products like cheese, cream or butter, other dairy farmers have been more creative in their efforts to acquire taxpayer money.

In Idaho, a dairy farm received grant funds to launch a marketing campaign in part to sell its ice cream.[1078] This will likely allow the farm to focus on maintaining the "drive-thru" where new customers can come and "get [their] milk, ice cream cones, bread or yogurt . . . ."[1079] Other farms have also used the funds to grow their ice cream businesses, including one in Oregon which plans to market a premium ice cream in its stores,[1080] and another in Washington which will help start up a store to sell ice cream.[1081] Sadly, however, the ice cream in Washington State will be for those with more sophisticated palates—the grantee will serve only a few "herbal" flavors at a time and will not offer any sprinkles since he is "not a sprinkles guy."[1082] In total, the USDA paid $267,703 of taxpayer money to ice cream producers.

Dairy farmers' creativity doesn't stop at artisanal ice cream. In Wisconsin and New York, a farmer cooperative and creamery received a grant to expand production and marketing of organic Greek yogurt.[1083] A Missouri farm will be using a grant it received also to produce yogurt, but from sheep's milk.[1084] A farm in Pennsylvania received a grant as well to expand its yogurt business but will use some of the money to build its Mexican chocolate business.[1085]

Other grantees really stretched their imagination to be awarded the grants. One grantee in New York used the money to develop "kosher artisanal raw milk cheese" produced from grass-fed cows.[1086] The cheeses are made under strict Rabbinic supervision.[1087] Another grantee in Florida will use the grant money it received to produce and market a line of "goat milk soap and other goat milk body care products."[1088] The soap is made from the farm's "own dairy goats [with] combinations of Olive, Coconut, and Palm Oils."[1089]

96. NASA's Near-Earth Object Program: The Comet that Keeps Chasing Its Tail

$40.5 million

Large objects may be hurtling toward Earth, but despite receiving a big budget for tracking efforts, NASA has no idea where most of them are.

NASA has operated the Near-Earth Object (NEO) Program since 1994, when Congress first required the agency start tracking all large NEOs within 28 million miles of Earth's orbit.[1090] The program is supposed to identify 90 percent of NEOs by 2020.

Funding for the program has grown exponentially from $4 million in 2009 to $40.5 million this year.[1091] NASA had been allocated $102 million in funding for this program since 2008 alone.[1092]

Despite the massive funding increases, earthlings are still in the dark about what objects are floating in space

NASA still has little capability to identify NEOs because it has completely mismanaged the program and will not make its 2020 goal, according to the Office of Inspector General (OIG).[1093] The OIG rung up NASA for a lack of collaboration, integration, and effective internal controls as reasons for the program's inability to accomplish its mission by 2020.[1094]

Like some comets in orbit, the NEO Program management keeps chasing its tail by not adopting measures to eliminate duplicative efforts between NASA-funded observatories. The NEO Program has not sought to establish alliances with other governmental agencies, NASA programs or foreign countries in conducting its work. For instance, both the Department of Defense and the National Science Foundation have Earth-based telescopes which could assist in identifying and tracking NEOs.[1095] Likewise, NASA's international partner could greatly enhance the program's capabilities.[1096]

Upon examining the NEO Program's long-term strategic approach, the OIG report disclosed that a lack of comprehensive "strategic plan, integrated master schedule, and cost estimates" have plagued program execution.[1097] In short, the program's management seem to be lost in space.

97. Medicaid Provider Taxes

$4 billion

States are taxing federal Medicaid payments to doctors and using the revenue to get even more federal funding, a trick that is worth billions of dollars a year.

The Medicaid program is jointly funded by the states and federal government. Uncle Sam matches a fraction of the funds that states allocate toward their programs. To boost the amount of funds they get from Uncle Sam, states use these "provider taxes." But in many cases, most of the revenue from the tax comes from federal payments already made by Medicaid.

Provider taxes cannot be applied specifically to Medicaid providers, but they can be levied against specific categories of medical providers. The most commonly taxed is one in which the federal government pays most of the bills: nursing homes. Medicaid covers almost half of the cost of all nursing home care nationwide, and Medicare covers almost one-quarter.[1098] Forty-four states use this tax on nursing homes to gather more federal dollars -- essentially a double benefit.[1099] Other oft-utilized tax categories include inpatient and outpatient hospital services and facilities for individuals with developmental disabilities.

Congress scaled back the use of this practice in the '90s, but the loophole continues to yield billions of dollars in unintended federal spending for states. In 2014 alone, its estimated cost is $4-5 billion annually.[1100]

All Americans should have access to quality health care, but the provider tax gimmick is indicative of Congress' ineptitude in addressing the real issues facing the Medicaid program.

98. Earmark Spends Taxpayer Money to Send Coal to Germany

$638,910

What some have called "a felony theft of the taxpayers' money," the United States is forced by law to pay for the mining and shipping of anthracite coal to U.S. military bases in Germany.[1101]

Thanks to an earmark in defense appropriations bills, the U.S. Air Force must use American anthracite coal to heat military bases in Germany.[1102] Introduced in the 1960s by the late Senator Daniel Flood, the earmark was an effort to preserve his Pennsylvania district's anthracite coal industry.[1103] The provision allows the DOD to implement "cost-effective agreements" that include anthracite coal for heating military based in Germany.[1104] But the Department of Defense (DOD) has tried for decades to end this earmark because it wasted hundreds of millions of dollars annually.[1105] Over thirty years ago, the DOD complained that the military had no use for the anthracite coal and that it had to expend additional resources just to protect the coal from the elements.[1106] The DOD also argued that it was more cost-effective to purchase energy from local suppliers overseas.[1107]

Ignoring the DOD's calls to end this anthracite coal mandate, the provision still remains in annual appropriations bills.[1108] According to a civilian contracting officer for the U.S. Air Force in Germany, taxpayers purchased about 9,000 tons of anthracite coal in 2013,[1109] amounting to $638,910 in cost to taxpayers.[1110]

99. Marketing Money for Little-Used Wisconsin Airport

$150,000

Officials at the Chippewa Valley Regional Airport are "pretty convinced" that the reason only 12% of air travelers in the region choose the airport is because the others who do not are "just not aware of the services available."[1111] Most travelers in the region choose to fly out of the Delta hub Minneapolis-St. Paul International Airport just 90 minutes away.[1112]

That explanation was good enough for the Federal Aviation Administration, which awarded the airport $150,000 to market the airport's services.[1113]

But what really drives airport choice? Cost and convenience.

Because the airport only serves Chicago O'Hare International Airport, any destination other than Chicago requires a connection there, driving up the cost and inconvenience of the travel choice.

For example, a nonstop round trip weekend ticket in December from Minneapolis to Denver cost around $145.[1114] The same ticket departing from Chippewa Valley Airport costs $433 and requires an hour layover in Chicago.[1115] It is understandable that locals would choose a 90 minute drive and a cheaper nonstop ticket over a shorter drive and a more expensive ticket with a layover.

Even a round trip ticket to Chippewa Valley's only destination, Chicago O'Hare, is cheaper out of Minneapolis ($92) than out of the regional airport ($178).

Chippewa Valley Regional Airport can market their services, but in an age where online price-comparison for airfare is a click away, savvy travelers will always pick cheaper, more convenient airfare despite any federally funded marketing scheme.

100. Farmers Get Grant to Produce "Worm Power" Compost

$199,000

These earthworms are not just eating through manure. They are also digesting taxpayer dollars.

Worm Power received two new grants this year, in part to study whether its novel worm-digested compost is good for plants.[1116] These grants are the eighth and ninth the private company has received from the federal government in the last decade. Though the grants came from federal programs that are only supposed to consider the merits, they did receive overt assistance from U.S. Senators Chuck Schumer and Kirsten Gillibrand in securing the grant.[1117]

Worm Power created a process called vermicomposting, in which worms eat through cow manure and produce a disease-preventing mixture of soil and fertilizer. "If I want to have eight million worms," said the company's president, "I kinda gotta make sure everything is really running to keep them fat, dumb, and happy [sp]."[1118]

Even though the company appears to have success on the market, it continues to worm its way through the federal dole. This year's grants – both coming from the U.S. Department of Agriculture (USDA) – are intended to help the company make its patented system more mainstream.[1119] One grant provided $100,000 to help the company "improve the profitability of hydroponic baby leaf spinach production."[1120] The other gave the company $99,994 to aid its development of a novel seed treatment product.[1121]

Worm Power has sold organic plant food products for years, and it has previously seen more demand than it can handle.[1122] The plant food sells on the website from $6.95 to $129.95.[1123] Development of a seed treatment may help the worms break into an industry worth over $3 billion annually.[1124]

With that kind of success, these worms should be able to eat their own dirt rather than taxpayers'.

ENDNOTES

1 Eldridge, David. "113th Congress Could Yield Fewest Laws in 60 Years." Web log post. *218 Blog*. Roll Call, 22 Sept. 2014. Web. 17 Oct. 2014. <http://blogs.rollcall.com/218/113th-congress-legacy-shutdowns-shoutdowns-gridlock/?dcz>.

2 Dupree, Jaimee. "This is the earliest departure by the Congress for the elections since 1960, when lawmakers left DC on September 1."18 September 2014, 5:45p.m. Tweet. <https://twitter.com/jamiedupree/status/512764338520604672>.

3 Isikoff, Michael. "DOJ Accuses Firm that Vetted Snowden of Faking 665,000 Background Checks." *Nbcnews.com*. NBC News. 23 January 2014. Web. <http://investigations.nbcnews.com/_news/2014/01/23/.UuLBsYpJl1M.twitter>.

4 The White House. Office of the Press Secretary. FACT SHEET: Emergency Supplemental Request to Address the Increase in Child and Adult Migration from Central America in the Rio Grande Valley Areas of the Southwest Border. Whitehouse.gov. N.p., 8 July 2014. Web. <http://www.whitehouse.gov/the-press-office/2014/07/08/fact-sheet-emergency-supplemental-request-address-increase-child-and-adu>.

5 Cowan, Richard. "Waves of Immigrant Minors Present Crisis for Obama, Congress." *Reuters.com*. Reuters. 28 May 2014. <http://www.reuters.com/article/2014/05/28/us-usa-immigration-children-idUSKBN0E814T20140528>.

6 Department of Homeland Security, Office of Inspector General. *U.S. Immigration and Customs Enforcement's Management of the Federal Employees' Compensation Act Program*. DHS-OIG. Rep. No.: OIG-14-105. Washington, D.C.: July 2014. Web. <http://www.oig.dhs.gov/assets/Mgmt/2014/OIG_14-105_Jul14.pdf>.

7 Stein, Sam. "Ebola Vaccine Would Likely Have Been Found By Now If Not For Budget Cuts: NIH Director." *Huffingtonpost.com*. TheHuffingtonPost.com Inc. 12 October 2014. Web. <http://www.huffingtonpost.com/2014/10/12/ebola-vaccine_n_5974148.html>.

8 Johnson, Judith. *A History of NIH Funding*. Congressional Research Service. 7 March 2014.

9 Little, Joe. "Perceptions of Americans Change after 3-week Visit from Pakistani journalists." *10news.com*. ABC10 NEWS. 31 March 2014. Web. <http://www.10news.com/news/perceptions-of-americans-change-after-3-week-visit-from-pakistani-journalists-03312014>.

10 "Historical Tables," The White House Office of Management and Budget, accessed 9 October 2014. Web. <http://www.whitehouse.gov/omb/budget/historicals>.

11" Monthly Budget Review for September 2014," Congressional Budget Office, September 2014; <http://www.cbo.gov/sites/default/files/cbofiles/attachments/49450-MBR.pdf >.

12 U.S. Senate Roll Call Votes 109th Congress – 1st Session. Vote on Coburn Amendment No. 2165 to H.R. 3058 As Modified. Web. <http://www.senate.gov/legislative/LIS/roll_call_lists/roll_call_vote_cfm.cfm?congress=109&session=1&vote=00262>.

13 "Oklahoma keeps unused airport open to collect federal checks – (OK) $450,000," Wastebook 2012, Office of Senator Tom Coburn, M.D., October 2012. <http://www.coburn.senate.gov/public/index.cfm?a=Files.Serve&File_id=b7b23f66-2d60-4d5a-8bc5-8522c7e1a40e>.

14 Correspondence from the Deputy Assistant Secretary for Grant Programs at the U.S. Department of Housing and Urban Development to the Executive Director of the Community Development Commission of the County of Los Angeles, October 16, 2012.

"16) California towns sell federal grants to neighbors – (CA) $206,426," Wastebook 2012, Office of Senator Tom Coburn, M.D., October 2012 <http://www.coburn.senate.gov/public/index.cfm?a=Files.Serve&File_id=b7b23f66-2d60-4d5a-8bc5-8522c7e1a40e>.

15 "#35, Science research dollars go to musical about biodiversity and climate change – (NY) $697,177," Wastebook 2012, Office of Senator Tom Coburn, M.D., October 2012; <http://www.coburn.senate.gov/public/index.cfm?a=Files.Serve&File_id=b7b23f66-2d60-4d5a-8bc5-8522c7e1a40e>.

16 USAspending.gov. "Prime Award Spending Data: US Department of State." PIID No. SBH20014M0253. <http://www.usaspending.gov/explore?fiscal_year=all&comingfrom=searchresults&piid=SBH20014M0253&typeofview=complete>.

17 Rein, Lisa. "Civil Servants Put On Paid Administrative Leave Can Get Stuck In an Ill-Defined Limbo." *Washingtonpost.com*. The Washington Post. 30 December 2012. <http://www.washingtonpost.com/lifestyle/style/civil-servants-accused-of-rule-breaking-can-get-stuck-in-an-ill-defined-limbo/2012/12/29/450ffc68-37e4-11e2-8a97-363b0f9a0ab3_story.html>.

18 "Pay & Leave Reference Materials." Office of Personnel Management. Accessed via web. 26 September 2014. <http://www.opm.gov/policy-data-oversight/pay-leave/reference-materials/>.

19 This is an extremely low estimate. The actual amount of money federal agencies spent paying the salaries of employees on administrative leave status is likely much higher. This number is based on a small sample of data we received from 11 agencies.

20 Data provided by the Government Accountability Office, October 2014.

21 Rein, Lisa. "Civil Servants Put On Paid Administrative Leave Can Get Stuck In an Ill-Defined Limbo." *Washingtonpost.com*. The Washington Post. 30 December 2012. <http://www.washingtonpost.com/lifestyle/style/civil-servants-accused-of-rule-breaking-can-get-stuck-in-an-ill-defined-limbo/2012/12/29/450ffc68-37e4-11e2-8a97-363b0f9a0ab3_story.html>.

22 U.S. Department of Defense, Office of Inspector General. *Alleged Misconduct: Mr. Stephen E. Calvery, Senior Executive Service, Director, Pentagon Force Protection Agency*. Report No. 20121204-000911, 20 February 2013.Web. <http://www.dodig.mil/FOIA/err/CalveryROI(Redacted).pdf>.

23 Data provided by the Government Accountability Office, October 2014.

24 Data provided by the Government Accountability Office, October 2014.

25 Data provided by the Government Accountability Office, October 2014.

26 Data provided by the Government Accountability Office, October 2014.

27 Authority for administrative leave comes from the federal statute governing annual and sick leave and its accompanying Office of Personnel Management (OPM) regulations that guideline removal and suspension procedures for employees facing adverse actions. See 5 U.S.C. § 6104, 6302(a); 5 C.F.R. § 752.404(b)(3)(iv).

28 Data provided by the Government Accountability Office, October 2014.

29 Data provided by the Government Accountability Office, October 2014.

30 Data provided by the Government Accountability Office, October 2014.

31 Martosko, David. "Lois Lerner, Embattled Official at the Heart of IRS Tea Party Scandal, Retires With Full Pension Likely Worth More Than $50,000 as an Internal Review Called for Her Firing." *Dailymail.co.uk*. Associated Newspapers Ltd. 23 September 2013. <http://www.dailymail.co.uk/news/article-2430174/Lois-Lerner-

embattled-official-heart-IRS-tea-party-scandal-retire-pension-likely-50-000-year-Congress-seeks-answers.html#ixzz3EFn3RAQY>.

32 Dilanian, Ken. "CIA Suspends Chief of Iran Operations Over Workplace Issues." *Latimes.com*. Los Angeles Times. 16 March 2014. < http://articles.latimes.com/2014/mar/16/nation/la-na-cia-workplace-20140317>.

33 Leonnig, Carol D. and David Nakamura. "Secret Service Agents Sent Home From Netherlands Were Warned To Avoid Trouble." *Washingtonpost.com*. The Washington Post. 26 March 2014. <http://www.washingtonpost.com/politics/secret-service-agents-on-obama-detail-sent-home-from-netherlands-after-night-of-drinking/2014/03/26/86d1a8a6-b4e6-11e3-8020-b2d790b3c9e1_story.html?clsrd>.

34 Subcommittee on Financial and Contracting Oversight. "Investigation into Allegations of Misconduct by the Former Acting and Deputy Inspector General of the Department of Homeland Security." United States Senate Committee on Homeland Security and Governmental Affairs. 24 April 2014. <http://www.ronjohnson.senate.gov/public/_cache/files/4f916bda-8373-4ac8-b2cd-4d0ba115e279/fco-report-investigation-into-allegations-of-misconduct-by-the-former-acting-and-deputy-inspector-general-of-the-department-of-homeland.pdf>.

35 Hicks, Josh. "Commerce Inspector General Places Two Officials on Leave After Call for Firings." *Washingtonpost.com*. The Washington Post. 7 August 2014. <http://www.washingtonpost.com/blogs/federal-eye/wp/2014/08/07/commerce-inspector-general-places-two-officials-on-leave-after-call-for-firings/>.

36 Kachmar, Kala. "Ala. VA Employee Accused of Sexually Abusing Patient." *Montgomeryadvertiser.com*. Gannett. 25 August 2014. <http://www.montgomeryadvertiser.com/story/news/2014/08/25/tuskegee-va-employee-arrested-for-sexually-abusing-patient/14583555/>.

37 Kachmar, Kala. "Tuskegee VA Employee Charged with DUI, Still Employed." *Montgomeryadvertiser.com*. Gannett. 21 September 2014. <http://www.montgomeryadvertiser.com/story/news/local/2014/09/21/tuskegee-va-employee-charged-dui-still-employed/15998469/>.

38 Troyan, Mary. "Nashville VA Employee Resigned before Facing Disciplinary Measures." *Tennessean.com*. Gannett. 7 September 2014. <http://www.tennessean.com/story/news/2014/09/08/nashville-va-employee-resigned-facing-disciplinary-measures/15269411/>.

39 Troyan, Mary. "Nashville VA Employee Resigned before Facing Disciplinary Measures." *Tennessean.com*. Gannett. 7 September 2014. <http://www.tennessean.com/story/news/2014/09/08/nashville-va-employee-resigned-facing-disciplinary-measures/15269411/>.

40 Kachmar, Kala. "Report: VA Employee Took Recovering Vet to Crack House." *Montgomeryadvertiser.com*. Gannett. 16 August 2014. <http://www.montgomeryadvertiser.com/story/news/local/alabama/2014/08/17/report-va-employee-took-recovering-vet-crack-house/14190573/>.

41 Gore, Leada. "Director, Chief of Staff of Central Alabama VA Placed on Administrative Leave." *Al.com*. Alabama Media Group. 21 August 2014. <http://www.al.com/news/index.ssf/2014/08/director_chief_of_staff_of_cen.html>.

42 Veterans Access, Choice, and Accountability Act of 2014, Public Law No: 113-146, 7 August 2014.

43 The White House. Office of the Press Secretary. *Remarks by the President at the Signing of the Veterans Access, Choice and Accountability Act*. 7 August 2014. <http://www.whitehouse.gov/the-press-office/2014/08/07/remarks-president-signing-veterans-access-choice-and-accountability-act>.

44 Troyan, Mary. "Law Making It Easier to Fire VA Executives Still Unused." *Montgomeryadvertiser.com*. Gannett. 5 September 2014. <http://www.montgomeryadvertiser.com/story/news/local/alabama/2014/09/05/law-making-easier-fire-va-executives-still-unused/15115237/>.

45 U.S. Department of Veterans Affairs, Office of Inspector General. *Administrative Investigation: Failure to Properly Supervise, Misuse of Official Time and Resources, and Prohibited Personnel Practice VA Center for Innovation VA Central Office*. Report No. 13-01488-86, 24 February 2014. Web. <http://www.va.gov/oig/pubs/VAOIG-13-01488-86r.pdf>.

46 Letter from SSA to Senator Coburn, August 20, 2014.

47 Letter from SSA to Senator Coburn, August 20, 2014.

48 Letter from DHS to Senator Coburn, August 21, 2014.

49 Letter from DHS to Senator Coburn, August 21, 2014.

50 Letter from DHS to Senator Coburn, August 21, 2014.

51 Leonnig, Carol D. and David Nakamura. "Secret Service Agents Sent Home From Netherlands Were Warned To Avoid Trouble." *Washingtonpost.com*. The Washington Post. 26 March 2014. <http://www.washingtonpost.com/politics/secret-service-agents-on-obama-detail-sent-home-from-netherlands-after-night-of-drinking/2014/03/26/86d1a8a6-b4e6-11e3-8020-b2d790b3c9e1_story.html?clsrd>.

52 Leonnig, Carol D., David Nakamura, and Michael Birnbaum. "Secret Service Incident in Netherlands Was on Heels of Car Wreck During Obama's Miami Trip." *Washingtonpost.com*. The Washington Post. 26 March 2014. <http://www.washingtonpost.com/politics/secret-service-agents-sent-home-from-netherlands-were-warned-to-avoid-trouble/2014/03/26/ff01c618-b54e-11e3-8020-b2d790b3c9e1_story.html>.

53 Lederman, Josh. "Secret Service Agent Found Drunk in Hotel Room." *Ap.org*. The Associated Press. 26 March 2014. <http://bigstory.ap.org/article/3-secret-service-agents-benched-obama-trip-0>.

54 Leonnig, Carol D., David Nakamura, and Michael Birnbaum. "Secret Service Incident in Netherlands Was on Heels of Car Wreck During Obama's Miami Trip." *Washingtonpost.com*. The Washington Post. 26 March 2014. <http://www.washingtonpost.com/politics/secret-service-agents-sent-home-from-netherlands-were-warned-to-avoid-trouble/2014/03/26/ff01c618-b54e-11e3-8020-b2d790b3c9e1_story.html>.

55 Leonnig, Carol D., David Nakamura, and Michael Birnbaum. "Secret Service Incident in Netherlands Was on Heels of Car Wreck During Obama's Miami Trip." *Washingtonpost.com*. The Washington Post. 26 March 2014. <http://www.washingtonpost.com/politics/secret-service-agents-sent-home-from-netherlands-were-warned-to-avoid-trouble/2014/03/26/ff01c618-b54e-11e3-8020-b2d790b3c9e1_story.html>.

56 "SALARY TABLE 2014-GS INCORPORATING THE 1% GENERAL SCHEDULE INCREASE EFFECTIVE JANUARY 2014." Office of Personnel Management. Accessed via web. 23 September 2014. <http://www.opm.gov/policy-data-oversight/pay-leave/salaries-wages/salary-tables/pdf/2014/saltbl.pdf>.

57 Leonnig, Carol D. and David Nakamura. "Secret Service Agents Sent Home From Netherlands Were Warned To Avoid Trouble." *Washingtonpost.com*. The Washington Post. 26 March 2014. <http://www.washingtonpost.com/politics/secret-service-agents-on-obama-detail-sent-home-from-netherlands-after-night-of-drinking/2014/03/26/86d1a8a6-b4e6-11e3-8020-b2d790b3c9e1_story.html?clsrd>.

58 Leonnig, Carol D., David Nakamura, and Michael Birnbaum. "Secret Service Incident in Netherlands Was on Heels of Car Wreck During Obama's Miami Trip." *Washingtonpost.com*. The Washington Post. 26 March 2014. <http://www.washingtonpost.com/politics/secret-service-agents-sent-home-from-netherlands-were-warned-to-avoid-trouble/2014/03/26/ff01c618-b54e-11e3-8020-b2d790b3c9e1_story.html>.

59 Martosko, David "'How much pornography would it take for an EPA employee to lose their job?' Congress fumes as daily porn-surfing worker is STILL collecting $120,000 Salary." *Dailymail.co.uk*. Associated Newspapers Ltd. 7 May 2014. <http://www.dailymail.co.uk/news/article-2622503/How-pornography-EPA-employee-lose-job-Congress-fumes-daily-porn-surfing-EPA-employee-STILL-collecting-120-000-salary.html>.

60 Statement by Allan Williams, Deputy Assistant Inspector General for Investigations, before the Committee on Oversight and Government Reform U.S. House of Representatives. "The Office of Inspector General's Cases of Employee Misconduct at the Environmental Protection Agency." 7 May 2014 <http://oversight.house.gov/wp-content/uploads/2014/05/Williams-Statement.pdf>.

61 Martosko, David "'How much pornography would it take for an EPA employee to lose their job?' Congress fumes as daily porn-surfing worker is STILL collecting

$120,000 Salary." *Dailymail.co.uk*. Associated Newspapers Ltd. 7 May 2014. <http://www.dailymail.co.uk/news/article-2622503/How-pornography-EPA-employee-lose-job-Congress-fumes-daily-porn-surfing-EPA-employee-STILL-collecting-120-000-salary.html>.

62 Martosko, David "'How much pornography would it take for an EPA employee to lose their job?' Congress fumes as daily porn-surfing worker is STILL collecting $120,000 Salary." *Dailymail.co.uk*. Associated Newspapers Ltd. 7 May 2014. <http://www.dailymail.co.uk/news/article-2622503/How-pornography-EPA-employee-lose-job-Congress-fumes-daily-porn-surfing-EPA-employee-STILL-collecting-120-000-salary.html>.

63 Martosko, David "'How much pornography would it take for an EPA employee to lose their job?' Congress fumes as daily porn-surfing worker is STILL collecting $120,000 Salary." *Dailymail.co.uk*. Associated Newspapers Ltd. 7 May 2014. <http://www.dailymail.co.uk/news/article-2622503/How-pornography-EPA-employee-lose-job-Congress-fumes-daily-porn-surfing-EPA-employee-STILL-collecting-120-000-salary.html>.

64 Wagner, Dennis. "Auditor Ties VA Waits to Deaths." *AZcentral.com*. The Republic. 17 September 2014. <http://www.azcentral.com/story/news/politics/investigations/2014/09/17/va-inspector-general-delayed-care-may-have-contributed-deaths/15793641/>.

65 Skoloff, Brian "3 On Leave Over Allegations On Phoenix Vet Care," ap.org. The Associated Press. 1 May 2014 <http://bigstory.ap.org/article/3-leave-over-allegations-phoenix-vet-care>.

66 Harris, Craig. "Phoenix VA: Ousted Exec Keeps Salary While on Leave." *AZcentral.com*. The Republic. 20 June 2014. <http://www.azcentral.com/story/news/politics/2014/06/20/phoenix-va-ousted-exec-keeps-salary-leave/11101981/>.

67 U.S. Treasury Inspector General. *Inappropriate Criteria Were Used to Identify Tax-Exempt Applications for Review*. Reference No. 2013-10-053. 14 May 2013. <http://www.treasury.gov/tigta/auditreports/2013reports/201310053fr.pdf>.

68 Stein, Sam. "Obama On IRS Scandal: 'I Have Got No Patience' For It," huffingtonpost.com. TheHuffingtonPost.com, Inc. 13 May 2014; <http://www.huffingtonpost.com/2013/05/13/obama-irs-scandal_n_3266577.html>.

69 U.S. Treasury Inspector General. *Inappropriate Criteria Were Used to Identify Tax-Exempt Applications for Review*. Reference No. 2013-10-053. 14 May 2013. <http://www.treasury.gov/tigta/auditreports/2013reports/201310053fr.pdf>.

70 McKinnon, John K. "U.S. Judge Orders IRS to Explain Lost Emails." *Wsj.com*. Wall Street Journal. 10 July 2014. <http://online.wsj.com/articles/u-s-judge-orders-irs-to-explain-lost-emails-1405015820>.

71 Martosko, David. "Unearthed emails show embattled IRS official knew her agency was secretly targeting conservative groups," dailymail.co.uk. Associated Newspapers, Ltd. 12 September 2013. <http://www.dailymail.co.uk/news/article-2419512/Lois-Lerner-emails-IRS-official-knew-agency-targeted-conservative-groups.html>.

72 Bade, Rachel. "Timeline of IRS Scandal." *Politico.com*. Politico LLC. 22 September 2014. <http://www.politico.com/story/2014/09/timeline-of-the-irs-scandal-111185.html>.

73 Foster, Daniel. "Firing Lois Lerner." *Nationalreview.org*. National Review Online. 23 May 2013. <http://www.nationalreview.com/article/349115/firing-lois-lerner-daniel-foster/>.

74 Martosko, David. "Lois Lerner, Embattled Official at the Heart of IRS Tea Party Scandal, Retires with Full Pension Likely Worth More than $50,000 as an Internal Review Called for Her Firing." *Dailymail.co.uk*. Associated Newspapers, Ltd. 23 September 2013. <http://www.dailymail.co.uk/news/article-2430174/Lois-Lerner-embattled-official-heart-IRS-tea-party-scandal-retire-pension-likely-50-000-year-Congress-seeks-answers.html#ixzz3EFn3RAQY>.

75 Kachmar, Kala. "Report: VA Employee Took Recovering Vet to Crack House." *Montgomeryadvertiser.com*. Gannett. 16 August 2014. <http://www.montgomeryadvertiser.com/story/news/local/alabama/2014/08/17/report-va-employee-took-recovering-vet-crack-house/14190573/>.

76 Kachmar, Kala. "Report: VA Employee Took Recovering Vet to Crack House." *Montgomeryadvertiser.com*. Gannett. 16 August 2014. <http://www.montgomeryadvertiser.com/story/news/local/alabama/2014/08/17/report-va-employee-took-recovering-vet-crack-house/14190573/>.

77 Hicks, Josh. "Commerce Inspector General Places Two Officials on Leave After Call for Firings." *Washingtonpost.com*. The Washington Post. 7 August 2014. <http://www.washingtonpost.com/blogs/federal-eye/wp/2014/08/07/commerce-inspector-general-places-two-officials-on-leave-after-call-for-firings/>.

78 Leada Gore, "Director, chief of staff of Central Alabama VA placed on administrative leave," AL.com, August 21, 2014; http://www.al.com/news/index.ssf/2014/08/director_chief_of_staff_of_cen.html .

79 Rawls, Phillip. "VA Worker in Alabama Charged with Sexual Abuse." *Washingtontimes.com*. Associated Press. 19 August 2014. <http://www.washingtontimes.com/news/2014/aug/19/va-employee-in-alabama-charged-with-sexual-abuse/#ixzz3E9poxAwe>.

80 Kachmar, Kala. "Ala. VA Employee Accused of Sexually Abusing Patient." *Montgomeryadvertiser.com*. Gannett. 25 August 2014. <http://www.montgomeryadvertiser.com/story/news/2014/08/25/tuskegee-va-employee-arrested-for-sexually-abusing-patient/14583555/>.

81 Kachmar, Kala "Tuskegee VA Patient Charged with Sexual Abuse." *Montgomeryadvertiser.com*. Gannett. 19 August 2014. <http://www.montgomeryadvertiser.com/story/news/2014/08/19/tuskegee-va-employee-charged-with-sexual-abuse/14285917/>.

82 Kachmar, Kala. "Tuskegee VA Employee Charged with DUI, Still Employed." *Montgomeryadvertiser.com*. Gannett. 21 September 2014. <http://www.montgomeryadvertiser.com/story/news/local/2014/09/21/tuskegee-va-employee-charged-dui-still-employed/15998469/>.

83 Kachmar, Kala. "Tuskegee VA Employee Charged with DUI, Still Employed." *Montgomeryadvertiser.com*. Gannett. 21 September 2014. <http://www.montgomeryadvertiser.com/story/news/local/2014/09/21/tuskegee-va-employee-charged-dui-still-employed/15998469/>.

84 Kachmar, Kala. "Ala. VA Employee Accused of Sexually Abusing Patient." *Montgomeryadvertiser.com*. Gannett. 25 August 2014. <http://www.montgomeryadvertiser.com/story/news/2014/08/25/tuskegee-va-employee-arrested-for-sexually-abusing-patient/14583555/>.

85 Kachmar, Kala. "Ala. VA Employee Accused of Sexually Abusing Patient." *Montgomeryadvertiser.com*. Gannett. 25 August 2014. <http://www.montgomeryadvertiser.com/story/news/2014/08/25/tuskegee-va-employee-arrested-for-sexually-abusing-patient/14583555/>.

86 Kachmar, Kala. "Ala. VA Employee Accused of Sexually Abusing Patient." *Montgomeryadvertiser.com*. Gannett. 25 August 2014. <http://www.montgomeryadvertiser.com/story/news/2014/08/25/tuskegee-va-employee-arrested-for-sexually-abusing-patient/14583555/>.

87 Tschida, Stephen. "NIH Police Officer Accused of Road Rage." *Wjla.com*. WJLA ABC 7. 6 June 2014 <http://www.wjla.com/articles/2014/06/nih-police-officer-accused-of-road-rage-103868.html>.

88 Tschida, Stephen. "NIH Police Officer Accused of Road Rage." *Wjla.com*. WJLA ABC 7. 6 June 2014 <http://www.wjla.com/articles/2014/06/nih-police-officer-accused-of-road-rage-103868.html>.

89 Dilanian, Ken. "CIA Suspends Chief of Iran Operations Over Workplace Issues." *Latimes.com*. Los Angeles Times. 16 March 2014. < http://articles.latimes.com/2014/mar/16/nation/la-na-cia-workplace-20140317>.

90 Dilanian, Ken. "CIA Suspends Chief of Iran Operations Over Workplace Issues." *Latimes.com*. Los Angeles Times. 16 March 2014. < http://articles.latimes.com/2014/mar/16/nation/la-na-cia-workplace-20140317>.

91 Dilanian, Ken. "Bad Management Drives Talent from CIA, Internal Reports Suggest." *Latimes.com*. Los Angeles Times. 29 July 2013. <http://articles.latimes.com/2013/jul/29/nation/la-na-cia-management-20130730>.

92 Dilanian, Ken. "Bad Management Drives Talent from CIA, Internal Reports Suggest." *Latimes.com*. Los Angeles Times. 29 July 2013. <http://articles.latimes.com/2013/jul/29/nation/la-na-cia-management-20130730>.

93 Troyan, Mary. "Nashville VA Employee Resigned before Facing Disciplinary Measures." *Tennessean.com*. Gannett. 7 September 2014. <http://www.tennessean.com/story/news/2014/09/08/nashville-va-employee-resigned-facing-disciplinary-measures/15269411/>.

94 U.S. Department of Veterans Affairs, Office of Inspector General. *Administrative Investigation: Failure to Properly Supervise, Misuse of Official Time and Resources, and Prohibited Personnel Practice VA Center for Innovation VA Central Office*. Report No. 13-01488-86, 24 February 2014. Web. <http://www.va.gov/oig/pubs/VAOIG-13-01488-86r.pdf>.

95 Shane, Leo, III. "IG: Managers Let VA Employee Get Away with Cheating Agency." *Militarytimes.com*. Gannett. 4 March 2014. <http://www.militarytimes.com/article/20140304/NEWS/303040012/IG-Managers-let-VA-employee-get-away-cheating-agency>.

96 U.S. Department of Veterans Affairs, Office of Inspector General. *Administrative Investigation: Failure to Properly Supervise, Misuse of Official Time and Resources, and Prohibited Personnel Practice VA Center for Innovation VA Central Office*. Report No. 13-01488-86, 24 February 2014. Web. <http://www.va.gov/oig/pubs/VAOIG-13-01488-86r.pdf>.

97 U.S. Department of Veterans Affairs, Office of Inspector General. *Administrative Investigation: Failure to Properly Supervise, Misuse of Official Time and Resources, and Prohibited Personnel Practice VA Center for Innovation VA Central Office*. Report No. 13-01488-86, 24 February 2014. Web. <http://www.va.gov/oig/pubs/VAOIG-13-01488-86r.pdf>.

98 U.S. Department of Veterans Affairs, Office of Inspector General. *Administrative Investigation: Failure to Properly Supervise, Misuse of Official Time and Resources, and Prohibited Personnel Practice VA Center for Innovation VA Central Office*. Report No. 13-01488-86, 24 February 2014. Web. <http://www.va.gov/oig/pubs/VAOIG-13-01488-86r.pdf>.

99 U.S. Department of Veterans Affairs, Office of Inspector General. *Administrative Investigation: Failure to Properly Supervise, Misuse of Official Time and Resources, and Prohibited Personnel Practice VA Center for Innovation VA Central Office*. Report No. 13-01488-86, 24 February 2014. Web. <http://www.va.gov/oig/pubs/VAOIG-13-01488-86r.pdf>.

100 U.S. Department of Veterans Affairs, Office of Inspector General. *Administrative Investigation: Failure to Properly Supervise, Misuse of Official Time and Resources, and Prohibited Personnel Practice VA Center for Innovation VA Central Office*. Report No. 13-01488-86, 24 February 2014. Web. <http://www.va.gov/oig/pubs/VAOIG-13-01488-86r.pdf>.

101 This amount is an extremely low estimate. The actual amount of money federal agencies spent on the salaries of employees on administrative leave status is likely much higher. This number is based on a small sample of data we received from 11 agencies.

118 Lukits, Ann. "After Exercise, Massage as Fast as a Rabbit." *Wsj.com*. Wall Street Journal. 10 June 2013. <http://online.wsj.com/news/articles/SB10001424127887324634304578537492538857534>.

119 *Massage Therapy in Eccentric Exercise Induced Muscle Weakness and Inflammation*. "Project Information 5R01AT004922-04," National Institutes of Health Research Portfolio Online Reporting Tools website, page last updated on 15 October 2014, accessed 15 October 2014 <http://projectreporter.nih.gov/project_info_details.cfm?aid=8290073&icde=21622004>.

120 Haas, Caroline, Timothy Butterfield, Sarah Abshire, Yi Zhao, Xiaoli Zhang, David Jarjoura, and Thomas Best. "Massage Timing Affects Postexercise Muscle Recovery and Inflammation in a Rabbit Model." *Medicine & Science in Sports & Exercise*. 2013 June; 45(6): 1105-1112. Epub 1 June 2014. <http://www.ncbi.nlm.nih.gov/pmc/articles/PMC3632662/>.

121 Haas, Caroline, Timothy Butterfield, Sarah Abshire, Yi Zhao, Xiaoli Zhang, David Jarjoura, and Thomas Best. "Massage Timing Affects Postexercise Muscle Recovery and Inflammation in a Rabbit Model." *Medicine & Science in Sports & Exercise*. 2013 June; 45(6): 1105-1112. Epub 1 June 2014. <http://www.ncbi.nlm.nih.gov/pmc/articles/PMC3632662/>.

122 Wang, Qian, Hansong Zeng, Thomas M. Best, Caroline Haas, Ned T. Heffner, Sudha Agarwal, and Yi Zhao. "A Mechatronic System for Quantitative Application and Assessment of Massage-Like Actions in Small Animals." *Annals of Biomedical Engineering* 42.1 (2014): 36-49. Web. <http://www.ncbi.nlm.nih.gov/pubmed/23943071>.

123 *Massage Therapy in Eccentric Exercise Induced Muscle Weakness and Inflammation*. "Project Information 5R01AT004922-04," National Institutes of Health Research Portfolio Online Reporting Tools website, page last updated on 15 October 2014, accessed 15 October 2014. <http://projectreporter.nih.gov/project_info_details.cfm?aid=8290073&icde=21622004>.

124 Caldwell, Emily. "Study: Massaging Muscles Facilitates Recovery After Exercise." *Researchnews.osu.edu*. The Ohio State University. 12 August 2008. <http://researchnews.osu.edu/archive/compload.htm>.

125 Caldwell, Emily. "Study: Massaging Muscles Facilitates Recovery After Exercise." *Researchnews.osu.edu*. The Ohio State University. 12 August 2008. <http://researchnews.osu.edu/archive/compload.htm>.

126 Haas, Caroline, Timothy Butterfield, Sarah Abshire, Yi Zhao, Xiaoli Zhang, David Jarjoura, and Thomas Best. "Massage Timing Affects Postexercise Muscle Recovery and Inflammation in a Rabbit Model." *Medicine & Science in Sports & Exercise*. 2013 June; 45(6): 1105-1112. Epub 1 June 2014. <http://www.ncbi.nlm.nih.gov/pmc/articles/PMC3632662/>.

127 *Massage Therapy in Eccentric Exercise Induced Muscle Weakness and Inflammation*. "Project Information 5R01AT004922-04," National Institutes of Health Research Portfolio Online Reporting Tools website, page last updated on 15 October 2014, accessed 15 October 2014. <http://projectreporter.nih.gov/project_info_details.cfm?aid=8290073&icde=21622004>.

128 *Massage Therapy in Eccentric Exercise Induced Muscle Weakness and Inflammation*. "Project Information 5R01AT004922-04," National Institutes of Health Research Portfolio Online Reporting Tools website, page last updated on 15 October 2014, accessed 15 October 2014. <http://projectreporter.nih.gov/project_info_details.cfm?aid=8290073&icde=21622004>.

129 Brown, T.C. "Rx: Engineering." *Engineering.osu.edu*. The Ohio State University College of Engineering. 22 December 2011. <https://engineering.osu.edu/news/2011/12/rx-engineering>.

130 Sinclair, Brendan, "America's Army Bill: $32.8 Million," *GameSpot.com*, CBS Interactive Inc. 8 December 2009. <http://www.gamespot.com/articles/americas-army-bill-328-million/1100-6242635/>.

131 Hodes, Jacob, and Emma Ruby-Sachs, "'America's Army' Targets Youth," *TheNation.com*, The Nation. 23 August 2002. <http://www.thenation.com/article/americas-army-targets-youth#>.

132 Email from the Congressional Research Service to minority staff of the Homeland Security and Governmental Affairs Committee on October 8, 2014.

133 Sinclair, Brendan, "America's Army Bill: $32.8 Million," *GameSpot.com*, CBS Interactive Inc. 8 December 2009. <http://www.gamespot.com/articles/americas-army-bill-328-million/1100-6242635/>.

134 "Topic: Exploiting Terrorist Use of Games & Virtual Environments," NSA, 2007, http://cryptome.org/2013/12/nsa-spy-games.pdf, accessed September 26, 2014.

135 Kyle Orland, "Snowden leak examines gaming as a terrorist propaganda and training tool," ARS Tecnica, December 9, 2013, http://arstechnica.com/gaming/2013/12/snowden-leak-examines-gaming-as-a-terrorist-propaganda-and-training-tool/

136 "Topic: Exploiting Terrorist Use of Games & Virtual Environments," NSA, 2007, http://cryptome.org/2013/12/nsa-spy-games.pdf, accessed September 26, 2014.

137 News Release, "RFI-4 New Mission: Intercept." *Americasarmy.com*. America's Army. 24 September 24, 2014, http://news.americasarmy.com/rfi-4-new-mission-intercept/.

138 "America's Army: The Official U.S. Army Game," Facebook page, September 24, 2014 post, <https://www.facebook.com/pages/Americas-Army-The-Official-US-Army-Game/81797167460>. accessed September 26, 2014.

139 Tim Stephens, "Study of mountain lion energetics shows the power of the pounce," University of California-Santa Cruz News Center, October 2, 2014; http://news.ucsc.edu/2014/10/puma-energetics.html .

140 "The National Science Foundation: Under the Microscope," Office of Senator Tom Coburn, M.D., April 2011; http://www.coburn.senate.gov/public/index.cfm?a=Files.serve&File_id=2dccf06d-65fe-4087-b58d-b43ff68987fa .

141 Justin D Foster, et. al., "A freely-moving monkey treadmill model," Journal of *Neural Engineering, August 6, 2014;* http://iopscience.iop.org/1741-2552/11/4/046020/pdf/1741-2552_11_4_046020.pdf .

142 "Veterinary Student Spends the Summer Studying Hypertension," Louisiana State University School of Veterinary Medicine 2009-2010 Research Report, https://www1.vetmed.lsu.edu/PDFs/item22608.pdf .

143 J. A. Davidson and D. K. Beede, "Exercise training of late-pregnant and nonpregnant dairy cows affects physical fitness and acid-base homeostasis," Journal of Dairy Science, Vol. 92, No. 2, 2009; http://www.journalofdairyscience.org/article/S0022-0302(09)70359-5/pdf .

144 Arnold, Allison S; Lee, David V; Biewener, Andrew A, "Modulation of joint moments and work in the goat hindlimb with locomotor speed and surface grade," The Journal of experimental biology. 2013 Jun 15; 216 (Pt 12) :2201-12. http://projectreporter.nih.gov/project_info_description.cfm?aid=7080442&icde=22168695

145 "ANIMA (Accelerometer Network Integrator for Mobile Animals), a New Instrument Package for Integrating Behavior, Physiology and Ecology of Wild Mammals," Award Abstract #0963022, National Science Foundation award database website, accessed October 17, 2014; http://www.nsf.gov/awardsearch/showAward?AWD_ID=0963022&HistoricalAwards=false .

146 Tim Stephens, "Study of mountain lion energetics shows the power of the pounce," University of California-Santa Cruz News Center, October 2, 2014; http://news.ucsc.edu/2014/10/puma-energetics.html .

147 Tim Stephens, "Study of mountain lion energetics shows the power of the pounce," University of California-Santa Cruz News Center, October 2, 2014; http://news.ucsc.edu/2014/10/puma-energetics.html .

148 Tim Stephens, "Study of mountain lion energetics shows the power of the pounce," University of California-Santa Cruz News Center, October 2, 2014; http://news.ucsc.edu/2014/10/puma-energetics.html .

149 Tim Stephens, "Study of mountain lion energetics shows the power of the pounce," University of California-Santa Cruz News Center, October 2, 2014; http://news.ucsc.edu/2014/10/puma-energetics.html .

150 Tim Stephens, "Study of mountain lion energetics shows the power of the pounce," University of California-Santa Cruz News Center, October 2, 2014; http://news.ucsc.edu/2014/10/puma-energetics.html .

151 "ANIMA (Accelerometer Network Integrator for Mobile Animals), a New Instrument Package for Integrating Behavior, Physiology and Ecology of Wild Mammals," Award Abstract #0963022, National Science Foundation award database website, accessed October 17, 2014; http://www.nsf.gov/awardsearch/showAward?AWD_ID=0963022&HistoricalAwards=false .

152 "ANIMA (Accelerometer Network Integrator for Mobile Animals), a New Instrument Package for Integrating Behavior, Physiology and Ecology of Wild Mammals," Award Abstract #0963022, National Science Foundation award database website, accessed October 17, 2014; http://www.nsf.gov/awardsearch/showAward?AWD_ID=0963022&HistoricalAwards=false .

153 Shenon, Philip and Kevin Flynn. "THREATS AND RESPONSES: WITNESSES; Mayor Tells Panel 'Pork Barrel Politics' Is Increasing Risk of Terrorism for City." *Nyimes.com*. The New York Times Company. 20 May 2004. <http://www.nytimes.com/2004/05/20/nyregion/threats-responses-witnesses-mayor-tells-panel-pork-barrel-politics-increasing.html>.

154 "Notice of Availability of State and Federal Funds: Fiscal Year 2013 Tactical Team Grant Program." *Ny.gov*. Website of the State of New York. 11 September 2013. <http://docs.dos.ny.gov/info/register/2013/sept11/pdf/availability.pdf>.

155 Davies, Jerry. "Eighth Annual Farmers Insurance Study Ranks the Most Secure Places to Live in the U.S." Farmers Insurance. Press Release. 15 December 2011. Web. http://www.farmers.com/12_15_11_SecureCities.html>.

156 Davies, Jerry. "Eighth Annual Farmers Insurance Study Ranks the Most Secure Places to Live in the U.S." Farmers Insurance. Press Release. 15 December 2011. Web. http://www.farmers.com/12_15_11_SecureCities.html>.

157 Website of the Ithaca Police Department, accessed 15 October 2014. <http://cityofithaca.org/departments/ipd/index.cfm>.

158 Williamson, Jamie. "Ithaca Swat Team Receives Federal Grant." Media Release. Ithaca Police Department, 23 January 2014. <http://www.egovlink.com/public_documents300/ithaca/published_documents/Ithaca_Police_Department/Press%20Releases/2014/01-23-2014%20Ithaca%20SWAT%20Team%20Receives%20Federal%20Grant.pdf>.

159 Davies, Jerry. "Eighth Annual Farmers Insurance Study Ranks the Most Secure Places to Live in the U.S." Farmers Insurance. Press Release. 15 December 2011. Web. http://www.farmers.com/12_15_11_SecureCities.html>.

160 Regan, Michal. "Twin Cities SWAT Team Gets Grant." *Tonawanda-news.com*. Tonawanda News, 23 January 2014. <http://www.tonawanda-news.com/news/local_news/article_78402010-dd07-5b41-90ab-bea80fd464c0.html>.

161 Total amount of funding obligated under OPM Contract Number OPM1511C0015 from February 2014 to the most recent reported data from July 2014, as reported in the Federal Procurement Data System-Next Generation.

162 NEED CITE

163 Isikoff, Michael. "DOJ Accuses Firm That Vetted Snowden Of Faking 665,000 Background Checks." *Nbcnews.com*. NBC News. 23 January 2014. <http://investigations.nbcnews.com/_news/2014/01/23/22401812-doj-accuses-firm-that-vetted-snowden-of-faking-665000-background-checks?lite>.

164 Hamburger, Tom and Debbi Wilgoren. "Justice Department Says USIS Submitted 665,000 Incomplete Background Checks." *Washingtonpost.com*. The Washington Post. 23 January 2014. <http://www.washingtonpost.com/world/national-security/justice-department-joins-lawsuit-against-usis-over-background-checks/2014/01/23/db16e244-8432-11e3-8099-9181471f7aaf_story.html>.

165 Office of the Director of National Intelligence. *2013 Report on Security Clearance Determinations*. <http://www.dni.gov/files/documents/2013%20Report%20on%20Security%20Clearance%20Determinations.pdf>. p4.

166 *Percival v. U.S. Investigations Services Inc.*, Civil Action No. 11-CV-527-WKW, M.D. AL. N.D. Doc. 26 Filed 22 January 2013. <http://s3.documentcloud.org/documents/1008869/justice-department-joins-suit-against-usis.pdf>. p5.

167 *Percival v. U.S. Investigations Services Inc.*, Civil Action No. 11-CV-527-WKW, M.D. AL. N.D. Doc. 26 Filed 22 January 2013. <http://s3.documentcloud.org/

documents/1008869/justice-department-joins-suit-against-usis.pdf>. p10.

168 *Percival v. U.S. Investigations Services Inc.*, Civil Action No. 11-CV-527-WKW, M.D. AL. N.D. Doc. 26 Filed 22 January 2013. <http://s3.documentcloud.org/documents/1008869/justice-department-joins-suit-against-usis.pdf>. p11

169 *Percival v. U.S. Investigations Services Inc.*, Civil Action No. 11-CV-527-WKW, M.D. AL. N.D. Doc. 26 Filed 22 January 2013. <http://s3.documentcloud.org/documents/1008869/justice-department-joins-suit-against-usis.pdf>. p5

170 *Percival v. U.S. Investigations Services Inc.*, Civil Action No. 11-CV-527-WKW, M.D. AL. N.D. Doc. 26 Filed 22 January 2013. <http://s3.documentcloud.org/documents/1008869/justice-department-joins-suit-against-usis.pdf>. p15.

171 *Percival v. U.S. Investigations Services Inc.*, Civil Action No. 11-CV-527-WKW, M.D. AL. N.D. Doc. 26 Filed 22 January 2013. <http://s3.documentcloud.org/documents/1008869/justice-department-joins-suit-against-usis.pdf>. p16.

172 *Percival v. U.S. Investigations Services Inc.*, Civil Action No. 11-CV-527-WKW, M.D. AL. N.D. Doc. 26 Filed 22 January 2013. <http://s3.documentcloud.org/documents/1008869/justice-department-joins-suit-against-usis.pdf>. p16.

173 Bushman, Brad J., C. Nathan DeWall, Richard S. Pond Jr., and Michael D. Hanus. "Low glucose relates to greater aggression in married couples." Proceedings of the National Academy of Sciences of the United States of America 111.17 (2014): 6254-6257. ProQuest. Web. 16 Oct. 2014.

174 Bushman, Brad J., C. Nathan DeWall, Richard S. Pond Jr., and Michael D. Hanus. "Low glucose relates to greater aggression in married couples." Proceedings of the National Academy of Sciences of the United States of America 111.17 (2014): 6254-6257. ProQuest. Web. 16 Oct. 2014.

175 Bushman, Brad J., C. Nathan DeWall, Richard S. Pond Jr., and Michael D. Hanus. "Low glucose relates to greater aggression in married couples." Proceedings of the National Academy of Sciences of the United States of America 111.17 (2014): 6254-6257. ProQuest. Web. 16 Oct. 2014.

176 Borenstein, Seth. "Study: Snack might help avoid fight with spouse," *ap.org*. Associated Press. 14 April 2014. <http://bigstory.ap.org/article/study-snack-might-help-avoid-fight-spouse>.

177 Bushman, Brad J., C. Nathan DeWall, Richard S. Pond Jr., and Michael D. Hanus. "Low glucose relates to greater aggression in married couples." Proceedings of the National Academy of Sciences of the United States of America 111.17 (2014): 6254-6257. ProQuest. Web. 16 Oct. 2014.

178 Borenstein, Seth. "Study: Snack might help avoid fight with spouse," *ap.org*. Associated Press. 14 April 2014. <http://bigstory.ap.org/article/study-snack-might-help-avoid-fight-spouse>.

179 NSF Grant 1104118 (http://www.nsf.gov/awardsearch/showAward?AWD_ID=1104118).

180 Hagen, Susan. "Monkeys Also Believe in Winning Streaks, Study Shows." *Rochester.edu*. University of Rochester Newscenter. 27 June 2014. <http://www.rochester.edu/newscenter/monkeys-also-believe-in-winning-streaks-study-shows/>.

181 "Hagen, Susan. "Monkeys Also Believe in Winning Streaks, Study Shows." *Rochester.edu*. University of Rochester Newscenter. 27 June 2014. <http://www.rochester.edu/newscenter/monkeys-also-believe-in-winning-streaks-study-shows/>.

182 Hagen, Susan. "Monkeys Also Believe in Winning Streaks, Study Shows." *Rochester.edu*. University of Rochester Newscenter. 27 June 2014. <http://www.rochester.edu/newscenter/monkeys-also-believe-in-winning-streaks-study-shows/>.

183 Hagen, Susan. "Monkeys Also Believe in Winning Streaks, Study Shows." *Rochester.edu*. University of Rochester Newscenter. 27 June 2014. <http://www.rochester.edu/newscenter/monkeys-also-believe-in-winning-streaks-study-shows/>.

184 Blanchard, Tommy C., Andreas Wilke, and Benjamin Y. Hayden. "Hot-Hand Bias in Rhesus Monkeys." Journal of Experimental Psychology 40.3 (2014): 280-286. ProQuest. Web. 16 Oct. 2014.

185 Hagen, Susan. "Monkeys Also Believe in Winning Streaks, Study Shows." *Rochester.edu*. University of Rochester Newscenter. 27 June 2014. <http://www.rochester.edu/newscenter/monkeys-also-believe-in-winning-streaks-study-shows/>.

186 Blanchard, Tommy C., Andreas Wilke, and Benjamin Y. Hayden. "Hot-Hand Bias in Rhesus Monkeys." Journal of Experimental Psychology 40.3 (2014): 280-286. ProQuest. Web. 16 Oct. 2014.

187 Hagen, Susan. "Monkeys Also Believe in Winning Streaks, Study Shows." *Rochester.edu*. University of Rochester Newscenter. 27 June 2014. <http://www.rochester.edu/newscenter/monkeys-also-believe-in-winning-streaks-study-shows/>.

188 NSF Grant. "CAREER: Flexible control of reward based decisions," Award Abstract #125357 <http://www.nsf.gov/awardsearch/showAward?AWD_ID=1253576&HistoricalAwards=false>.

189 Kuriloff, Aaron and Darrell Preston. "In Stadium Building Spree, U.S. Taxpayers Lose $4 Billion." *Bloomberg.com*. Bloomberg L.P. 5 September 2012. <http://www.bloomberg.com/news/2012-09-05/in-stadium-building-spree-u-s-taxpayers-lose-4-billion.html>.

190 Kuriloff, Aaron and Darrell Preston. "In Stadium Building Spree, U.S. Taxpayers Lose $4 Billion." *Bloomberg.com*. Bloomberg L.P. 5 September 2012. <http://www.bloomberg.com/news/2012-09-05/in-stadium-building-spree-u-s-taxpayers-lose-4-billion.html>.

191 Kuriloff, Aaron and Darrell Preston. "In Stadium Building Spree, U.S. Taxpayers Lose $4 Billion." *Bloomberg.com*. Bloomberg L.P. 5 September 2012. <http://www.bloomberg.com/news/2012-09-05/in-stadium-building-spree-u-s-taxpayers-lose-4-billion.html>.

192 "11 Most Expensive Stadiums In The World." Total Pro Sports RSS. N.p., 26 May 2014. Web. 15 Oct. 2014. <http://www.totalprosports.com/2011/10/27/11-most-expensive-stadiums-in-the-world/>.

193 Henchman, Joseph and Travis Greaves. "From the House That Ruth Building to the House the IRS Built." *Taxfoundation.org*. The Tax Foundation. 9 April 2009. <http://taxfoundation.org/article/house-ruth-built-house-irs-built>.

194 Kuriloff, Aaron and Darrell Preston. "In Stadium Building Spree, U.S. Taxpayers Lose $4 Billion." *Bloomberg.com*. Bloomberg L.P. 5 September 2012. <http://www.bloomberg.com/news/2012-09-05/in-stadium-building-spree-u-s-taxpayers-lose-4-billion.html>.

195 Brostek, Michael. *Tax Policy: Tax-Exempt Status of Certain Bonds Merits Reconsideration, and Apparent Noncompliance with Issuance Cost Limitations Should Be Addressed*. Rep. no. GAO-08-364. Report to Congressional Committees. Governmental Accountability Office, February 2008. Web. <http://www.gao.gov/assets/280/272369.pdf>. p29.

196 Brostek, Michael. *Tax Policy: Tax-Exempt Status of Certain Bonds Merits Reconsideration, and Apparent Noncompliance with Issuance Cost Limitations Should Be Addressed*. Rep. no. GAO-08-364. Report to Congressional Committees. Governmental Accountability Office, February 2008. Web. <http://www.gao.gov/assets/280/272369.pdf>. p3.

197 OCTportland. "NEA Sample: Zombie in Love." YouTube. YouTube, 17 Mar. 2014. Web. 16 Oct. 2014. <https://www.youtube.com/watch?v=1e_9myLSL_s>.

198 National Endowment for the Arts. "*Oregon Children's Theatre to Present World Premiere ZOMBIE IN LOVE, 3/1-23,*" Grant No. 14-3200-7046. Web. <http://apps.nea.gov/GrantSearch/SearchResults.aspx>.

199 BWW News Desk. "Oregon Children's Theatre to Present World Premiere ZOMBIE IN LOVE, 3/1-23." BroadwayWorld.com. N.p., 5 Feb. 2014. Web. 16 Oct. 2014. <http://www.broadwayworld.com/portland/article/Oregon-Childrens-Theatre-to-Present-World-Premiere-ZOMBIE-IN-LOVE-31-23-20140205#.>.

200 Dennis Sparks. (2014, March 10). Zombie in Love – Oregon Children's Theatre at the Winningstad – downtown Portland. (Web log post). Retrieved from <http://

dennissparksreviews.blogspot.com/2014/03/zombie-in-loveoregon-childrens-theatre.html>.

201 "A World Premiere Musical: March 4-21, 2014." Oregon Children's Theatre. N.p., n.d. Web. 28 February 2014. <http://octc.org/schoolservices/zombieinlove>.

202 National Endowment for the Arts. "*Oregon Children's Theatre to Present World Premiere ZOMBIE IN LOVE, 3/1-23*," Grant No. 14-3200-7046. Web. <http://apps.nea.gov/GrantSearch/SearchResults.aspx>.

202 BWW News Desk. "Oregon Children's Theatre to Present World Premiere ZOMBIE IN LOVE, 3/1-23." BroadwayWorld.com. N.p., 5 Feb. 2014. Web. 16 Oct. 2014

203 "Zombie in Love." Oregon Children's Theatre. N.p., n.d. Web. 28 Feb. 2014. <http://octc.org/onstage/zombieinlove>..

204 Vorenberg, Sue. "Bits 'n' Pieces: Kids' Show Has Heart, Braaaaains." *Columbian*.com. The Columbian. 28 February 2014. <http://www.columbian.com/news/2014/feb/28/kids-show-has-heart-brains-zombie-love/>.

205 Oregon Children's Theatre. "Zombie in Love: Teacher Resource Guide." <http://octc.org/pdf/guides/zombieinlove_rg_before.pdf>.

206 Oregon Children's Theatre. "Zombie in Love: Teacher Resource Guide." <http://octc.org/pdf/guides/zombieinlove_rg_before.pdf>.

207 BWW News Desk. "Oregon Children's Theatre to Present World Premiere ZOMBIE IN LOVE, 3/1-23." BroadwayWorld.com. N.p., 5 Feb. 2014. Web. 16 Oct. 2014. <http://www.broadwayworld.com/portland/article/Oregon-Childrens-Theatre-to-Present-World-Premiere-ZOMBIE-IN-LOVE-31-23-20140205#.>.

208 Burke, Becky, "Review: Oregon Children's Theatre Presents – Zombie in Love." *Portlandstagereviews.com*. Portland Stage Reviews. 4 March 2014. <http://portlandstagereviews.com/2014/03/04/review-oregon-childrens-theatre-presents-zombie-in-love/>.

209 Schulze, John. "The Appropriate Age for Kids to Watch 'The Walking Dead' is Up for Debate." *Examiner.com*. AXS Digital Group LLC. 25 March 2014. <http://www.examiner.com/article/the-appropriate-age-for-kids-to-watch-the-walking-dead-is-up-for-debate>.

210 ""Night of the Living Dead 3D: Reanimation - Parents' Guide." IMDb. IMDb.com, n.d. Web. 16 Oct. 2014. <http://www.imdb.com/title/tt1879012/parentalguide?ref_=tt_stry_pg>.

b211 Patterson, Steve. "In Guana Marsh, Research Sheds New Light On Old Florida Environment."*Jacksonville.com*. The Florida Times-Union. 11 August 2014. <http://jacksonville.com/news/metro/2014-08-11/story/guana-marsh-research-sheds-new-light-old-florida-environment>.

212 University of Rhode Island Environmental Data Center. "Smooth Cordgrass (Spartina alterniflora)." *Edc.uri.edu*. The University of Rhode Island Habitat Restoration. Accessed 29 September 2014. <http://www.edc.uri.edu/restoration/html/gallery/plants/smooth.htm>.

213 Patterson, Steve. "In Guana Marsh, Research Sheds New Light On Old Florida Environment."*Jacksonville.com*. The Florida Times-Union. 11 August 2014. <http://jacksonville.com/news/metro/2014-08-11/story/guana-marsh-research-sheds-new-light-old-florida-environment>.

214 Patterson, Steve. "In Guana Marsh, Research Sheds New Light On Old Florida Environment."*Jacksonville.com*. The Florida Times-Union. 11 August 2014. <http://jacksonville.com/news/metro/2014-08-11/story/guana-marsh-research-sheds-new-light-old-florida-environment>.

215 Patterson, Steve. "In Guana Marsh, Research Sheds New Light On Old Florida Environment."*Jacksonville.com*. The Florida Times-Union. 11 August 2014. <http://jacksonville.com/news/metro/2014-08-11/story/guana-marsh-research-sheds-new-light-old-florida-environment>.

216 Patterson, Steve. "In Guana Marsh, Research Sheds New Light On Old Florida Environment."*Jacksonville.com*. The Florida Times-Union. 11 August 2014. <http://jacksonville.com/news/metro/2014-08-11/story/guana-marsh-research-sheds-new-light-old-florida-environment>.

217 Patterson, Steve. "In Guana Marsh, Research Sheds New Light On Old Florida Environment."*Jacksonville.com*. The Florida Times-Union. 11 August 2014. <http://jacksonville.com/news/metro/2014-08-11/story/guana-marsh-research-sheds-new-light-old-florida-environment>..

218 Stoeckel, Luke E., et al. "Patterns of Brain Activation when Mothers View their Own Child and Dog: An fMRI Study." PLoS One 9.10 (2014): e107205. ProQuest. Web. 16 Oct. 2014.

219 Stoeckel, Luke E., et al. "Patterns of Brain Activation when Mothers View their Own Child and Dog: An fMRI Study." PLoS One 9.10 (2014): e107205. ProQuest. Web. 16 Oct. 2014

220 Stoeckel, Luke E., et al. "Patterns of Brain Activation when Mothers View their Own Child and Dog: An fMRI Study." PLoS One 9.10 (2014): e107205. ProQuest. Web. 16 Oct. 2014

221 Stoeckel, Luke E., et al. "Patterns of Brain Activation when Mothers View their Own Child and Dog: An fMRI Study." PLoS One 9.10 (2014): e107205. ProQuest. Web. 16 Oct. 2014

222 Stoeckel, Luke E., et al. "Patterns of Brain Activation when Mothers View their Own Child and Dog: An fMRI Study." PLoS One 9.10 (2014): e107205. ProQuest. Web. 16 Oct. 2014

223 Stoeckel, Luke E., et al. "Patterns of Brain Activation when Mothers View their Own Child and Dog: An fMRI Study." PLoS One 9.10 (2014): e107205. ProQuest. Web. 16 Oct. 2014

224 Stoeckel, Luke E., et al. "Patterns of Brain Activation when Mothers View their Own Child and Dog: An fMRI Study." PLoS One 9.10 (2014): e107205. ProQuest. Web. 16 Oct. 2014.

225 Stoeckel, Luke E., et al. "Patterns of Brain Activation when Mothers View their Own Child and Dog: An fMRI Study." PLoS One 9.10 (2014): e107205. ProQuest. Web. 16 Oct. 2014

226 Stoeckel, Luke E., et al. "Patterns of Brain Activation when Mothers View their Own Child and Dog: An fMRI Study." PLoS One 9.10 (2014): e107205. ProQuest. Web. 16 Oct. 2014

227 Stoeckel, Luke E., et al. "Patterns of Brain Activation when Mothers View their Own Child and Dog: An fMRI Study." PLoS One 9.10 (2014): e107205. ProQuest. Web. 16 Oct. 2014

228 Stoeckel, Luke E., et al. "Patterns of Brain Activation when Mothers View their Own Child and Dog: An fMRI Study." PLoS One 9.10 (2014): e107205. ProQuest. Web. 16 Oct. 2014

229 NIH Award No. 5K23DA032612; Award No. 5K24DA030443

230 Wagstaff, Keith. "This is Your Mom's Brain On Babies – And Dogs. Science Shows the Love," *Today.com*, NBC News. 3 October 2014. <http://www.today.com/health/your-moms-brain-babies-dogs-science-shows-love-2D80192080>.

231 Szabo, Liz. "NIH director: Budget cuts put U.S. Science at Risk." *USAtoday.com*. Gannett. 23 April 2014. <http://www.usatoday.com/story/news/nation/2014/04/23/nih-budget-cuts/8056113/>.

232 Bostwick, William, "The 50 Best Craft Beers Every Man Must Try." *GQ.com*. Condé Nast. 19 September 2014. September 19, 2014. <http://www.gq.com/food-travel/201409/the-50-best-craft-beers-as-chosen-by-experts>.

233 Kass, Sam. "Ale to the Chief: White House Beer Recipe." The White House. The White House, 1 Sept. 2012. Web. 16 Oct. 2014. <http://www.whitehouse.gov/blog/2012/09/01/ale-chief-white-house-beer-recipe>.

234 Website of the Empire Brewing Company, <http://empirebrew.com/beer/>.

235 Weiner, Mark. "USDA awards $200,000 to Empire Brewing Co. for new Farmstead brewery in Cazenovia." *Syracuse.com*. The Syracuse Post-Standard. 20 August

2014. <http://www.syracuse.com/news/index.ssf/2014/08/usda_awards_200000_to_empire_brewing_co_for_new_farmstead_brewery_in_cazenovia.html#incart_river>.

236 Office of Senator Charles Schumer. U.S. Senate. *Schumer, Gillibrand, Maffei Announce Nearly $500,000 in Value-Added Produce Grants for Three Farms in Central New York & Empire Brewery in Syracuse. Schumer.senate.gov.* Press Release.. 20 August 2014. <http://www.schumer.senate.gov/Newsroom/record.cfm?id=355225>.

237 Website of the Empire Brewing Company. <http://empirebrew.com/farmstead-brewery/>.

238 Website of the Empire Brewing Company. <http://empirebrew.com/farmstead-brewery/>.

239 Abbott, Ellen, "Empire Brewing Company Says New Brewery Will Create Distinctive Craft Beers." *WRVO.org.* WRVO Public Media. 23 July 2014. <http://wrvo.org/post/empire-brewing-company-says-new-brewery-will-create-distinctive-craft-beers>.

240 The Brewers Association. Press Room. *Brewers Association Announces 2013 Craft Beer Growth. Brewersassociation.org.* Brewers Association. 13 March 2014. <http://www.brewersassociation.org/press-releases/brewers-association-announces-2013-craft-brewer-growth>.

241 Office of Senator Charles Schumer. U.S. Senate. *Schumer, Gillibrand, Maffei Announce Nearly $500,000 in Value-Added Produce Grants for Three Farms in Central New York & Empire Brewery in Syracuse. Schumer.senate.gov.* Press Release.. 20 August 2014. <http://www.schumer.senate.gov/Newsroom/record.cfm?id=355225>.

242 Cazentre, Don, "Empire Farmstead Brewery in Cazenovia Will Be Among the State's Largest Craft Beer Makers." *Syracuse.com.* 15 July 2014., <http://www.syracuse.com/drinks/index.ssf/2014/07/empire_brewery_in_cazenovia_wi.html>.

243 Cazentre, Don, "Empire Farmstead Brewery in Cazenovia Will Be Among the State's Largest Craft Beer Makers." *Syracuse.com.* 15 July 2014., <http://www.syracuse.com/drinks/index.ssf/2014/07/empire_brewery_in_cazenovia_wi.html>.

244 Colorado Symphony. "Classically Cannabis: The High Note Series." *Coloradosymphony.org.* CSO. Accessed 16 October 2014. <http://www.coloradosymphony.org/Events/Classically-Cannabis>.

245 Wenzel, John, "Colorado Symphony Orchestra Rolls Out First Cannabis-Linked Concert."*denverpost.com.* The Denver Post. 23 May 2014. <http://www.denverpost.com/entertainment/ci_25827194/colorado-symphony-orchestras-first-pot-concert-classical-gas>.

246 Mobley, Mark. "Coming Soon To Colorado: Wolfgang And Weed." NPR. NPR, 30 Apr. 2014. Web. 16 Oct. 2014. <http://www.npr.org/blogs/deceptivecadence/2014/04/30/308351387/coming-soon-to-colorado-wolfgang-and-weed>.

247 Nestel, M.L., "Symphony for Stoners Is Not a Hit with Donors." *Vocativ.com.* Vocative. 2 May 2014. <http://www.vocativ.com/culture/music/colorado-symphony-wooing-stoners-donors-arent-happy/>.

248 National Endowment for the Arts. Grant #14-3100-7208.

249 National Endowment for the Arts. "Grants, Art Works." *Arts.gov.* National Endowment for the Arts. Accessed 16 October 2014. <http://arts.gov/grants-organizations/art-works>.

250 Rittiman, Brandon. "Marijuana Concerts Will Not Jeopardize Symphony's Federal Grants." *9news.com.* KUSA Multimedia Holdings Corporation. 14 May 2014. <http://www.9news.com/story/news/local/politics/2014/05/14/colorado-symphony-marijuana-themed-concerts-funding/9086855/>.

251 Rittiman, Brandon. "Marijuana Concerts Will Not Jeopardize Symphony's Federal Grants." *9news.com.* KUSA Multimedia Holdings Corporation. 14 May 2014. <http://www.9news.com/story/news/local/politics/2014/05/14/colorado-symphony-marijuana-themed-concerts-funding/9086855/>.

252 Nestel, M.L., "Symphony for Stoners Is Not a Hit with Donors." *Vocativ.com.* Vocative. 2 May 2014. <http://www.vocativ.com/culture/music/colorado-symphony-wooing-stoners-donors-arent-happy/>.

253 Nestel, M.L., "Symphony for Stoners Is Not a Hit with Donors." *Vocativ.com.* Vocative. 2 May 2014. <http://www.vocativ.com/culture/music/colorado-symphony-wooing-stoners-donors-arent-happy/>.

254 Warner, Joel, "Puff Puff Brass." *Slate.com.* The Slate Group LLC. 29 May 2014. <http://www.slate.com/articles/arts/culturebox/2014/05/classically_cannabis_concert_review_colorado_symphony_orchestra_s_high_note.html>.

255 "U.S. Coast Guard: Organization and Missions." *Seapowermagazine.org.* SEAPOWER Magazine. January Almanac 2006. <http://www.seapowermagazine.org/archives/january/2006/us_coast_guard.html>.

256 Christofferson, John. "Taxpayers Cover Coast Guard's Private-Party Patrols." *Nypost.com.* Associated Press. 14 September 2014. <http://nypost.com/2014/09/09/taxpayers-cover-coast-guards-private-party-patrols/>.

257 Christofferson, John. "Taxpayers Cover Coast Guard's Private-Party Patrols." *Nypost.com.* Associated Press. 14 September 2014. <http://nypost.com/2014/09/09/taxpayers-cover-coast-guards-private-party-patrols/>.

258 Christofferson, John. "Taxpayers Cover Coast Guard's Private-Party Patrols." *Nypost.com.* Associated Press. 14 September 2014. <http://nypost.com/2014/09/09/taxpayers-cover-coast-guards-private-party-patrols/>.

259 Christofferson, John. "Taxpayers Cover Coast Guard's Private-Party Patrols." *Nypost.com.* Associated Press. 14 September 2014. <http://nypost.com/2014/09/09/taxpayers-cover-coast-guards-private-party-patrols/>.

260 Christofferson, John. "Taxpayers Cover Coast Guard's Private-Party Patrols." *Nypost.com.* Associated Press. 14 September 2014. <http://nypost.com/2014/09/09/taxpayers-cover-coast-guards-private-party-patrols/>.

261 Christofferson, John. "Taxpayers Cover Coast Guard's Private-Party Patrols." *Nypost.com.* Associated Press. 14 September 2014. <http://nypost.com/2014/09/09/taxpayers-cover-coast-guards-private-party-patrols/>.

262 Christofferson, John. "Taxpayers Cover Coast Guard's Private-Party Patrols." *Nypost.com.* Associated Press. 14 September 2014. <http://nypost.com/2014/09/09/taxpayers-cover-coast-guards-private-party-patrols/>.

263 Christofferson, John. "Taxpayers Cover Coast Guard's Private-Party Patrols." *Nypost.com.* Associated Press. 14 September 2014. <http://nypost.com/2014/09/09/taxpayers-cover-coast-guards-private-party-patrols/>.

264 Christofferson, John. "Taxpayers Cover Coast Guard's Private-Party Patrols." *Nypost.com.* Associated Press. 14 September 2014. <http://nypost.com/2014/09/09/taxpayers-cover-coast-guards-private-party-patrols/>.

265 Christofferson, John. "Taxpayers Cover Coast Guard's Private-Party Patrols." *Nypost.com.* Associated Press. 14 September 2014. <http://nypost.com/2014/09/09/taxpayers-cover-coast-guards-private-party-patrols/>.

266 Christofferson, John. "Taxpayers Cover Coast Guard's Private-Party Patrols." *Nypost.com.* Associated Press. 14 September 2014. <http://nypost.com/2014/09/09/taxpayers-cover-coast-guards-private-party-patrols/>.

267 Christofferson, John. "Taxpayers Cover Coast Guard's Private-Party Patrols." *Nypost.com.* Associated Press. 14 September 2014. <http://nypost.com/2014/09/09/taxpayers-cover-coast-guards-private-party-patrols/>.

268 Christofferson, John. "Taxpayers Cover Coast Guard's Private-Party Patrols." *Nypost.com.* Associated Press. 14 September 2014. <http://nypost.com/2014/09/09/taxpayers-cover-coast-guards-private-party-patrols/>.

269 Sharples, Tiffany. "Get into Trouble Outdoors — Who Pays for the Rescue?" *time.com*. Time Inc. 25 April 2009. <http://content.time.com/time/nation/article/0,8599,1892621,00.html>.

270 Bleyer, Bill. "Coast Guard to Cut Operations Around LI." *Newsday.com*. Newsday. 28 March 2013. <http://www.newsday.com/long-island/coast-guard-to-cut-operations-around-li-1.4932678>.

271 Subcommittee on Border and Maritime Security. "Future of the Homeland Security Missions of the Coast Guard." Hearing Transcript. *Homeland.house.gov/subcommittee-BMS*. House Committee on Homeland Security. 4 February 2014. <http://www.gpo.gov/fdsys/pkg/CHRG-113hhrg88023/html/CHRG-113hhrg88023.htm>.

272 Fornicola, Jason. "Sequestration Forces Coast Guard to Get Creative." *Federalnewsradio.com*. Federal News Radio. 13 March 2014. <http://www.federalnewsradio.com/474/3580913/Sequestration-forces-Coast-Guard-to-get-creative>.

273 Bleyer, Bill. "Coast Guard to Cut Operations Around LI." *Newsday.com*. Newsday. 28 March 2013. <http://www.newsday.com/long-island/coast-guard-to-cut-operations-around-li-1.4932678>.

274 Sullivan, Julia Howe. "Vermont Historical Society Awarded Grant To Research Vermont's 1970s Counterculture Movement," *ShelburneNews.com*. Shelburne News. 24 September 2014. <http://shelburnenews.com/?p=17942>.

275 Website of the Institute for Museum and Library Services, Grant Announcement, accessed October 8, 2014, h <http://www.imls.gov/recipients/grantsearch.aspx>.

276 Website of the Institute for Museum and Library Services, Grant Announcement, accessed October 8, 2014, h <http://www.imls.gov/recipients/grantsearch.aspx>.

277 Vermont Historical Society, "Back to the Land: Communes in Vermont," <http://vermonthistory.org/research/research-resources-online/green-mountain-chronicles/back-to-the-land-communes-in-vermont-1968>.

278 Potter, Jon, "Hippies from the '70s." *reformer.com*. Brattleboro Reformer. 14 July 2010. <http://www.reformer.com/localnews/ci_15509617>.

279 Johnson, Sally, "Excesses Blamed for Demise of the Commune Movement," *nytimes.com*. The New York Times. 3 August 1998. <http://www.nytimes.com/1998/08/03/us/excesses-blamed-for-demise-of-the-commune-movement.html>.

280 Green, Susan, "Life on a Vermont Commune: Poet Verandah Porche Remembers Back-to-the Land Living." *Burlingtonfreepress.com*. Burlington Free Press. Gannett. 6 June 2013. <http://archive.burlingtonfreepress.com/article/20130106/ARTS/301060004/Life-on-a-Vermont-commune-Poet-Verandah-Porche-remembers-back-to-the-land-living>.

281 "Value-Added Producer Grant Awards Fiscal Year 2014," USDA website, accessed October 7, 2014; http://www.rurdev.usda.gov/supportdocuments/RD_2014VAPGRecipients.pdf .

282 "Who Am I?," Mary's Alpaca website, accessed October 7, 2014; http://www.maryspoop.com/who-am-i/mary-forte/marysalpaca/alpaca-compost-tea/Virginia .

283 "20 MARY'S PREMIUM ALPACA POOP REFILLS – 20 POOP PAKS," Mary's Alpaca website, accessed October 7, 2014; **http://www.maryspoop.com/20-marys-premium-alpaca-poop-refills-20-poop-paks/** .

284 "20 MARY'S PREMIUM ALPACA POOP REFILLS – 20 POOP PAKS," Mary's Alpaca website, accessed October 7, 2014; http://www.maryspoop.com/20-marys-premium-alpaca-poop-refills-20-poop-paks/ .

285 "Awards," Mary's Alpaca website, accessed October 7, 2014; http://www.marysalpaca.com/eventsAwards.aspx .

286 "Our Farm," Mary's Alpaca website, accessed October 7, 2014; http://www.marysalpaca.com/AboutUs.aspx .

287 Mary's Alpaca At Cedar Hill Farm Facebook page, posted June 14, 2012; https://www.facebook.com/122961277761405/photos/pb.122961277761405.-2207520000.1412699129./384167854974078/?type=1&theater .

288 Douglas Martin, "Harold von Braunhut, Seller of Sea Monkeys, Dies at 77," New York Times, December 21, 2003; **http://www.nytimes.com/2003/12/21/national/21BRAU.html** .

289 Classic Sea-Monkey advertisement. California State University Archives. Accessed 16 October 2014. <http://library.csun.edu/sites/default/files/Exhibitions/sea_monkeys.jpg>.

290 Martin, Douglas. "Harold von Braunhut, Seller of Sea Monkeys, Dies at 77." *NYtimes.com*. The New York Times. 21 December 2003. <http://www.nytimes.com/2003/12/21/national/21BRAU.html>.

291 Williams-Hedges, Deborah. "Swimming Sea-Monkeys Reveal How Zooplankton May Help Drive Ocean Circulation | Caltech." The California Institute of Technology. Press Release. 30 Sept. 2014. Web. 16 Oct. 2014. <http://www.caltech.edu/content/swimming-sea-monkeys-reveal-how-zooplankton-may-help-drive-ocean-circulation>.

292 Williams-Hedges, Deborah. "Swimming Sea-Monkeys Reveal How Zooplankton May Help Drive Ocean Circulation | Caltech." The California Institute of Technology. Press Release. 30 Sept. 2014. Web. 16 Oct. 2014.
<http://www.caltech.edu/content/swimming-sea-monkeys-reveal-how-zooplankton-may-help-drive-ocean-circulation>.

293 Williams-Hedges, Deborah. "Swimming Sea-Monkeys Reveal How Zooplankton May Help Drive Ocean Circulation | Caltech." The California Institute of Technology. Press Release. 30 Sept. 2014. Web. 16 Oct. 2014. <http://www.caltech.edu/content/swimming-sea-monkeys-reveal-how-zooplankton-may-help-drive-ocean-circulation>.

294 Williams-Hedges, Deborah. "Swimming Sea-Monkeys Reveal How Zooplankton May Help Drive Ocean Circulation | Caltech." The California Institute of Technology. Press Release. 30 Sept. 2014. Web. 16 Oct. 2014. <http://www.caltech.edu/content/swimming-sea-monkeys-reveal-how-zooplankton-may-help-drive-ocean-circulation>.

295 Boyle, Alan. "Laser-Guided Sea-Monkeys Reveal How Critters Boost Ocean's Waves." *NBCnews.com*. NBC News. 30 September 2014. <http://www.nbcnews.com/science/weird-science/laser-guided-sea-monkeys-reveal-how-critters-boost-oceans-waves-n215066>.

296 Lee, Jane J. "Laser-Guided Sea-Monkeys Show That Tiny Animals Can Move Mountains of Seawater." *Nationalgeographic.com*. National Geographic Society. 30 September 2014. <http://news.nationalgeographic.com/news/2014/09/140930-sea-monkeys-laser-ocean-animals-science/>.

297 Geggel, Laura. "Tiny Sea Monkeys Create Giant Ocean Currents." *Livescience.com*. Purch. 30 September 2014. <http://www.livescience.com/48069-sea-monkeys-swirl-ocean.html>.

298 Lee, Jane J. "Laser-Guided Sea-Monkeys Show That Tiny Animals Can Move Mountains of Seawater." *Nationalgeographic.com*. National Geographic Society. 30 September 2014. <http://news.nationalgeographic.com/news/2014/09/140930-sea-monkeys-laser-ocean-animals-science/>.

299 Geggel, Laura. "Tiny Sea Monkeys Create Giant Ocean Currents." *Livescience.com*. Purch. 30 September 2014. <http://www.livescience.com/48069-sea-monkeys-swirl-ocean.html>.

300 Williams-Hedges, Deborah. "Swimming Sea-Monkeys Reveal How Zooplankton May Help Drive Ocean Circulation | Caltech." The California Institute of Technology. Press Release. 30 Sept. 2014. Web. 16 Oct. 2014. <http://www.caltech.edu/content/swimming-sea-monkeys-reveal-how-zooplankton-may-help-drive-

ocean-circulation>.

301 Wilhelmus, Monica M. and John O. Dabiri. *Observations of Large-Scale Fluid Transport by Laser-Guided Plankton Aggregations.* Physics of Fluids, 26 . Art. No. 101302. ISSN 1070-6631, September 2014; *Caltech.edu.* <http://resolver.caltech.edu/CaltechAUTHORS:20140926-103222105>.

302 National Science Foundation. "Collaborative Research: Turbulence and Suspension Feeding - a New Approach using the Lobate Ctenophore Mnemiopsis Leidyi," Award Abstract #1061268. Accessed 16 October 2014. <http://www.nsf.gov/awardsearch/showAward?AWD_ID=1061268&HistoricalAwards=false>

303 Amazon.com, accessed 16 October 2014. <http://www.amazon.com/s/ref=nb_sb_noss_1?url=search-alias%3Daps&field-keywords=sea+monkeys>.

304 ToysRus.com, accessed 16 October 2014 <http://www.toysrus.com/search/index.jsp?kwCatId=&kw=seamonkey&keywords=seamonkey&origkw=seamonkey&sr=1>.

305 Williams-Hedges, Deborah. "Swimming Sea-Monkeys Reveal How Zooplankton May Help Drive Ocean Circulation | Caltech." The California Institute of Technology. Press Release. 30 Sept. 2014. Web. 16 Oct. 2014. <http://www.caltech.edu/content/swimming-sea-monkeys-reveal-how-zooplankton-may-help-drive-ocean-circulation>.

306 Moyer, Josh. "Penn State's Postseason Ban Over." *ESPN.com.* ESPN Internet Ventures. 10 September 2014. <http://espn.go.com/college-football/story/_/id/11489258/ncaa-drops-postseason-ban-penn-state-nittany-lions>.

307 ESPN.com News Service. "Penn State Sanctions: $60M, Bowl Ban." *ESPN.com.* ESPN Internet Ventures. 24 July 2012. <http://espn.go.com/college-football/story/_/id/8191027/penn-state-nittany-lions-hit-60-million-fine-4-year-bowl-ban-wins-dating-1998>.

308 National Science Foundation. "RAPID: When Pride Becomes Shame: Organizational Identification and Self-Presentation During Scandal." Award Abstract #1260929. Accessed 16 October 2014. http://www.nsf.gov/awardsearch/showAward?AWD_ID=1260929 .

309 National Science Foundation. "RAPID: When Pride Becomes Shame: Organizational Identification and Self-Presentation During Scandal." Award Abstract #1260929. Accessed 16 October 2014. http://www.nsf.gov/awardsearch/showAward?AWD_ID=1260929 .

310 National Science Foundation. "RAPID: When Pride Becomes Shame: Organizational Identification and Self-Presentation During Scandal." Award Abstract #1260929. Accessed 16 October 2014. http://www.nsf.gov/awardsearch/showAward?AWD_ID=1260929 .

311 Joe Little, *Perceptions of Americans change after 3-week visit from Pakistani journalists*, ABC10 NEWS (Mar. 31, 2014) http://www.10news.com/news/perceptions-of-americans-change-after-3-week-visit-from-pakistani-journalists-03312014.

312 Joe Little, *Perceptions of Americans change after 3-week visit from Pakistani journalists*, ABC10 NEWS (Mar. 31, 2014) http://www.10news.com/news/perceptions-of-americans-change-after-3-week-visit-from-pakistani-journalists-03312014.

313 *About the Bureau*, DEP'T OF STATE, http://eca.state.gov/about-bureau.

314 Congressional Budget Justification FY15, DEP'T OF STATE, at 401, http://www.state.gov/documents/organization/223495.pdf.

315 About American Music Abroad, American Voices (last accessed Aug. 13, 2014) http://amvoices.org/ama/about/.

316 Email from grantee (July 18, 2014) (on file with the Office of Senate Coburn).

317 Email from grantee (July 18, 2014) (on file with the Office of Senate Coburn).

318 Email from grantee (July 18, 2014) (on file with the Office of Senate Coburn).

319 *See The Nose Flute*, Youtube (last accessed Oct. 1, 2014), https://www.youtube.com/watch?v=0dpVpPIg-IU.

320 *See* Arkansas Bo & Big Piph, *Dem Shawts*, Audiomack (last accessed Oct. 1, 2014), https://www.audiomack.com/song/arkansas-bo-big-piph/3-them-shawts-master

321 *See* Big Piph, *The Calm (EP)* (last accessed Oct. 1, 2014), http://www.bigpiph.com/music/.

322 *See OneBeat*, Bang on A Can (last accessed Oct. 1, 2014), http://bangonacan.org/found_sound_nation/one_beat

323 *See OneBeat*, Bang on A Can (last accessed Oct. 1, 2014), http://bangonacan.org/found_sound_nation/one_beat

324 Found Sound Nation, *OneBeat 2012 - Walmart Ruckus*, Youtube (last accessed Oct. 1, 2014), https://www.youtube.com/watch?v=w3KuFJCOsM4&list=PLkLzOTNw7TRTsUS9lol3WrrCQQplPRdXc

325 Found Sound Nation, *OneBeat 2013 - Making Instruments*, Youtube (last accessed Oct. 1, 2014), https://www.youtube.com/watch?v=vptM3aBjs_s&index=4&list=PLkLzOTNw7TRQ28XnTjOGYpT8TtSlE5P9B.

326 Found Sound Nation, *OneBeat 2013 - Washington*, Youtube (last accessed Oct. 1, 2014), https://www.youtube.com/watch?v=M6MXBE_odTA&list=PLkLzOTNw7TRQ28XnTjOGYpT8TtSlE5P9B#t=184.

327 *See, e.g.,* ACYPL; Bang on a Can; Global Nomads Group.

328 *See, e.g.,* Association of American Voices; Bang on a Can.

329 "Department of Homeland Security. DHS Press Office. Secretary Johnson Announces Fiscal Year 2015 Budget Request. Official Website of the Department of Homeland Security. DHS, 4 May 2014. Web. 16 Oct. 2014. <http://www.dhs.gov/news/2014/03/04/secretary-johnson-announces-fiscal-year-2015-budget-request>.

330 DHS Immigration and Customs Enforcement Solicitation. "Gym Membership Services." FedBizOpps.gov. Solicitation No. ICE-OAQ-GYM-FY14. 18 June 2014. <https://www.fbo.gov/index?s=opportunity&mode=form&id=19887c0c9564ed74d89a68936f96e87a&tab=core&_cview=0>.

331 Website of Vida Fitness, "About Vida Fitness." *Vidafitness.com.* Accessed 30 September 2014. <http://vidafitness.com/about>.

332 Harrington, Elizabeth, "Homeland Security Spends $450,000 on 'State of the Art' Gym Memberships." *Freebeacon.com.* The Washington Free Beacon 6 August 2014. <http://freebeacon.com/issues/homeland-security-spends-450000-on-state-of-the-art-gym-memberships/>.

333 DHS Immigration and Customs Enforcement Solicitation. "Gym Membership Services." FedBizOpps.gov. Solicitation No. ICE-OAQ-GYM-FY14. 18 June 2014. <https://www.fbo.gov/index?s=opportunity&mode=form&id=19887c0c9564ed74d89a68936f96e87a&tab=core&_cview=0>.

334 Distance from VIDA Fitness, 999 9th St. NW, Washington DC, to ICE offices at 801 I Street NW, Washington, DC, measured by http://maps.google.com, 7 August 2014.

335 BloombergTV."The Most Expensive Object Ever (Lives in Space)." *Bloomberg.com.* Bloomberg L.P. 12 May 2014. <http://www.bloomberg.com/video/the-most-expensive-object-ever-lives-in-space-oKuCsqCLR3akanG_eCWXUQ.html>.

336 President Reagan's Statement on the International Space Station, January 25, 1984; http://history.nasa.gov/printFriendly/reagan84.htm .

337 NASA Office of Inspector General. *Extending the Operational Life of the International Space Station Until 2024.* Report No. IG-14-031. 14 September 2014. Web. < http://www.hq.nasa.gov/office/oig/hq/audits/reports/FY14/IG-14-031.pdf >.

338 NASA Office of Inspector General. *Extending the Operational Life of the International Space Station Until 2024.* Report No. IG-14-031. 14 September 2014. Web. < http://www.hq.nasa.gov/office/oig/hq/audits/reports/FY14/IG-14-031.pdf >.

339 NASA Office of Inspector General. *Extending the Operational Life of the International Space Station Until 2024.* Report No. IG-14-031. 14 September 2014. Web. <

http://www.hq.nasa.gov/office/oig/hq/audits/reports/FY14/IG-14-031.pdf >.

340 NASA Office of Inspector General. *Extending the Operational Life of the International Space Station Until 2024.* Report No. IG-14-031. 14 September 2014. Web. < http://www.hq.nasa.gov/office/oig/hq/audits/reports/FY14/IG-14-031.pdf >.

341 Holdren, John P., and Charles Bolden. "Obama Administration Extends International Space Station until at Least 2024." Web log post. The White House. Office of Science and Technology Policy, 8 Jan. 2014. Web. 16 Oct. 2014. <http://www.whitehouse.gov/blog/2014/01/08/obama-administration-extends-international-space-station-until-least-2024>.

342 Morgan, Daniel. *NASA Appropriations and Authorizations: A Fact Sheet.* Rep. No. R43419. Washington, D.C.: Congressional Research Service, 26 June 2013. <http://www.crs.gov/pages/Reports.aspx?PRODCODE=R43419&Source=search>.

343 Holdren, John P., and Charles Bolden. "Obama Administration Extends International Space Station until at Least 2024." Web log post. The White House. Office of Science and Technology Policy, 8 Jan. 2014. Web. 16 Oct. 2014. <http://www.whitehouse.gov/blog/2014/01/08/obama-administration-extends-international-space-station-until-least-2024>.

344 Achenbach, Joel. "The Skies. The Limits. The International Space Station is One of Humanity's Great Engineering Triumphs. But What is it for?" W*ashingtonpost.com* The Washington Post. 14 September 2013. <http://www.washingtonpost.com/sf/national/2013/09/14/the-skies-the-limits/>.

345 Bond, Peter. The Continuing Story of the International Space Station. London: Springer, 2002. p279.

346 "The New York Times Op-Ed." Editorial. Nytimes.com. The New York Times, 14 Aug. 2005. Web. 16 Oct. 2014. <http://www.nytimes.com/2005/08/14/opinion/14sun1.html?pagewanted=all&_r=1&>..

347 "NASA'S EFFORTS TO MAXIMIZE RESEARCH ON THE INTERNATIONAL SPACE STATION," National Aeronautics and Space Administration Office of Inspector General, July 8, 2013; http://oig.nasa.gov/audits/reports/FY13/IG-13-019.pdf .

348 Mohler, Brenda. "Cobra Puma Tests Golf Clubs in Space." *Golf.com.* TI Golf Holdings Inc. 1 October 2014. <http://www.golf.com/tour-and-news/cobra-puma-golf-conducting-experiments-aboard-international-space-station>.

349 Center for the Advancement of Science in Space. "About CASIS." *Iss-casis.org.* Accessed 7 October 2014; <http://www.iss-casis.org/About/AboutCASIS.aspx>.

350 Mohler, Brenda. "Cobra Puma Tests Golf Clubs in Space." *Golf.com.* TI Golf Holdings Inc. 1 October 2014. <http://www.golf.com/tour-and-news/cobra-puma-golf-conducting-experiments-aboard-international-space-station>.

351 Mohler, Brenda. "Cobra Puma Tests Golf Clubs in Space." *Golf.com.* TI Golf Holdings Inc. 1 October 2014. <http://www.golf.com/tour-and-news/cobra-puma-golf-conducting-experiments-aboard-international-space-station>.

352 Than, Ker. "Astronauts Whack Golf Ball and Outfit Station in Spacewalk." *Space.com.* Purch. 23 November 2006. <http://www.space.com/3149-astronauts-whack-golf-ball-outfit-station-spacewalk.html>.

353 Gaskill, Melissa. "From Antibiotics to Yeast: Latest Student Science Heads For Space." *NASA.gov.* NASA International Space Station Program Office. 7 July 2014. <http://www.nasa.gov/mission_pages/station/research/news/ssep_mission5/#.VEBGtfldV8E>.

354 "Gaskill, Melissa. "From Antibiotics to Yeast: Latest Student Science Heads For Space." *NASA.gov.* NASA International Space Station Program Office. 7 July 2014. <http://www.nasa.gov/mission_pages/station/research/news/ssep_mission5/#.VEBGtfldV8E>.

355 "Gaskill, Melissa. "From Antibiotics to Yeast: Latest Student Science Heads For Space." *NASA.gov.* NASA International Space Station Program Office. 7 July 2014.

356 NASA Office of Inspector General. *Extending the Operational Life of the International Space Station Until 2024.* Report No. IG-14-031. 14 September 2014. Web. < http://www.hq.nasa.gov/office/oig/hq/audits/reports/FY14/IG-14-031.pdf >.

357 Chaplain, Cristina T. *NASA: Significant Challenges Remain for Access, Use, and Sustainment of the International Space Station.* Testimony Before the Subcommittee on Science, Space, and Technology. U.S. House of Representatives. Rep. No. GAO-12-587T. 28 March 2012. <http://www.gao.gov/products/GAO-12-587T>.

358 NASA Office of Inspector General. *2013 Report on NASA's Top Management and Performance Challenges.* 2 December 2013. Web. <http://oig.nasa.gov/NASA2013ManagementChallenges.pdf>.

359 NASA Office of Inspector General. *Extending the Operational Life of the International Space Station Until 2024.* Report No. IG-14-031. 14 September 2014. Web. < http://www.hq.nasa.gov/office/oig/hq/audits/reports/FY14/IG-14-031.pdf >.

360 Achenbach, Joel. "The Skies. The Limits. The International Space Station is One of Humanity's Great Engineering Triumphs. But What is it for?" W*ashingtonpost.com* The Washington Post. 14 September 2013. <http://www.washingtonpost.com/sf/national/2013/09/14/the-skies-the-limits/>.

361 NASA Office of Inspector General. *2013 Report on NASA's Top Management and Performance Challenges.* 2 December 2013. Web. <http://oig.nasa.gov/NASA2013ManagementChallenges.pdf>.

362 "The proportion of NASA funds dedicated to aeronautics research has declined from approximately 6 percent in fiscal year (FY) 2005 to 3 percent today, dwarfed by the Agency's focus on space exploration and operations (44 percent) and scientific investments (22 percent)," according to the NASA OIG.

NASA Office of Inspector General. *The Aeronautics Research Mission Directorate's Management Strategy for Conducting Aeronautics Research.* Report No. IG-14-012, 30 January 2014. Web. <http://oig.nasa.gov/audits/reports/FY14/IG-14-012.pdf>.

363 Salant, Jonathan D. "Congress Makes NASA Finish Useless $350 Million Structure," *Bloomberg.com.* Bloomberg L.P. 8 January 2014. Web. <http://www.bloomberg.com/news/2014-01-08/congress-makes-nasa-finish-useless-350-million-structure.html>.

364 Office of Senator Roger Wicker. Newsroom. Wicker Says NASA Reauthorization Provides Stability for Future of Human Space Flight. Wicker.senate.gov. N.p., 30 Sept. 2010. Web. 16 Oct. 2014. <http://www.wicker.senate.gov/public/index.cfm/press-releases?ID=63def9a4-07ee-8c4c-e23f-b3de54e30b61>.

365 Rayman, Noah. "The NASA Launchpad To Nowhere," *swampland.time.com.* Time Inc. 8 January 2014. Web. <http://swampland.time.com/2014/01/08/the-nasa-launchpad-to-nowhere/>.

366 Salant, Johnathan D. "In Mississippi, NASA's $350 Million Tower of Pork." *Businessweek.com.* Bloomberg L.P. 9 January 2014. Web. <http://www.businessweek.com/articles/2014-01-09/in-mississippi-nasas-350-million-tower-of-pork>.

367 Salant, Jonathan D. "Congress Makes NASA Finish Useless $350 Million Structure," *Bloomberg.com.* Bloomberg L.P. 8 January 2014. Web. <http://www.bloomberg.com/news/2014-01-08/congress-makes-nasa-finish-useless-350-million-structure.html>.

368 Salant, Jonathan D. "Congress Makes NASA Finish Useless $350 Million Structure," *Bloomberg.com.* Bloomberg L.P. 8 January 2014. Web. <http://www.bloomberg.com/news/2014-01-08/congress-makes-nasa-finish-useless-350-million-structure.html>.

369 Salant, Jonathan D. "Congress Makes NASA Finish Useless $350 Million Structure," *Bloomberg.com.* Bloomberg L.P. 8 January 2014. Web. <http://www.bloomberg.com/news/2014-01-08/congress-makes-nasa-finish-useless-350-million-structure.html>.

370 "U.S. Sheep Experiment Station to remain open," *LocalNews8.com.* ABC. 16 July 2014. <http://www.localnews8.com/news/us-sheep-experiment-station-to-remain-open/26982086>.

371 U.S. Department of Agriculture, Agricultural Research Service. "Range Sheep Production Efficiency Research." *Ars.usda.gov.* Accessed 17 October 2014. <http://www.ars.usda.gov/main/site_main.htm?modecode=53-64-05-00>.

372 Gilman, Sarah. "Sheep vs. Bear, Agency vs. Agency." *HCN.org*. High Country News 18 January 2012. <http://www.hcn.org/ blogs/goat/sheep-versus-bear-agency-versus-agency>.

373 Letter from Thomas J. Vilsack, Secretary of the U.S. Department of Agriculture to Congressman Robert B. Aderholt, Chairman of the U.S. House of Representatives Subcommittee on Agriculture, Rural Development, Food and Drug Administration, and Related Agencies, Committee on Appropriations. 17 June 2014, <http://amhealthmaster.http.internapcdn.net/AMHealthMaster/DOCUMENT/SheepUSA/USSES_Vilsack_to_Aberholt.pdf>.

374 Sakariassen, Alex. "USDA Approves Proposal to Close Sheep Station in Centennial Mountains." *Missoulanews.com*. Missoula Independent. 27 June 2014. <http://missoulanews.bigskypress.com/IndyBlog/archives/2014/06/27/usda-approves-proposal-to-close-sheep-station-in-centennial-mountains>.

375 Barker, Rocky. "Tough Times Out There for Idaho's Sheep Ranchers." *Idahostatesman.com*. Idaho Statesman. 27 June 2004. <http://www.idahostatesman.com/2014/06/27/3256761/tough-times-out-there-for-idahos.html>.

376 Associated Press. "Groups Sue Federal Agency Over Sheep Research Station after Grizzly Deaths." *Missoulian.com*. Associated Press. 18 May 2013. <http://missoulian.com/news/state-and-regional/groups-sue-federal-agency-over-sheep-research-station-after-grizzly/article_7b390052-c004-11e2-9ccf-001a4bcf887a.html>.

377 Letter from Thomas J. Vilsack, Secretary of the U.S. Department of Agriculture to Congressman Robert B. Aderholt, Chairman of the U.S. House of Representatives Subcommittee on Agriculture, Rural Development, Food and Drug Administration, and Related Agencies, Committee on Appropriations. 17 June 2014, <http://amhealthmaster.http.internapcdn.net/AMHealthMaster/DOCUMENT/SheepUSA/USSES_Vilsack_to_Aberholt.pdf>.

378 Letter from Representatives Mike Simpson, Doc Hastings, Greg Walden, Cathy McMorris-Rodgers, Steve Daines, and Raul Labrador to Representative Robert Aderholt, Chairman of the U.S. House of Representatives Subcommittee on Agriculture, Rural Development, Food and Drug Administration, and Related Agencies, Committee on Appropriations, June 26, 2014, <http://amhealthmaster.http.internapcdn.net/AMHealthMaster/DOCUMENT/SheepUSA/Dubois_USSES_6_26_14.pdf>.

379 Wieber, Aubrey. "Clark County Employer Likely Closing Down." *Postregister.com*. Post Register. 26 June 2014. <http://www.postregister.com/articles/news-todays-headlines/2014/06/26/clark-county-employer-likely-closing-down>.

380 Western Watershed Project. *Sheep Experiment Station Closure Thwarted by Political Interference*. Thewildlifenews.com. N.p., 16 July 2014. Web. 17 Oct. 2014. <http://www.thewildlifenews.com/2014/07/16/sheep-experiment-station-closure-thwarted-by-political-interference/>.

381 Western Watershed Project. *Sheep Experiment Station Closure Thwarted by Political Interference*. Thewildlifenews.com. N.p., 16 July 2014. Web. 17 Oct. 2014. <http://www.thewildlifenews.com/2014/07/16/sheep-experiment-station-closure-thwarted-by-political-interference/>.

382 "Idaho Press-Tribune Editorial Board. "Simpson, Sheep Station Contribute to Growing Debt Crisis." *Idahopress.com*. Idaho Press-Tribune. <http://m.idahopress.com/members/simpson-sheep-station-contribute-to-growing-debt-crisis/article_65251040-1200-11e4-82ee-001a4bcf887a.html?mode=jqm>.

383 Knight, Phil, "Letter to the editor: Sheep Station a Waste of Money, Should be Closed." *Bozemandailychronicle.com*. Bozeman Daily Chronicle. February 2014. <http://www.bozemandailychronicle.com/opinions/letters_to_editor/article_6efe383c-9404-11e3-b585-0019bb2963f4.html?mode=jqm>.

384 Department of Housing and Urban Development, HUD Exchange. "CDBG Entitlement Program Eligibility Requirements." *Hudexchange.info*. Accessed 14 October 2014, <https://www.hudexchange.info/cdbg-entitlement/cdbg-entitlement-program-eligibility-requirements/>.

385 Curtin, Eugene. "City Gives Final Approval to Installing Splash Pad at Hastings Banner Park." *Omaha.com*. Bellevue Leader. 31 July 2014. <http://www.omaha.com/sarpy/bellevue/city-gives-final-approval-to-installing-splash-pad-at-hastings/article_216caf3d-b951-53fb-8529-08a4a97b971e.html>.

386 City of Bellevue. "2013 Comprehensive Aquatics Study," 22 July 2013. <www.bellevue.net>

387 Curtin, Eugene. "City Gives Final Approval to Installing Splash Pad at Hastings Banner Park." *Omaha.com*. Bellevue Leader. 31 July 2014. <http://www.omaha.com/sarpy/bellevue/city-gives-final-approval-to-installing-splash-pad-at-hastings/article_216caf3d-b951-53fb-8529-08a4a97b971e.html>.

388 Powell, Andy. "Water Feature Coming to East Gadsden Rec Center." *Gadsentimes.com*. Gadsden Times. 12 August 2014. <http://www.gadsdentimes.com/article/20140812/NEWS/140819945?p=1&tc=pg>.

389 Savage, Lisa Rogers. "Council Approves Splash Pad Grant for East Gadsden." *Gadsentimes.com*. Gadsden Times. 19 August 2014. <http://www.gadsdentimes.com/article/20140819/NEWS/140819777?tc=ar>.

390 Martins, Andrew. "Grant Received for Spray Park." *Tri.gmnews.com* Tri-Town News. 2 October 2014. <http://tri.gmnews.com/news/2014-10-02/Front_Page/Grant_received_for_spray_park.html>.

391 "Burnham's Field to reopen with a splash," *glouster.wickedlocal.com*. Gatehouse Media, Inc. 4 September 2014. <http://gloucester.wickedlocal.com/article/20140904/NEWS/140908617>.

392 Wilson, Jeff. "Splash Park Construction Under Way." *Thesouthern.com*. Southern Illinoisan. 24 July 2014. <http://thesouthern.com/news/local/communities/carbondale/splash-park-construction-under-way/article_09ddca29-bd77-5d55-9b04-e8d09ecee24f.html>.

393 Website of the Carbondale Park District. "A Case for Support 2014." Accessed 17 October 2014. <http://www.cpkd.org/supersplashpark/images/case-for-support.pdf>.

394 Williams, Leah. "Carbondale Park District's Super Splash Park Blues: Fundraising Continues for the Outdoor Aquatic Center." *Carbondalerocks.com*. Carbondale Nightlife. <http://www.carbondalerocks.com/node/120565>.

395 The TEAM Plays. "RoosevElvis Press Kit and Touring Info." *Theteamplays.org*. The TEAM. Accessed 17 October 2014. <http://theteamplays.org/wp-content/uploads/2012/01/RoosevElvis-press-kit.pdf>.

396 The TEAM Plays. "RoosevElvis Press Kit and Touring Info." *Theteamplays.org*. The TEAM. Accessed 17 October 2014. <http://theteamplays.org/wp-content/uploads/2012/01/RoosevElvis-press-kit.pdf>.

397 The TEAM Plays. "RoosevElvis Press Kit and Touring Info." *Theteamplays.org*. The TEAM. Accessed 17 October 2014. <http://theteamplays.org/wp-content/uploads/2012/01/RoosevElvis-press-kit.pdf>.

398 The TEAM Plays. "RoosevElvis Press Kit and Touring Info." *Theteamplays.org*. The TEAM. Accessed 17 October 2014. <http://theteamplays.org/wp-content/uploads/2012/01/RoosevElvis-press-kit.pdf>.

399 The TEAM "About Us" webpage. *Available at:* http://theteamplays.org/about/about-the-company/

400 The TEAM. "RoosevElvis blog." *Theteamplays.org*. The TEAM. <http://theteamplays.org/category/team-blog/roosevelvis/>.

401 National Endowment for the Arts Grant. Award Number: 14-3200-7086.

402 Brantley, Ben. "*Finding Your Flair, Pompadour Optional*." *Nytimes.com*. The New York Times. 18 October 2013. <http://www.nytimes.com/2013/10/19/theater/reviews/roosevelvis-mashes-identities-at-the-bushwick-starr.html>.

403 *Roosevelvis Final Performances*. The TEAM. Vimeo.com. 25 October 2013. Web. <*http://vimeo.com/album/1953386/video/77812652*>.

404 Brantley, Ben. "*Finding Your Flair, Pompadour Optional*." *Nytimes.com*. The New York Times. 18 October 2013. <http://www.nytimes.com/2013/10/19/theater/reviews/roosevelvis-mashes-identities-at-the-bushwick-starr.html>.

405 Office of Senator Jeff Flake. Press Office. #PRIMECUTS: Elvis and Teddy Roosevelt Walk into a Bar.... Flake.senate.gov, 16 July 2014. Web. 17 Oct. 2014. <www.

flake.senate.gov/public/index.cfm/press-releases?ID=d03cff46-3fe4-4153-9537-76e1b56ce913>.

406 McKenna, Barrie. "Canadian Steel Used in U.S. Bridge Triggers 'Buy America' Fiasco." *Theglobeandmail.com.* The Globe and Mail Inc. 18 September 2014. Web. <http://www.theglobeandmail.com/report-on-business/international-business/us-business/buy-america-act-provides-punishment-for-small-colorado-town/article20660211/>.

407 Mitchell David, and Ashley Michels. "New Bridge May be Torn Up Because Steel was Manufactured in Canada." *Kdvr.com.* FOX31 Denver. 26 August 2014. Web. <http://kdvr.com/2014/08/26/brand-new-bridge-in-morrison-may-have-to-be-ripped-out/>.

408 Mitchell David, and Ashley Michels. "New Bridge May be Torn Up Because Steel was Manufactured in Canada." *Kdvr.com.* FOX31 Denver. 26 August 2014. Web. <http://kdvr.com/2014/08/26/brand-new-bridge-in-morrison-may-have-to-be-ripped-out/>.

409 Klemaier, Josie. "Canadian Steel Could Doom Repairs Made to Historic Morrison Bridge." *Denverpost.com.* Denver Post, 26 August 2014. <http://www.denverpost.com/golden/ci_26408442/canadian-steel-could-doom-repairs-made-historic-morrison>.

410 Klemaier, Josie. "Canadian Steel Could Doom Repairs Made to Historic Morrison Bridge." *Denverpost.com.* Denver Post, 26 August 2014. <http://www.denverpost.com/golden/ci_26408442/canadian-steel-could-doom-repairs-made-historic-morrison>.

411 Klemaier, Josie. "Canadian Steel Could Doom Repairs Made to Historic Morrison Bridge." *Denverpost.com.* Denver Post, 26 August 2014. <http://www.denverpost.com/golden/ci_26408442/canadian-steel-could-doom-repairs-made-historic-morrison>..

412 Klemaier, Josie. "Canadian Steel Could Doom Repairs Made to Historic Morrison Bridge." *Denverpost.com.* Denver Post, 26 August 2014. <http://www.denverpost.com/golden/ci_26408442/canadian-steel-could-doom-repairs-made-historic-morrison>.

413 Klemaier, Josie. "Canadian Steel Could Doom Repairs Made to Historic Morrison Bridge." *Denverpost.com.* Denver Post, 26 August 2014. <http://www.denverpost.com/golden/ci_26408442/canadian-steel-could-doom-repairs-made-historic-morrison>.

414 Klemaier, Josie. "Canadian Steel Could Doom Repairs Made to Historic Morrison Bridge." *Denverpost.com.* Denver Post, 26 August 2014. <http://www.denverpost.com/golden/ci_26408442/canadian-steel-could-doom-repairs-made-historic-morrison>.

415 Klemaier, Josie. "Canadian Steel Could Doom Repairs Made to Historic Morrison Bridge." *Denverpost.com.* Denver Post, 26 August 2014. <http://www.denverpost.com/golden/ci_26408442/canadian-steel-could-doom-repairs-made-historic-morrison>.

416 Klemaier, Josie. "Canadian Steel Could Doom Repairs Made to Historic Morrison Bridge." *Denverpost.com.* Denver Post, 26 August 2014. <http://www.denverpost.com/golden/ci_26408442/canadian-steel-could-doom-repairs-made-historic-morrison>.

417 Klemaier, Josie. "Canadian Steel Could Doom Repairs Made to Historic Morrison Bridge." *Denverpost.com.* Denver Post, 26 August 2014. <http://www.denverpost.com/golden/ci_26408442/canadian-steel-could-doom-repairs-made-historic-morrison>.

418 Klemaier, Josie. "Canadian Steel Could Doom Repairs Made to Historic Morrison Bridge." *Denverpost.com.* Denver Post, 26 August 2014. <http://www.denverpost.com/golden/ci_26408442/canadian-steel-could-doom-repairs-made-historic-morrison>.

419 Mitchell David, and Ashley Michels. "New Bridge May be Torn Up Because Steel was Manufactured in Canada." *Kdvr.com.* FOX31 Denver. 26 August 2014. Web. <http://kdvr.com/2014/08/26/brand-new-bridge-in-morrison-may-have-to-be-ripped-out/>.

420 Mitchell David, and Ashley Michels. "New Bridge May be Torn Up Because Steel was Manufactured in Canada." *Kdvr.com.* FOX31 Denver. 26 August 2014. Web. <http://kdvr.com/2014/08/26/brand-new-bridge-in-morrison-may-have-to-be-ripped-out/>.

421 McKenna, Barrie. "Canadian Steel Used in U.S. Bridge Triggers 'Buy America' Fiasco." *Theglobeandmail.com.* The Globe and Mail Inc. 18 September 2014. Web. <http://www.theglobeandmail.com/report-on-business/international-business/us-business/buy-america-act-provides-punishment-for-small-colorado-town/article20660211/>.

422 Grossman, Marcy. "'Buy America' is a Hindrance to Expanding Trade," *denverpost.com.* Denver Post. 13 September 2014. <http://www.denverpost.com/opinion/ci_26520336/buy-america-is-hindrance-expanding-trade>.

423 McKenna, Barrie. "Canadian Steel Used in U.S. Bridge Triggers 'Buy America' Fiasco." *Theglobeandmail.com.* The Globe and Mail Inc. 18 September 2014. Web. <http://www.theglobeandmail.com/report-on-business/international-business/us-business/buy-america-act-provides-punishment-for-small-colorado-town/article20660211/>.

424 McKenna, Barrie. "Canadian Steel Used in U.S. Bridge Triggers 'Buy America' Fiasco." *Theglobeandmail.com.* The Globe and Mail Inc. 18 September 2014. Web. <http://www.theglobeandmail.com/report-on-business/international-business/us-business/buy-america-act-provides-punishment-for-small-colorado-town/article20660211/>.

425 Philpott, Tom, "Sleep Apnea Boom Splits Vet Community." *Militaryadvantage.military.com.* Military Advantage. 25 February 2014. <http://militaryadvantage.military.com/2014/02/sleep-apnea-boom-splits-vet-community/>.

426 Philpott, Tom, "Sleep Apnea Boom Splits Vet Community." *Militaryadvantage.military.com.* Military Advantage. 25 February 2014. <http://militaryadvantage.military.com/2014/02/sleep-apnea-boom-splits-vet-community/>.

427 National Sleep Foundation. "Sleep Apnea." *Sleepfoundation.org.* National Sleep Foundation. <http://sleepfoundation.org/sleep-disorders-problems/sleep-apnea>.

428 National Sleep Foundation. "Sleep Apnea." *Sleepfoundation.org.* National Sleep Foundation. <http://sleepfoundation.org/sleep-disorders-problems/sleep-apnea>.

429 National Sleep Foundation. "Sleep Apnea." *Sleepfoundation.org.* National Sleep Foundation. <http://sleepfoundation.org/sleep-disorders-problems/sleep-apnea>.

430 Department of Veterans Affairs. "Benefit Rates." *Benefits.va.gov.* U.S. Department of Veterans Affairs. Web. <http://www.benefits.va.gov/compensation/rates-index.asp#combined>.

431 Chumley, Cheryl K. "Rep. Tammy Duckworth, Double Amputee, Slams IRS Worker on Disability." *Washingtontimes.com.* The Washington Times, LLC. 27 June 2013. Web. <http://www.washingtontimes.com/news/2013/jun/27/rep-tammy-duckworth-double-amputee-slams-irs-worke/>.

432 Chumley, Cheryl K. "Rep. Tammy Duckworth, Double Amputee, Slams IRS Worker on Disability." *Washingtontimes.com.* The Washington Times, LLC. 27 June 2013. Web. <http://www.washingtontimes.com/news/2013/jun/27/rep-tammy-duckworth-double-amputee-slams-irs-worke/>.

433 Philpott, Tom, "Sleep Apnea Boom Splits Vet Community." *Militaryadvantage.military.com.* Military Advantage. 25 February 2014. <http://militaryadvantage.military.com/2014/02/sleep-apnea-boom-splits-vet-community/>.

434 Philpott, Tom, "Sleep Apnea Boom Splits Vet Community." *Militaryadvantage.military.com.* Military Advantage. 25 February 2014. <http://militaryadvantage.military.com/2014/02/sleep-apnea-boom-splits-vet-community/>.

435 Philpott, Tom. "Attorney Urges End to Sleep Apnea Claims 'Abuse.'" *Military.com.* Military Advantage. Web. <http://www.military.com/benefits/2013/05/30/attorney-urges-an-end-to-sleep-apnea-claims-abuse.html>.

436 Philpott, Tom, "Sleep Apnea Boom Splits Vet Community." *Militaryadvantage.military.com.* Military Advantage. 25 February 2014. <http://militaryadvantage.military.com/2014/02/sleep-apnea-boom-splits-vet-community/>.

437 Philpott, Tom, "Sleep Apnea Boom Splits Vet Community." *Militaryadvantage.military.com.* Military Advantage. 25 February 2014. <http://militaryadvantage.military.com/2014/02/sleep-apnea-boom-splits-vet-community/>.

438 Philpott, Tom, "Sleep Apnea Boom Splits Vet Community." *Militaryadvantage.military.com*. Military Advantage. 25 February 2014. <http://militaryadvantage.military.com/2014/02/sleep-apnea-boom-splits-vet-community/>.

439 U.S. Army. "Benefits – Basic Pay: Active Duty Soldiers." *Goarmy.com*. The United States Army. Web. Accessed 9 October 2014. <http://www.goarmy.com/benefits/money/basic-pay-active-duty-soldiers.html>.

440 Merritt, Zina D. *Defense Logistics: Actions Needed to Improve Department-Wide Management of Conventional Ammunition Survey*. Rep. no. GAO-14-182. Report to the Chairman, Committee on Homeland Security and Governmental Affairs. U.S. Senate, Washington, D.C.: Government Accountability Office. March 2014. <http://www.gao.gov/assets/670/662161.pdf>.

441 Vanden Brook, Tom. "Pentagon Refutes Senators' Charges of Wasted Ammo." *Usatoday.com*. Gannett. 8 August 2014. <http://www.usatoday.com/story/news/nation/2014/07/01/pentagon-ammunition-senate/11797375/>.

442 Merritt, Zina D. *Defense Logistics: Actions Needed to Improve Department-Wide Management of Conventional Ammunition Survey*. Rep. no. GAO-14-182. Report to the Chairman, Committee on Homeland Security and Governmental Affairs. U.S. Senate, Washington, D.C.: Government Accountability Office. March 2014. <http://www.gao.gov/assets/670/662161.pdf>.

443 Merritt, Zina D. *Defense Logistics: Actions Needed to Improve Department-Wide Management of Conventional Ammunition Survey*. Rep. no. GAO-14-182. Report to the Chairman, Committee on Homeland Security and Governmental Affairs. U.S. Senate, Washington, D.C.: Government Accountability Office. March 2014. <http://www.gao.gov/assets/670/662161.pdf>.

444 Merritt, Zina D. *Defense Logistics: Actions Needed to Improve Department-Wide Management of Conventional Ammunition Survey*. Rep. no. GAO-14-182. Report to the Chairman, Committee on Homeland Security and Governmental Affairs. U.S. Senate, Washington, D.C.: Government Accountability Office. March 2014. <http://www.gao.gov/assets/670/662161.pdf>.

445 Vakoch, Douglas A., "Archaeology, Anthropology, and Interstellar Communication." *Nasa.gov*. Web. Accessed 17 October 2014. <http://www.nasa.gov/connect/ebooks/archaeology_anthropology_and_interstellar_communication.html>.

446 Vakoch, Douglas A., "Archaeology, Anthropology, and Interstellar Communication," NASA website. http://www.nasa.gov/connect/ebooks/archaeology_anthropology_and_interstellar_communication.html

447 Vakoch, Douglas A., "Archaeology, Anthropology, and Interstellar Communication." *Nasa.gov*. Web. Accessed 17 October 2014. <http://www.nasa.gov/connect/ebooks/archaeology_anthropology_and_interstellar_communication.html>.

448 Vakoch, Douglas A., "Archaeology, Anthropology, and Interstellar Communication." *Nasa.gov*. Web. Accessed 17 October 2014. <http://www.nasa.gov/connect/ebooks/archaeology_anthropology_and_interstellar_communication.html>.

p248.

449 Vakoch, Douglas A., "Archaeology, Anthropology, and Interstellar Communication." *Nasa.gov*. Web. Accessed 17 October 2014. <http://www.nasa.gov/connect/ebooks/archaeology_anthropology_and_interstellar_communication.html>.

p248.

450 Barry, William P. "From the Chief Historian." *Nasa.gov*. NASA News & Notes. Web. Accessed 17 October 2014. <http://history.nasa.gov/nltr31-1.pdf>. p1-2

451 Information provided by NASA to the Congressional Research Service on July 7, 2014.

452 Isherwood, Charles. "A Dragon Returns, This Time Onstage." *Nytimes.com*. The New York Times. 24 February 2014. <http://www.nytimes.com/2014/02/25/theater/david-henry-hwangs-kung-fu-opens-at-signature-theater.html?_r=0>.

453 McElroy, Steven. "Fighting (and Dancing) Like Bruce Lee." *Nytimes.com*. The New York Times. February 17, 2014. <http://www.nytimes.com/2014/02/18/theater/for-the-play-kung-fu-choreographing-combat.html?_r=1>.

454 National Endowment for the Arts. <http://arts.gov/>.

455 Stasio, Marilyn. "Off Broadway Review: Bruce Lee Bio-Drama 'Kung Fu'." 24 February 2014. <http://variety.com/2014/legit/reviews/off-broadway-review-bruce-lee-bio-drama-kung-fu-1201116963/>.

456 Isherwood, Charles. "A Dragon Returns, This Time Onstage." *Nytimes.com*. The New York Times. 24 February 2014. <http://www.nytimes.com/2014/02/25/theater/david-henry-hwangs-kung-fu-opens-at-signature-theater.html?_r=0>.

457 Isherwood, Charles. "A Dragon Returns, This Time Onstage." *Nytimes.com*. The New York Times. 24 February 2014. <http://www.nytimes.com/2014/02/25/theater/david-henry-hwangs-kung-fu-opens-at-signature-theater.html?_r=0>.

458 "Support Signature Theatre." Signature Theatre. <http://www.signaturetheatre.org/support/index.aspx>

459 "Federal Award Identifier: 14-3200-7100." *Usaspending.gov*. <http://www.usaspending.gov/explore?frompage=assistance&tab=By%20Prime%20Awardee&comingfrom=searchresults&federal_award_id=14-3200-7100&fiscal_year=all&typeofview=complete>.

460 U.S. Department of Transportation, "Tiger Awards, 2013." *dot.gov*. Connecticut Department of Transportation. Web. <http://www.dot.gov/sites/dot.gov/files/docs/TIGER_2013_FactSheets.pdf>.

461 The City of Fresno. "The (Broken) Heart of Our City: A Fulton Mall Timeline." 8 February 2013. Web. <http://www.fresno.gov/NR/rdonlyres/2AD4C88B-9C6B-4581-BF39-57DC024DBA89/26488/FultonMallTimeline.pdf>.

462 Mumma, Linda. "Luftenburgs Bridal leaving Fulton Mall." *Abclocal.go.com*. KFSN-TV ABC. 29 June 2013. <http://abclocal.go.com/kfsn/story?section=news/local&id=9156394>.

463 Website of the City of Fresno. "Fresno Fulton Corridor Specific Plan, City of Fresno, California (Public Draft)." 14 October 2011. <http://webapp.fresno.gov/FresnoPlans/FultonCorridor/FCSP_Ch_04_Fulton_Mall_0.pdf>.

464 Website of the City of Fresno. "Fresno Fulton Corridor Specific Plan, City of Fresno, California (Public Draft)." 14 October 2011. <http://webapp.fresno.gov/FresnoPlans/FultonCorridor/FCSP_Ch_04_Fulton_Mall_0.pdf>.

465 Wozniacka, Gosia. "Fresno Moving to Tear Up Historic Pedestrian Mall." *Ap.org*. The Associated Press. 28 September 2013. <http://bigstory.ap.org/article/fresno-moving-tear-historic-pedestrian-mall>.

466 Oz, Mike. "Fulton Mall: Kill it? Rename it? Preserve it?" *FresnoBeehive.com*. The Bee. 3 September 2010. Web. <http://fresnobeehive.com/archives/7524>.

467 Nolte, Carl. "Sprawl, Clutter Define Fresno/Civic Corruption has Splotched the City's Image." *Sfgate.com*. The San Francisco Chronicle. 1 September 1999. <http://www.sfgate.com/news/article/Sprawl-Clutter-Define-Fresno-Civic-corruption-2911067.php>.

468 Nolte, Carl. Fresno Council of Government, "Downtown Transportation and Infrastructure Study (Prepared for the City of Fresno," October 2007 <http://www.fresnocog.org/files/TransitDocs/Fresno%20Downtown%20Transportation%20and%20Infrastructure%20Study-Final.pdf>.

469 The City of Fresno. Newsroom. *Mayor Swearengin: 'Historic' Federal Grant Will Help Return Downtown Fresno to Prosperity*. *Fresno.com*. N.p., 9 June 2013. Web. 17 Oct. 2014. <Mayor Swearengin: 'Historic' Federal Grant Will Help Return Downtown Fresno to Prosperity>.

470 Hostetter, George. "Reopen Fresno's Fulton Mall to traffic, City Council says in historic vote." *FresnoBee*.com. The Bee. 27 February 2014. Web. <http://www.fresnobee.com/2014/02/27/3794420/fresno-city-council-takes-key.html>.

471 The City of Fresno. Newsroom. *Mayor Swearengin: 'Historic' Federal Grant Will Help Return Downtown Fresno to Prosperity*. Fresno.com. N.p., 9 June 2013. Web. 17 Oct. 2014. <Mayor Swearengin: 'Historic' Federal Grant Will Help Return Downtown Fresno to Prosperity>.

472 U.S. Postal Service Office of Inspector General. *Alaska Bypass: Beyond Its Original Purpose*. Report No. RARC-WP-12-005. Washington, D.C.: USPSOIG, 28 November 2011. Web. <http://www.uspsoig.gov/sites/default/files/document-library-files/2013/rarc-wp-12-005.pdf>.

473 Rein, Lisa. "U.S. Postal Service losing tens of millions annually subsidizing shipments to Alaska." *Washingtonpost.com*. The Washington Post. 28 June 2014. Web. <http://www.washingtonpost.com/politics/us-postal-service-losing-tens-of-millions-annually-subsidizing-shipments-to-alaska/2014/06/28/3d007fd6-e51a-11e3-afc6-a1dd9407abcf_story.html?hpid=z1>.

474 Whitcomb, Tammy. Oral Statement at a "Hearing before Subcommittee on Federal Workforce, U.S. Postal Service and the Census, Committee on Oversight and Government Reform, House of Representatives." 4 March 2014. Web. < http://oversight.house.gov/wp-content/uploads/2014/03/Whitcomb-Testimony.pdf>.

475 Rein, Lisa. "U.S. Postal Service losing tens of millions annually subsidizing shipments to Alaska." *Washingtonpost.com*. The Washington Post. 28 June 2014. Web. <http://www.washingtonpost.com/politics/us-postal-service-losing-tens-of-millions-annually-subsidizing-shipments-to-alaska/2014/06/28/3d007fd6-e51a-11e3-afc6-a1dd9407abcf_story.html?hpid=z1>.

476 Rein, Lisa. "U.S. Postal Service losing tens of millions annually subsidizing shipments to Alaska." *Washingtonpost.com*. The Washington Post. 28 June 2014. Web. <http://www.washingtonpost.com/politics/us-postal-service-losing-tens-of-millions-annually-subsidizing-shipments-to-alaska/2014/06/28/3d007fd6-e51a-11e3-afc6-a1dd9407abcf_story.html?hpid=z1>.

477 "GRAMMY Museum Mississippi Breaks Ground; NEW GRAMMY MUSEUM SET TO OPEN IN CLEVELAND, MISS., IN SUMMER 2015,"*Grammy.com*. The Recording Academy. 12 June 2013. <http://www.grammy.com/news/grammy-museum-mississippi-breaks-ground>.

478 "GRAMMY Museum Mississippi Breaks Ground; NEW GRAMMY MUSEUM SET TO OPEN IN CLEVELAND, MISS., IN SUMMER 2015,"*Grammy.com*. The Recording Academy. 12 June 2013. <http://www.grammy.com/news/grammy-museum-mississippi-breaks-ground>.

479 Gallo, Phil. "Grammy Museum in Mississippi Set to Break Ground Next Month, Open in 2015." *Billboard.com*. Billboard. 8 February 2013. <http://www.billboard.com/biz/articles/news/1538573/grammy-museum-in-mississippi-set-to-break-ground-next-month-open-in-2015>.

480 Associated Press. "Miss. Grammy Museum gets $1.25M federal grant," *cdispatch.com*. The Commercial Dispatch Company. 10 September 2014. <http://www.cdispatch.com/news/article.asp?aid=36210>.

481 Gallo, Phil. "Grammy Museum in Mississippi Set to Break Ground Next Month, Open in 2015." *Billboard.com*. Billboard. 8 February 2013. <http://www.billboard.com/biz/articles/news/1538573/grammy-museum-in-mississippi-set-to-break-ground-next-month-open-in-2015>.

482 U.S. Economic Development Administration. Public Affairs Department. *U.S. Department of Commerce Invests Nearly $2.75 Million to Upgrade Critical Infrastructure to Support Business Growth and Tourism in Mississippi. EDA.gov*. Department of Commerce, 9 Sept. 2014. Web. 17 Oct. 2014. <http://www.eda.gov/news/press-releases/2014/09/09/ms.htm>.

483 Associated Press. "Miss. Grammy Museum gets $1.25M federal grant," *cdispatch.com*. The Commercial Dispatch Company. 10 September 2014. <http://www.cdispatch.com/news/article.asp?aid=36210>.

484 Wood, Robert. "Behind The Grammys Taxes," *Forbes*.com. Forbes. 26 January 2014. Web. <http://www.forbes.com/sites/robertwood/2014/01/26/behind-the-grammys-taxes/>.

485 Wood, Robert. "Behind The Grammys Taxes," *Forbes*.com. Forbes. 26 January 2014. Web. <http://www.forbes.com/sites/robertwood/2014/01/26/behind-the-grammys-taxes/>.

486 Wood, Robert. "Behind The Grammys Taxes," *Forbes*.com. Forbes. 26 January 2014. Web. <http://www.forbes.com/sites/robertwood/2014/01/26/behind-the-grammys-taxes/>.

487 Wood, Robert. "Behind The Grammys Taxes," *Forbes*.com. Forbes. 26 January 2014. Web. <http://www.forbes.com/sites/robertwood/2014/01/26/behind-the-grammys-taxes/>.

488 Wood, Robert. "Behind The Grammys Taxes," *Forbes*.com. Forbes. 26 January 2014. Web. <http://www.forbes.com/sites/robertwood/2014/01/26/behind-the-grammys-taxes/>.

489 "FutureCoast." *FutureCoast*. Future Voices. Web. 17 Oct. 2014. <http://futurecoast.org/>.

490 http://www.futurevoices.net/about/

491 Pyper, Julia, "New Climate-Fiction (Cli-Fi) Game Sends Players Clues from the Future." *ScientificAmerican.com*. The Scientific American. 1 May 2014. Web. <http://www.scientificamerican.com/article/new-climate-fiction-cli-fi-game-sends-players-clues-from-the-future/>.

492 *See, e.g.*, FutureCoast, Twitter (June 2 2014, 3:03 PM EDT), https://twitter.com/FutrCoast/status/461206905655148544 (documenting the location of a chronofact in Paris).

493 *A Perfect 75° (Antarctica)*, FutureCoast, http://futurecoast.org/voicemail/56781-86134025/.

494 *Ten Feet of Snow*, FutureCoast, http://futurecoast.org/voicemail/60289-15386431/.

495 *The Food Riots (Chicago)*, FutureCoast, http://futurecoast.org/voicemail/56208-48137961/.

496 *The Neo-Luddites are Closing In*, FutureCoast, http://futurecoast.org/voicemail/93594-38625955/.

497 *When You See Them*, FutureCoast, http://futurecoast.org/voicemail/48305-29152180/.

498 Candy, Stuart. "Participatory Cli-fi: The Making of FutureCoast." Weblog post.*Situation Lab*. N.p., 12 Feb. 2014. Web. 17 Oct. 2014. <http://situationlab.org/2014/02/12/futurecoast/>.

499 Andersen, Michael."Voicemails from the Future Explore the Impact of Climate Change." *Wired.com*. Condé Nast. Web. 7 February 2014. <http://www.wired.com/2014/02/futurecoast-climate-change/>.

500 Andersen, Michael."Voicemails from the Future Explore the Impact of Climate Change." *Wired.com*. Condé Nast. Web. 7 February 2014. <http://www.wired.com/2014/02/futurecoast-climate-change/>.

501 Andersen, Michael."Voicemails from the Future Explore the Impact of Climate Change." *Wired.com*. Condé Nast. Web. 7 February 2014. <http://www.wired.com/2014/02/futurecoast-climate-change/>.

Andersen, Michael."Voicemails from the Future Explore the Impact of Climate Change." *Wired.com*. Condé Nast. Web. 7 February 2014. <http://www.wired.com/2014/02/futurecoast-climate-change/>.

503 Andersen, Michael."Voicemails from the Future Explore the Impact of Climate Change." *Wired.com*. Condé Nast. Web. 7 February 2014. <http://www.wired.com/2014/02/futurecoast-climate-change/>.

504 Pyper, Julia, "New Climate-Fiction (Cli-Fi) Game Sends Players Clues from the Future." *ScientificAmerican.com.* The Scientific American. 1 May 2014. Web. <http://www.scientificamerican.com/article/new-climate-fiction-cli-fi-game-sends-players-clues-from-the-future/>.

505 "Enduring Questions: Pilot Course Grants." *NEH.gov.* National Endowment for the Humanities. Web. <https://securegrants.neh.gov/PublicQuery/main.aspx?q=1&n=0&o=0&k=0&f=0&s=0&p=1&pv=269&d=0&y=0&pg=0&ob=year&or=DESC>.

506 "National Endowment For The Humanities Grant Awards And Offers." *NEH.gov.* National Endowment for the Humanities. March 2014. Web. <http://www.neh.gov/files/press-release/march2014grantsstatebystate.pdf>.

507 Allan, Marc. "Why Is It Funny? Professor Bungard Will Tell You." *Butler.edu.* Butler University. 2 June 2014. Web. <http://news.butler.edu/blog/2014/06/bungard/>.

508 "Enduring Questions: Pilot Course Grants." *NEH.gov.* National Endowment for the Humanities. Web. <https://securegrants.neh.gov/PublicQuery/main.aspx?q=1&n=0&o=0&k=0&f=0&s=0&p=1&pv=269&d=0&y=0&pg=0&ob=year&or=DESC>.

509 Allan, Marc. "Why Is It Funny? Professor Bungard Will Tell You." *Butler.edu.* Butler University. 2 June 2014. Web. <http://news.butler.edu/blog/2014/06/bungard/>.

510 Science, technology, engineering and mathematics.

511 Parker, Laura, "Luxury Jets Vie for Runways," USA Today, August 25, 2003, http://usatoday30.usatoday.com/travel/news/2003/08/25-suv-jets.htm

512 Moore, Greg, "Airport gets $18M for construction. *mtexpress.com.* Idaho Mountain Express and Guide. 16 April 2014. Web. <http://www.mtexpress.com/index2.php?ID=2007151588>.

513 Moore, Greg, "Airport gets $18M for construction. *mtexpress.com.* Idaho Mountain Express and Guide. 16 April 2014. Web. <http://www.mtexpress.com/index2.php?ID=2007151588>

514 Olmsted, Larry, "Hollywood's A-List Ski Resort is Now Top Golf Resort," *forbes.com.* Forbes. 9 June 2012. Web. <http://www.forbes.com/sites/larryolmsted/2012/06/09/hollywoods-a-list-ski-resort-is-now-top-golf-resort/>.

515 Stebner, Beth, "Summer Camp for Moguls! Throngs of Media and Tech Luminaries Descend Upon Idaho for Annual Sun Valley Conference." *Dailymail.co.uk.* Associated Newspapers Ltd. 11 July 2012. Web <http://www.dailymail.co.uk/news/article-2172172/Sun-Valley-conference-Media-tech-luminaries-descend-Idaho-annual-Sun-Valley-conference.html>.

516 "More than 1,600 homes evacuated in Idaho region where celebrities including Bruce Willis and Arnold Schwarzenegger have homes as winds whip up wildfires, Daily Mail UK,, August 17, 2013, <http://www.dailymail.co.uk/news/article-2396153/More-1-600-homes-evacuated-Idaho-region-celebrities-including-Bruce-Willis-Arnold-Schwarzenegger-homes-winds-whip-wildfires.html>; Bellamy, Steve, "Arnold Schwarzenegger, Maria Shriver, Tom Hanks, Bruce Willis, Ashton Kutcher and Clint Eastwood second home in Sun Valley," The Ski Channel, July 4, 2009, <http://www.theskichannel.com/news/20090704/arnold-schwarzenegger-maria-shriver-tom-hanks-bruce-willis-ashton-kutcher-and-clint-eastwood-second-home-in-sun-valley/>.

517 Olmsted, Larry, "Hollywood's A-List Ski Resort is Now Top Golf Resort." *Forbes.com.* Forbes. 9 June 2012. Web. <http://www.forbes.com/sites/larryolmsted/2012/06/09/hollywoods-a-list-ski-resort-is-now-top-golf-resort/>.

518 Olmsted, Larry, "Hollywood's A-List Ski Resort is Now Top Golf Resort." *Forbes.com.* Forbes. 9 June 2012. Web. <http://www.forbes.com/sites/larryolmsted/2012/06/09/hollywoods-a-list-ski-resort-is-now-top-golf-resort/>.

519 Olmsted, Larry, "Hollywood's A-List Ski Resort is Now Top Golf Resort." *Forbes.com.* Forbes. 9 June 2012. Web. <http://www.forbes.com/sites/larryolmsted/2012/06/09/hollywoods-a-list-ski-resort-is-now-top-golf-resort/>./

520 Flightstats website. Web. <http://www.flightstats.com/go/FlightStatus/flightStatusByAirport.do?airportCode=SUN&airportQueryType=0>

521 RRC Associates, Friedman Memorial Airport Passenger Survey: Winter 2013/14 Summary (Prepared for the Fly Sun Valley Alliance), May 2014, http://www.flysunvalleyalliance.com/documents/SUNWinter2013-14short.pdf

522 Moore, Greg, "Airport gets $18M for construction. *mtexpress.com.* Idaho Mountain Express and Guide. 16 April 2014. Web. <http://www.mtexpress.com/index2.php?ID=2007151588>

523 Jervis, Rick, "Historic Flash Flood Leaves Devastation in Austin," *usatoday.com.* Gannett. 7 November 2013. Web. <http://www.usatoday.com/story/news/nation/2013/11/07/flash-flood-austin-residents-killed-displaced/3459181/>.

524 KUT Staff. "Austin, Travis County Works to Rebuild from Devastating Halloween Floods." *Kut.org.* KUT. 4 November 2013. Web. <http://kut.org/post/austin-travis-county-works-rebuild-devastating-halloween-floods>.

525 Office of the Governor Rick Perry. News. *Gov. Perry Requests Presidential Disaster Declaration for Central Texas Flood Damage.Governor.state.tx.us.* N.p., 13 Dec. 2013. Web. 17 Oct. 2014. <http://governor.state.tx.us/news/press-release/19168/>.

526 Federal Emergency Management Agency, *Initial Notice, Texas; Major Disaster and Related Determinations,* 20 December 2013. Web. <http://www.fema.gov/disaster/4159/notices/initial-notice>.

527 Analysis of dataset available at: Federal Emergency Management Agency. *FEMA Public Assistance Funded Projects Detail – Open Government Initiative,* Publication Date: 11 August 2014. Web. <http://www.fema.gov/media-library/assets/documents/28331>.

528 City of Austin Department of Parks and Recreation, *Roy Kizer Golf Course.* Web. <http://www.austintexas.gov/department/roy-kizer-golf-course>. Austin Senior Golf Association, *COA Golf Course Flood Damage,* Message from City of Austin Golf Division. Web. <http://www.austinsga.org/News/COAGolfCourseFloodDamage.html>.

529 Analysis of dataset available at: Federal Emergency Management Agency. *FEMA Public Assistance Funded Projects Detail – Open Government Initiative,* Publication Date: 11 August 2014. Web. <http://www.fema.gov/media-library/assets/documents/28331>.

530 Analysis of dataset available at: Federal Emergency Management Agency. *FEMA Public Assistance Funded Projects Detail – Open Government Initiative,* Publication Date: 11 August 2014. Web. <http://www.fema.gov/media-library/assets/documents/28331>.

531 Austin City Council, *Questions and Answers for Thursday, March 20, 201.* Web. <http://www.austintexas.gov/edims/document.cfm?id=207248>/. p4.

532 Austin City Council, *Questions and Answers for Thursday, March 20, 201.* Web. <http://www.austintexas.gov/edims/document.cfm?id=207248>/. p4. Sikora, Edward et al. *Golf Course Nematodes- The Hidden Enemy.* Highlights of Agricultural Research, Vol. 46 No. 3: Fall 1999, Web. <http://www.aaes.auburn.edu/comm/pubs/highlightsonline/fall99/golf.html>.

533 Analysis of dataset available at: Federal Emergency Management Agency. *FEMA Public Assistance Funded Projects Detail – Open Government Initiative,* Publication Date: 11 August 2014. Web. <http://www.fema.gov/media-library/assets/documents/28331>.

534 Counsinorville.com. "Best Disney Resort for Teens." *Cousinorville.com.* 5 September 2013. <http://cousinorville.com/best-disney-resort-for-teens/>.

535 http://disneyparks.disney.go.com/blog/2013/08/ten-things-you-may-not-know-about-disneys-polynesian-resort-at-walt-disney-world-resort/

536 http://www.usaspending.gov/explore?frompage=assistance&tab=By%20Prime%20Awardee&comingfrom=searchresults&federal_award_id=14E0436212810001&fiscal_year=all&typeofview=complete

537 http://www.usaspending.gov/explore?frompage=assistance&tab=By%20Prime%20Awardee&comingfrom=searchresults&federal_award_

id=14E4536081400001&fiscal_year=all&typeofview=complete

538 http://fortune.com/fortune500/best-buy-co-inc-60/

Sylt ,Christian, "The Secrets Behind Disney's $2.2 Billion Theme Park Profits," *Forbes*, July 14, 2014, 539 http://www.forbes.com/sites/csylt/2014/07/14/the-secrets-behind-disneys-2-2-billion-theme-park-profits/.

540 http://wdwnews.com/releases/2014/05/15/walt-disney-world-resort-shares-new-details-on-renovations-at-disneys-polynesian-village-resort/

541 Montoya, Nestor, "Disney announces big changes for Polynesian Resort," *Fox (Orlando)*, May 22, 2014, http://www.myfoxorlando.com/story/25531051/disney-announces-big-changes-for-polynesian-resort.

542 https://disneyworld.disney.go.com/resorts/polynesian-resort/

543 https://disneyworld.disney.go.com/dining/polynesian-resort/disney-spirit-of-aloha-dinner-show/

544 Montoya, Nestor, "Disney announces big changes for Polynesian Resort," *Fox (Orlando)*, May 22, 2014, http://www.myfoxorlando.com/story/25531051/disney-announces-big-changes-for-polynesian-resort.

545 "What is Harvart-NTL?" Harvard-NASA Tournament Lab. Web. 6 October 2014. <http://projects.iq.harvard.edu/nasatournamentlab/home>.

546 Andrews, Evan. "10 Things You May Not Know About Genghis Khan." *History.com*, A&E Television Networks, LLC. 29 April 2014. <http://www.history.com/news/history-lists/10-things-you-may-not-know-about-genghis-khan>.

547 Andrews, Evan. "10 Things You May Not Know About Genghis Khan." *History.com*, A&E Television Networks, LLC. 29 April 2014. <http://www.history.com/news/history-lists/10-things-you-may-not-know-about-genghis-khan>.

548 Office of Management and Budget, USAspending.gov search, *available at http://www.usaspending.gov/search?form_fields={%22search_term%22%3A%22Tournament%22%2C%22dept%22%3A[%228000%22]%2C%22fyear%22%3A[%222014%22]}&sort_by=dollars&per_page=25*

549 TopCoder. "Collective Minds & Machines Exploration Challenge." *Topcoder.com*. UC San Diego. 6 October 2014. <http://www.topcoder.com/collectiveminds>.

550 TopCoder. "Collective Minds & Machines Exploration Challenge." *Topcoder.com*. UC San Diego. 6 October 2014. <http://www.topcoder.com/collectiveminds>.

551 TopCoder. (2013, September 3). *Collective Minds & Machines Exploration Challenge*.[Video File] *Topcoder*. Retrieved from: <https://www.youtube.com/watch?v=gJtbLhRHg09 >.

552 Doug Ramsey, "UC San Diego Research Scientist Teams with TopCoder, NASA for Coding Challenge." UC *ucsd.edu*. San Diego News Center. 13 September 2013. <http://ucsdnews.ucsd.edu/pressrelease/uc_san_diego_research_scientist_teams_with_topcoder_nasa_for_coding_challen>.

553 Doug Ramsey, "UC San Diego Research Scientist Teams with TopCoder, NASA for Coding Challenge." UC *ucsd.edu*. San Diego News Center. 13 September 2013. <http://ucsdnews.ucsd.edu/pressrelease/uc_san_diego_research_scientist_teams_with_topcoder_nasa_for_coding_challen>.

554 Davis, Carolyn. "The Long Road to a Failed Project in Norristown." Philly.com. Philadelphia Media Network LLC. 17 February 2014. Web. <http://articles.philly.com/2014-02-17/news/47382264_1_jerry-nugent-charles-gallub-norristown>.

555 Davis, Carolyn. "The Long Road to a Failed Project in Norristown." Philly.com. Philadelphia Media Network LLC. 17 February 2014. Web. <http://articles.philly.com/2014-02-17/news/47382264_1_jerry-nugent-charles-gallub-norristown>.

556 Davis, Carolyn. "The Long Road to a Failed Project in Norristown." Philly.com. Philadelphia Media Network LLC. 17 February 2014. Web. <http://articles.philly.com/2014-02-17/news/47382264_1_jerry-nugent-charles-gallub-norristown>.

557 Kostelni, Natalie. "How Montgomery County Gabled and Lost on a Film Studio. Bizjournals.com. American City Business Journals (Philadelphia Division). 21 June 2013. Web. <http://www.bizjournals.com/philadelphia/print-edition/2013/06/21/how-montgomery-county-gambled-and.html?page=all>.

558 Kostelni, Natalie. "How Montgomery County Gabled and Lost on a Film Studio. Bizjournals.com. American City Business Journals (Philadelphia Division). 21 June 2013. Web. <http://www.bizjournals.com/philadelphia/print-edition/2013/06/21/how-montgomery-county-gambled-and.html?page=all>.

559 Davis, Carolyn. "The Long Road to a Failed Project in Norristown." Philly.com. Philadelphia Media Network LLC. 17 February 2014. Web. <http://articles.philly.com/2014-02-17/news/47382264_1_jerry-nugent-charles-gallub-norristown>.

560 Wine and Vines Staff. "Ask Dr. Vinny." *Winesandvines.com*. Wine Spectator. 27 January 2014. Web. <http://www.winespectator.com/drvinny/show/id/46410>.

561 Wine and Vines Staff. "Number of Wineries Grows to 8,391 in North America. *Winesandvines.com*. Wine Spectator. 27 January 2014. Web. <http://www.winesandvines.com/template.cfm?section=news&content=127266>.

562 *Hatch Red Chile Wine*, Online Wine Store Accessed 18 October 2014. Web. <http://www.stclairwinery.com/online-wine-store/>.

563 USDA. "Value-Added Producer Grant Awards Fiscal Year 2014." *Rurdev.usda.gov*. USDA Rural Development. Accessed 18 September 2014/ <http://www.rurdev.usda.gov/supportdocuments/RD_2014VAPGRecipients.pdf>.

564 USDA. "Value-Added Producer Grants." *Rurdev.usda.gov*. USDA Rural Development. <http://www.rurdev.usda.gov/BCP_VAPG.html>.

565 Office of Senator Tom Udall. News Room. Udall Announces Funding to Help Deming Winery Expand Operations. N.p., 27 Aug. 2014. Web. 18 Oct. 2014. <http://www.tomudall.senate.gov/?p=press_release&id=1745>.

566 *Hatch Red Chile Wine*, Online Wine Store Accessed 18 October 2014. Web. <http://www.stclairwinery.com/online-wine-store/>.

567 Van Tieghem, Jen. "Southwest Wines' Hatch Green Chile Lacks Punch." *Sdcitybeat.com*. San Diego City Beat. 30 August 2013. Web. http://www.sdcitybeat.com/sandiego/article-12155-southwest-wines-hatch-green-chile-lacks-punch.html>.

568 Van Tieghem, Jen. "Southwest Wines' Hatch Green Chile Lacks Punch." *Sdcitybeat.com*. San Diego City Beat. 30 August 2013. Web. http://www.sdcitybeat.com/sandiego/article-12155-southwest-wines-hatch-green-chile-lacks-punch.html>.

569 USDA. "Value-Added Producer Grant Awards Fiscal Year 2014." *Rurdev.usda.gov*. USDA Rural Development. Accessed 18 September 2014/ <http://www.rurdev.usda.gov/supportdocuments/RD_2014VAPGRecipients.pdf>.

570 USDA. "Value-Added Producer Grant Awards Fiscal Year 2014." *Rurdev.usda.gov*. USDA Rural Development. Accessed 18 September 2014/ <http://www.rurdev.usda.gov/supportdocuments/RD_2014VAPGRecipients.pdf>.

571 USDA. "Value-Added Producer Grant Awards Fiscal Year 2014." *Rurdev.usda.gov*. USDA Rural Development. Accessed 18 September 2014/ <http://www.rurdev.usda.gov/supportdocuments/RD_2014VAPGRecipients.pdf>.

572 USDA. "Value-Added Producer Grant Awards Fiscal Year 2014." *Rurdev.usda.gov*. USDA Rural Development. Accessed 18 September 2014/ <http://www.rurdev.usda.gov/supportdocuments/RD_2014VAPGRecipients.pdf>.

573 Harris, Amy Julia. "Subsidized Squalor: Residents Live in Filth, Fear in Mismanaged Bay Area Public Housing." *Cir.org*. The Center for Investigative Reporting. 17 February 2014. <https://beta.cironline.org/reports/residents-live-in-filth-fear-in-mismanaged-bay-area-public-housing/>.

574 Resolution of the Board of Commissioners of the Housing Authority of the City of Richmond Accepting the Operating Budget for FY2014/2015." Resolution No. 1978. The City of Richmond, California. 17 June 2014. <http://www.ci.richmond.ca.us/ArchiveCenter/ViewFile/Item/5890>.

575 Harris, Amy Julia. "Subsidized Squalor: Residents Live in Filth, Fear in Mismanaged Bay Area Public Housing." *Cir.org*. The Center for Investigative Reporting. 17 February 2014. <https://beta.cironline.org/reports/residents-live-in-filth-fear-in-mismanaged-bay-area-public-housing/>.

576 Harris, Amy Julia. "Subsidized Squalor: Residents Live in Filth, Fear in Mismanaged Bay Area Public Housing." *Cir.org*. The Center for Investigative Reporting. 17 February 2014. <https://beta.cironline.org/reports/residents-live-in-filth-fear-in-mismanaged-bay-area-public-housing/>. .

577 Harris, Amy Julia. "Frustrated Residents Sound off on Richmond Public Housing." *Cir.org*. The Center for Investigative Reporting. 5 March 2014. <https://beta.cironline.org/reports/frustrated-public-housing-residents-give-lawmakers-an-earful-at-meeting/>.

578 Harris, Amy Julia. "Frustrated Residents Sound off on Richmond Public Housing." *Cir.org*. The Center for Investigative Reporting. 5 March 2014. <https://beta.cironline.org/reports/frustrated-public-housing-residents-give-lawmakers-an-earful-at-meeting/>.

579 Harris, Amy Julia. "Frustrated Residents Sound off on Richmond Public Housing." *Cir.org*. The Center for Investigative Reporting. 5 March 2014. <https://beta.cironline.org/reports/frustrated-public-housing-residents-give-lawmakers-an-earful-at-meeting/>.

580 Harris, Amy Julia. "Subsidized Squalor: Residents Live in Filth, Fear in Mismanaged Bay Area Public Housing." *Cir.org*. The Center for Investigative Reporting. 17 February 2014. <https://beta.cironline.org/reports/residents-live-in-filth-fear-in-mismanaged-bay-area-public-housing/>.

581 Harris, Amy Julia. "Subsidized Squalor: Residents Live in Filth, Fear in Mismanaged Bay Area Public Housing." *Cir.org*. The Center for Investigative Reporting. 17 February 2014. <https://beta.cironline.org/reports/residents-live-in-filth-fear-in-mismanaged-bay-area-public-housing/>.

582 Coburn, Tom. "To End Payments to landlords Who Are Endangering the Lives of Children and Needy Families." S. Amdt. 792 to S.Amdt. 738 to H.R. 2112. <http://www.coburn.senate.gov/public/index.cfm?a=Files.Serve&File_id=6842dfb5-9d28-42b2-a822-a02a976319bd>.

583 U.S. Senate Roll Call Votes 112th Congress – 1st Session. Vote on Coburn Amendment No. 792, As Modified. 21 October 2011. <http://www.senate.gov/legislative/LIS/roll_call_lists/roll_call_vote_cfm.cfm?congress=112&session=1&vote=00184>.

584 Rogers, Robert. "Embattled Richmond Housing Authority Funded Extensive Training Trips for Volunteer Advisers." *Contracostatimes.com*. Contra Costa Times. 18 April 2014. <http://www.contracostatimes.com/west-county-times/ci_25593579/embattled-richmond-housing-authority-funded-extensive-training-trips>.

585 Rogers, Robert. "Embattled Richmond Housing Authority Funded Extensive Training Trips for Volunteer Advisers." *Contracostatimes.com*. Contra Costa Times. 18 April 2014. <http://www.contracostatimes.com/west-county-times/ci_25593579/embattled-richmond-housing-authority-funded-extensive-training-trips>.

586 Rogers, Robert. "Embattled Richmond Housing Authority Funded Extensive Training Trips for Volunteer Advisers." *Contracostatimes.com*. Contra Costa Times. 18 April 2014. <http://www.contracostatimes.com/west-county-times/ci_25593579/embattled-richmond-housing-authority-funded-extensive-training-trips>.

587 Harris, Amy Julia. "Subsidized Squalor: Residents Live in Filth, Fear in Mismanaged Bay Area Public Housing." *Cir.org*. The Center for Investigative Reporting. 17 February 2014. <https://beta.cironline.org/reports/residents-live-in-filth-fear-in-mismanaged-bay-area-public-housing/>.

588 Harris, Amy Julia. "Frustrated Residents Sound off on Richmond Public Housing." *Cir.org*. The Center for Investigative Reporting. 5 March 2014. <https://beta.cironline.org/reports/frustrated-public-housing-residents-give-lawmakers-an-earful-at-meeting/>.

589 Department of Homeland Security Office of Inspector General *DHS Does Not Adequately Manage or Have Enforcement Authority Over Its Components' Vehicle Operations*. Report No. OIG-14-126, Washington, D.C.: DHS-OIG, August 2014. Web. <http://www.oig.dhs.gov/assets/Mgmt/2014/OIG_14-126_Aug14.pdf>.

590 An "underused" vehicle is a vehicle that is driven less than 12,000 miles per annum.

591 Department of Homeland Security Office of Inspector General *DHS Does Not Adequately Manage or Have Enforcement Authority Over Its Components' Vehicle Operations*. Report No. OIG-14-126, Washington, D.C.: DHS-OIG, August 2014. Web. <http://www.oig.dhs.gov/assets/Mgmt/2014/OIG_14-126_Aug14.pdf>.

592 Department of Homeland Security Office of Inspector General *DHS Does Not Adequately Manage or Have Enforcement Authority Over Its Components' Vehicle Operations*. Report No. OIG-14-126, Washington, D.C.: DHS-OIG, August 2014. Web. <http://www.oig.dhs.gov/assets/Mgmt/2014/OIG_14-126_Aug14.pdf>.

593 **Foumberg, Jason.** "Iñigo Manglano-Ovalle." *Frieze.com*. Frieze Magazine. 17 November 2013. Web. <http://www.frieze.com/issue/print_back/inigo-manglano-ovalle/>.

594 Hirschkorn, Phil. "Bird Sculpture Fetches Record $27million." *Cnn.com*. CNN. 5 May 2005. Web. <http://www.cnn.com/2005/US/05/04/sculpture.record/>.

595 **Foumberg, Jason.** "Iñigo Manglano-Ovalle." *Frieze.com*. Frieze Magazine. 17 November 2013. Web. <http://www.frieze.com/issue/print_back/inigo-manglano-ovalle/>.

596 **Foumberg, Jason.** "Iñigo Manglano-Ovalle." *Frieze.com*. Frieze Magazine. 17 November 2013. Web. <http://www.frieze.com/issue/print_back/inigo-manglano-ovalle/>.

597 Lorenz, Phillip, III. "Art Meets Science in Unique Tunnel 9 Test of a Bird…In Flight." *Arnold.af.mil*. Arnold Air Force Base. 25 January 2013. <http://www.arnold.af.mil/news/story.asp?id=123333920>.

598 Lorenz, Phillip, III. "Art Meets Science in Unique Tunnel 9 Test of a Bird…In Flight." *Arnold.af.mil*. Arnold Air Force Base. 25 January 2013. <http://www.arnold.af.mil/news/story.asp?id=123333920>.

599 USA Spending. Prime Award Spending Data. PIID: GS11P12MKC0023 6 May 2014. Web. <http://www.usaspending.gov/explore?fiscal_year=all&comingfrom=searchresults&piid=GS11P12MKC0023&modification=PS04&typeofview=complete>.

600 Vergun, David, "'Iron-Man-style Suit in Early Stages of Development." *Army.mil*. Army News Service. 17 October 2013. Web. <http://www.army.mil/article/113332/>.

601 Nissenbaum, Dion, "U.S. Military Turns to Hollywood to Outfit the Soldier of the Future." *Wsj.com*. Dow Jones & Company. 4 July 2014. Web. <http://online.wsj.com/articles/u-s-military-turns-to-hollywood-to-outfit-the-soldier-of-the-future-1404527893>.

602 Nissenbaum, Dion, "U.S. Military Turns to Hollywood to Outfit the Soldier of the Future." *Wsj.com*. Dow Jones & Company. 4 July 2014. Web. <http://online.wsj.com/articles/u-s-military-turns-to-hollywood-to-outfit-the-soldier-of-the-future-1404527893>.

603 Nissenbaum, Dion, "U.S. Military Turns to Hollywood to Outfit the Soldier of the Future." *Wsj.com*. Dow Jones & Company. 4 July 2014. Web. <http://online.wsj.com/articles/u-s-military-turns-to-hollywood-to-outfit-the-soldier-of-the-future-1404527893>.

604 Cox, Matt. "Congress Wants More Control of Special Ops Iron Man Suit." *DefenseTech.org*. Military Advantage. 29 April 2014. Web. <http://defensetech.org/2014/04/29/congress-wants-more-control-of-special-ops-iron-man-suit/>.

605 Strauss, Mark. "The Military Has Hired Hollywood to Help Build an Actual Iron Man Suit." *Io9.com*. Kinja. 7 July 2014. <http://io9.com/the-military-has-hired-hollywood-to-help-build-an-actua-1601102216/>.

606 Cox, Matt. "Congress Wants More Control of Special Ops Iron Man Suit." *DefenseTech.org*. Military Advantage. 29 April 2014. Web. <http://defensetech.org/2014/04/29/congress-wants-more-control-of-special-ops-iron-man-suit/>.

607 Nissenbaum, Dion, "U.S. Military Turns to Hollywood to Outfit the Soldier of the Future." *Wsj.com*. Dow Jones & Company. 4 July 2014. Web. <http://online.wsj.com/articles/u-s-military-turns-to-hollywood-to-outfit-the-soldier-of-the-future-1404527893>.

608 Committee on Making the Soldier Decisive on Future Battlefields; Board on Army Science and Technology ; Division on Engineering and Physical Sciences; National Research Council. *Making the Soldier Decisive on Future Battlefields*. Washington: National Academies, 2013. Web. <http://www.nap.edu/catalog.php?record_

id=18321>. P4.

609 Nissenbaum, Dion, "U.S. Military Turns to Hollywood to Outfit the Soldier of the Future." *Wsj.com*. Dow Jones & Company. 4 July 2014. Web. <http://online.wsj.com/articles/u-s-military-turns-to-hollywood-to-outfit-the-soldier-of-the-future-1404527893>.

610 Nissenbaum, Dion, "U.S. Military Turns to Hollywood to Outfit the Soldier of the Future." *Wsj.com*. Dow Jones & Company. 4 July 2014. Web. <http://online.wsj.com/articles/u-s-military-turns-to-hollywood-to-outfit-the-soldier-of-the-future-1404527893>.

611 Nissenbaum, Dion, "U.S. Military Turns to Hollywood to Outfit the Soldier of the Future." *Wsj.com*. Dow Jones & Company. 4 July 2014. Web. <http://online.wsj.com/articles/u-s-military-turns-to-hollywood-to-outfit-the-soldier-of-the-future-1404527893>.

612 Nissenbaum, Dion, "U.S. Military Turns to Hollywood to Outfit the Soldier of the Future." *Wsj.com*. Dow Jones & Company. 4 July 2014. Web. <http://online.wsj.com/articles/u-s-military-turns-to-hollywood-to-outfit-the-soldier-of-the-future-1404527893>.

613 Nissenbaum, Dion, "U.S. Military Turns to Hollywood to Outfit the Soldier of the Future." *Wsj.com*. Dow Jones & Company. 4 July 2014. Web. <http://online.wsj.com/articles/u-s-military-turns-to-hollywood-to-outfit-the-soldier-of-the-future-1404527893>.

614 Drug Enforcement Agency. "The History Behind the DEA Museum." *Deamuseum.org*. DEA Visitors Center. Web. <http://www.deamuseum.org/museum_mhistory.html>.

615 Friedersdorf, Conor. "Your Tax Dollars at Work: The DEA Renovates Its Propaganda Museum." *Theatlantic.com*. The Atlantic Monthly Group. 30 May 2013. Web. http://www.theatlantic.com/politics/archive/2013/05/your-tax-dollars-at-work-the-dea-renovates-its-propaganda-museum/276376/>.

616 USASpending.gov, "Prime Award Spending Data: DEA Office of Congressional & Public Affairs." Web. <http://www.usaspending.gov/explore?fiscal_year=all&comingfrom=searchresults&piid=DJD14HQP0715&typeofview=complete>.

617 USASpending.gov, "Prime Award Spending Data: DEA Office of Congressional & Public Affairs." Web. <http://www.usaspending.gov/explore?fiscal_year=all&comingfrom=searchresults&piid=DJD14HQP0715&typeofview=complete>.

618 USASpending.gov, "Prime Award Spending Data: DEA Office of Congressional & Public Affairs." Web. <http://www.usaspending.gov/explore?fiscal_year=all&comingfrom=searchresults&piid=DJD14HQP0715&typeofview=complete>.

619 "DEA Museum to Get Major Makeover in 2013." The Informant 7 (fall 2014): 1. Deaeducationalfoundation.org. Drug Enforcement Agency. Web. <http://www.deaeducationalfoundation.org/wp-content/uploads/2010/06/Informant-Fall-2012-Vol7-No1.pdf>.

620 Daniel, Dale. "Spoils From Drug War On Display in Disputed DEA Museum." *Chron.com*. Houston Chronicle Washington Bureau. 17 June 2007. Web. <http://www.chron.com/news/nation-world/article/Spoils-from-drug-war-on-display-in-disputed-DEA-1609954.php>.

621 U.S. Department of Justice. Press Room. DEA OPENS MUSEUM TO THE PUBLIC WITH INAUGURAL EXHIBIT ON "ILLEGAL DRUGS IN AMERICA: A MODERN HISTORY" Justice.gov. N.p., 30 Apr. 1999. Web. 18 Oct. 2014. <http://www.justice.gov/dea/pubs/pressrel/pr043099.htm>.

622 Drug Enforcement Agency. "Group Tours." *Deamuseum.org*. DEA Visitors Center. Web. <http://www.deamuseum.org/museum_gptours.html>.

623 Washington Post. "Going Out Guide – Museums." *Washingtonpost.com*. Reuters. Web. <http://www.washingtonpost.com/gog/museums/dea-museum,800290.html>.

624 Drug Enforcement Agency. "Education." *Deamuseum.org*. DEA Visitors Center. Web. <http://www.deamuseum.org/education/kids/>.

625 Website of DEA Educational Foundation Gift Shop (Archive). "Scout, DEA PLUSH GERMAN SHEPHERD, <http://www.apifederal.com/dea/default.aspx?p=viewitem&item=D2171&subno=&showpage=13&subcat>.

626 Daniel, Dale. "Spoils From Drug War On Display in Disputed DEA Museum." *Chron.com*. Houston Chronicle Washington Bureau. 17 June 2007. Web. <http://www.chron.com/news/nation-world/article/Spoils-from-drug-war-on-display-in-disputed-DEA-1609954.php>.

627 Drug Enforcement Agency. "The Informant." *Deaeducationalfoundation.org*. DEA Educational Foundation. Web. <http://www.deaeducationalfoundation.org/wp-content/uploads/2010/06/Informant-Fall-2012-Vol7-No1.pdf>.

628 Government Accountability Office, *Missile Defense: Opportunity to Refocus on Strengthening Acquisition Management, GAO-13-432, April 2013, http://www.gao.gov/assets/660/654233.pdf*.

629 "Missile Defense Agency." The Ballistic Missile Defense System. Department of Defense, 12 Dec. 2013. Web. 8 Oct. 2014. <http://www.mda.mil/system/system.html>.

630 "Ground-based Midcourse Defense." The Missile Defense Agency. Department of Defense, 4 June 2014. Web. <http://www.mda.mil/global/documents/pdf/gmdfacts.pdf>.

631 38 WCPD 2172 "Statement Announcing a Missile Defense Initiative." (December 17, 2002). Web. <http://www.gpo.gov/fdsys/pkg/PPP-2002-book2/pdf/PPP-2002-book2-doc-pg2198.pdf>.

632 Sullivan, Michael J. *Defense Acquisitions: Assessments of Selected Weapons*. Rep. no. GAO-12-400SP. Report to Congressional Committees. Washington, D.C.: Government Accountability Office, March 2012. Web. <http://www.gao.gov/products/GAO-12-400SP>.

633 Reif, Kingston. "Lather, Rinse, Repeat."*Nukes of Hazard Blog RSS*. 14 Jan. 2013. Web. 8 Oct. 2014. <http://www.nukesofhazardblog.com/story/2013/1/14/235731/021>.

634 Cirincione, Joe. "Alaskan Folly." *Foreign Policy*. The FP Group, 18 Mar. 2013. Web. 8 Oct. 2014. <http://www.foreignpolicy.com/articles/2013/03/18/alaskan_folly>.

635 Gilmore, J. Michael. Oral Statement Before the House Armed Services Committee, Subcommittee on Strategic Forces. 6 March 2012. Web. <http://www.gpo.gov/fdsys/pkg/CHRG-112hhrg73437/html/CHRG-112hhrg73437.htm>.

636 Government Accountability Office, *Defense Acquisitions: Assessments of Selected Weapons*. Rep. no. GAO-12-400SP. Report to Congressional Committees. Washington, D.C.: Government Accountability Office, March 2012. Web. <http://www.gao.gov/products/GAO-12-400SP>.

637 Government Accountability Office, *Missile Defense: Mixed Progress in Achieving Acquisition Goals and Improving Accountability*. Rep. no. GAO-14-351. Report to Congressional Committee. Washington, D.C.: Government Accountability Office. April 2014. Web. < http://www.gao.gov/products/GAO-14-351>.

638 Missile Defense Agency. News & Resources. *Target Missile Intercepted Over the Pacific Ocean During Missile Defense Exercise*. Mda.mil. U.S. Department of Defense, 22 June 2014. Web. 18 Oct. 2014. <http://www.mda.mil/news/14news0005.html>.

639 Chaplain, Cristina. *Missile Defense: DOD's Report Provides Limited Insight on Testing Options for the Ground-based Midcourse Defense System*. Letter to Congressional Committees. 30 April 2014. Web. <http://www.gao.gov/assets/670/662856.pdf>.

640 Department of Defense Office of Inspector General. *Exoatmospheric Kill Vehicle Quality Assurance and Reliability Assessment – Part A*. Report to Director, Missile Defense Agency. Washington, D.C.: DOD-OIG, 8 September 2014. Web. <http://www.dodig.mil/pubs/documents/DODIG-2014-111.pdf>.

641 National Resource Council. Making sense of ballistic missile defense: an assessment of concepts and systems for U.S. boost-phase missile defense in comparison to other alternatives. Washington, D.C.: National Academies Press, 2012.

642 Chaplain, Cristina. *Missile Defense: DOD's Report Provides Limited Insight on Testing Options for the Ground-based Midcourse Defense System*. Letter to

Congressional Committees. 30 April 2014. Web. 8 Oct. 2014. <http://www.gao.gov/assets/670/662856.pdf>.

643 National Resource Council. Making sense of ballistic missile defense: an assessment of concepts and systems for U.S. boost-phase missile defense in comparison to other alternatives. Washington, D.C.: National Academies Press, 2012.

644 Chaplain, Cristina. *Missile Defense: DOD's Report Provides Limited Insight on Testing Options for the Ground-based Midcourse Defense System.* Letter to Congressional Committees. 30 April 2014. Web. 8 Oct. 2014. <http://www.gao.gov/assets/670/662856.pdf>.

645 National Resource Council. Making sense of ballistic missile defense: an assessment of concepts and systems for U.S. boost-phase missile defense in comparison to other alternatives. Washington, D.C.: National Academies Press, 2012.

646 Lohr, Lynda. "Stimulus Money to Buy Two New Ferry Boats." *Stthomassource.com.* V.I. Source Publications, Inc. 16 July 2009. Web. http://stthomassource.com/content/news/local-news/2009/07/16/stimulus-money-buy-two-new-ferry-boats/>.

647 Lewin, Aldeth. "V.I.'S 2 New Ferries Finally in Service." *virginislandsdailynews.com.* Virgin Islands Daily News. 8 July 2014. Web. <http://virginislandsdailynews.com/news/v-i-s-2-new-ferries-finally-in-service-1.1715552>.

648 Blackburn, Joy, "Federal Grant To Help V.I. Acquire Two New Passenger Ferries." *virginislandsdailynews.com.* Virgin Islands Daily News. 18 August 2010. Web. <http://virginislandsdailynews.com/news/federal-grant-to-help-v-i-acquire-two-new-passenger-ferries-1.956418>.

649 Lewin, Aldeth. "V.I.'S 2 New Ferries Finally in Service." *virginislandsdailynews.com.* Virgin Islands Daily News. 8 July 2014. Web. <http://virginislandsdailynews.com/news/v-i-s-2-new-ferries-finally-in-service-1.1715552>.

650 Broom, Jack and Lindsay Toler. "Feds Snub State's Ferry Fleet." *Seattletimes.com.* The Seattle Times Company. 15 July 2009. http://seattletimes.com/html/politics/2009471834_ferrystimulus15m.htm>l.

651 Lewin, Aldeth. "V.I.'S 2 New Ferries Finally in Service." *virginislandsdailynews.com.* Virgin Islands Daily News. 8 July 2014. Web. <http://virginislandsdailynews.com/news/v-i-s-2-new-ferries-finally-in-service-1.1715552>.

652 Lewin, Aldeth, "New Ferries Are One Inspection Away from Starting Service." *virginislandsdailynews.com.* Virgin Islands Daily News. 8 March 2014. Web. <http://virginislandsdailynews.com/news/new-ferries-are-one-inspection-away-from-starting-service-1.1647074>.

653 Lewin, Aldeth, "New Ferries Are One Inspection Away from Starting Service." *virginislandsdailynews.com.* Virgin Islands Daily News. 8 March 2014. Web. <http://virginislandsdailynews.com/news/new-ferries-are-one-inspection-away-from-starting-service-1.1647074>.

654 Lewin, Aldeth. "V.I.'S 2 New Ferries Finally in Service." *virginislandsdailynews.com.* Virgin Islands Daily News. 8 July 2014. Web. <http://virginislandsdailynews.com/news/v-i-s-2-new-ferries-finally-in-service-1.1715552>.

655 Lewin, Aldeth, "New Ferries Out of Service for the Last Month," ." *virginislandsdailynews.com.* Virgin Islands Daily News. 4 September 2014. <http://virginislandsdailynews.com/news/new-ferries-out-of-service-for-the-last-month-1.1746775>.

656 Lewin, Aldeth, "New Ferries Out of Service for the Last Month," ." *virginislandsdailynews.com.* Virgin Islands Daily News. 4 September 2014. <http://virginislandsdailynews.com/news/new-ferries-out-of-service-for-the-last-month-1.1746775>.

657 Lewin, Aldeth, "New Ferries Out of Service for the Last Month," ." *virginislandsdailynews.com.* Virgin Islands Daily News. 4 September 2014. <http://virginislandsdailynews.com/news/new-ferries-out-of-service-for-the-last-month-1.1746775>.

658 Bell, Kay. "Pocketing Tax-Free Rental Income," *Bankrate.com.* Bankrate, Inc. 11 June 2013. Web. <http://www.bankrate.com/financing/taxes/pocketing-tax-free-rental-income/>.

659 Joint Committee on Taxation. *Options to Improve Tax Compliance and Reform Tax Expenditures." Staff Report.* Report No. JCS-02-05, Washington, D.C.: JCT Committee Staff. 27 January 2005. Web. <http://www.jct.gov/s-2-05.pdf>.

660 Craig, Giammona. "Super Bowl Homes Command $1,600 a Night as Listings Jump." *Bloomberg.com.* Bloomberg L.P. 24 January 2014. Web. <http://www.bloomberg.com/news/2014-01-24/super-bowl-homes-command-1-600-a-night-as-listings-jump.html>.

661 Air BNB home rental advertisement, https://www.airbnb.com/rooms/2241014?checkin=02%2F01%2F2014&checkout=02%2F02%2F2014&s=m56g.

662 Craig, Giammona. "Super Bowl Homes Command $1,600 a Night as Listings Jump." *Bloomberg.com.* Bloomberg L.P. 24 January 2014. Web. <http://www.bloomberg.com/news/2014-01-24/super-bowl-homes-command-1-600-a-night-as-listings-jump.html>.

663 Maresca, Rachel. "Kevin Jonas, Pregnant Wife List New Jersey Home to Rent for Week of Super Bowl at $20,000 a Night." *Nydailynews.com.* New York Daily News. 29 January 2014. Web. <http://www.nydailynews.com/life-style/real-estate/kevin-jonas-lists-home-rent-super-bowl-week-20-000-night-article-1.1595310>.

664 Maresca, Rachel. "Kevin Jonas, Pregnant Wife List New Jersey Home to Rent for Week of Super Bowl at $20,000 a Night." *Nydailynews.com.* New York Daily News. 29 January 2014. Web. <http://www.nydailynews.com/life-style/real-estate/kevin-jonas-lists-home-rent-super-bowl-week-20-000-night-article-1.1595310>.

665 Warner, Brian. "Kevin Jonas Net Worth." *Celebritynetworth.com.* Celebrity Networth. Web. <http://www.celebritynetworth.com/richest-celebrities/singers/kevin-jonas-net-worth/>.

666 Notte, Jason. "Super Bowl Home Rental Is a Tempting Gamble," *TheStreet.com.* The Street, Inc. 8 January 2014. <http://www.thestreet.com/story/12203549/1/super-bowl-home-rental-is-a-tempting-gamble.html>.

667 Notte, Jason. "Super Bowl Home Rental Is a Tempting Gamble," *TheStreet.com.* The Street, Inc. 8 January 2014. <http://www.thestreet.com/story/12203549/1/super-bowl-home-rental-is-a-tempting-gamble.html>.

668 Over the Cap. "Cooper Taylor." *Overthecap.com.* Over the Cap. Web. http://overthecap.com/cap.php?Name=Cooper%20Taylor&Position=S&Team=Giants>.

669 "Super Bowl Vacation Dream Home." *HomeAway.com.* HomeAway.com, Inc.Web. Accessed 30 January 2014. Web. <http://www.homeaway.com/vacation-rental/p508134vb#calendar>.

670 Bell, Kay. "Pocketing Tax-Free Rental Income," *Bankrate.com.* Bankrate, Inc. 11 June 2013. Web. <http://www.bankrate.com/financing/taxes/pocketing-tax-free-rental-income/>.

671 Information provided by Department of State.

672 U.S. Department of State. (ThinkAgain_DOS) Web. https://twitter.com/ThinkAgain_DOS>.

673 Information provided by Department of State.

674 Information provided by Department of State.

675 Information provided by Department of State.

676 Cushing, Tim. "State Dept. Now Trolling Twitter Terrorists." *TechDirt .* Floor64. 26 March 2014. Web. <https://www.techdirt.com/articles/20140322/10393226658/state-dept-now-trolling-twitter-terrorists.shtml>.

677 Katz, Rita. "The State Department's Twitter War with ISIS Is Embarrassing." *Time.com.* Time Inc.16 Sept. 2014. Web. <http://time.com/3387065/isis-twitter-war-state-department/>.

678 Katz, Rita. "The State Department's Twitter War with ISIS Is Embarrassing." *Time.com.* Time Inc.16 Sept. 2014. Web. <http://time.com/3387065/isis-twitter-war-

state-department/>.

679 Katz, Rita. "The State Department's Twitter War with ISIS Is Embarrassing." *Time.com*. Time Inc.16 Sept. 2014. Web. <http://time.com/3387065/isis-twitter-war-state-department/>.

680 Schake, Kori. "@ISIS Is #Winning: Why is a Barbaric Medieval Caliphate So Much Better At Social Media Than Washington?" *ForeignPolicy.com*. Foreign Policy Group. 9 July 2014. Web. <http://www.foreignpolicy.com/articles/2014/07/09/isis_is_winning_social_media_hashtag_diplomacy?utm_source=Sailthru&utm_medium=email&utm_term=*Situation%20Report&utm_campaign=SITREP%20JULY%2010%202014>.

681 Hicks, Josh, "U.S. Border Agency 'Vastly Overpaid' To Build Homes for Agents, Audit Says." *Washingtonpost.com*. The Washington Post. 12 September 2014. Web. <http://www.washingtonpost.com/blogs/federal-eye/wp/2014/09/12/u-s-border-agency-vastly-overpaid-to-build-homes-for-agents-audit-says/>.

682 U.S. Department of Homeland Security, Office of Inspector General. *CBP Did Not Effectively Plan and Manage Employee Housing in Ajo, Arizona*. Report No. OIG-14-131. Washington, D.C.: DHS OIG, 16 September 2014. Web. <http://www.oig.dhs.gov/assets/Mgmt/2014/OIG_SLP_14-131_Sep14.pdf>.

683 Hicks, Josh, "U.S. Border Agency 'Vastly Overpaid' To Build Homes for Agents, Audit Says." *Washingtonpost.com*. The Washington Post. 12 September 2014. Web. <http://www.washingtonpost.com/blogs/federal-eye/wp/2014/09/12/u-s-border-agency-vastly-overpaid-to-build-homes-for-agents-audit-says/>.

684 U.S. Department of Homeland Security, Office of Inspector General. *CBP Did Not Effectively Plan and Manage Employee Housing in Ajo, Arizona*. Report No. OIG-14-131. Washington, D.C.: DHS OIG, 16 September 2014. Web. <http://www.oig.dhs.gov/assets/Mgmt/2014/OIG_SLP_14-131_Sep14.pdf>.

685 U.S. Department of Homeland Security, Office of Inspector General. *CBP Did Not Effectively Plan and Manage Employee Housing in Ajo, Arizona*. Report No. OIG-14-131. Washington, D.C.: DHS OIG, 16 September 2014. Web. <http://www.oig.dhs.gov/assets/Mgmt/2014/OIG_SLP_14-131_Sep14.pdf>.

686 U.S. Department of Homeland Security, Office of Inspector General. *CBP Did Not Effectively Plan and Manage Employee Housing in Ajo, Arizona*. Report No. OIG-14-131. Washington, D.C.: DHS OIG, 16 September 2014. Web. <http://www.oig.dhs.gov/assets/Mgmt/2014/OIG_SLP_14-131_Sep14.pdf>.

687 U.S. Department of Homeland Security, Office of Inspector General. *CBP Did Not Effectively Plan and Manage Employee Housing in Ajo, Arizona*. Report No. OIG-14-131. Washington, D.C.: DHS OIG, 16 September 2014. Web. <http://www.oig.dhs.gov/assets/Mgmt/2014/OIG_SLP_14-131_Sep14.pdf>.

688 Goth, Brenna. "Feds Pay Millions for Border-Agent Housing in Ajo," azcentral.com. The Arizona Republic. 11 August 2013. Web. <http://www.azcentral.com/news/arizona/articles/20130811ajo-border-agent-housing.html>.

689 U.S. Department of Homeland Security, Office of Inspector General. *CBP Did Not Effectively Plan and Manage Employee Housing in Ajo, Arizona*. Report No. OIG-14-131. Washington, D.C.: DHS OIG, 16 September 2014. Web. <http://www.oig.dhs.gov/assets/Mgmt/2014/OIG_SLP_14-131_Sep14.pdf>.

690 U.S. Department of Homeland Security, Office of Inspector General. *CBP Did Not Effectively Plan and Manage Employee Housing in Ajo, Arizona*. Report No. OIG-14-131. Washington, D.C.: DHS OIG, 16 September 2014. Web. <http://www.oig.dhs.gov/assets/Mgmt/2014/OIG_SLP_14-131_Sep14.pdf>.

691 U.S. Department of Homeland Security, Office of Inspector General. *CBP Did Not Effectively Plan and Manage Employee Housing in Ajo, Arizona*. Report No. OIG-14-131. Washington, D.C.: DHS OIG, 16 September 2014. Web. <http://www.oig.dhs.gov/assets/Mgmt/2014/OIG_SLP_14-131_Sep14.pdf>.

692 U.S. Department of Homeland Security, Office of Inspector General. *CBP Did Not Effectively Plan and Manage Employee Housing in Ajo, Arizona*. Report No. OIG-14-131. Washington, D.C.: DHS OIG, 16 September 2014. Web. <http://www.oig.dhs.gov/assets/Mgmt/2014/OIG_SLP_14-131_Sep14.pdf>.

693 Garris, Blake. "Level Up With Marvel's Avengers S.T.A.T.I.O.N. Tickets."*marvel.com*. Marvel. 1 May 2014. Web. <http://marvel.com/news/live_events/2014/5/1/22437/level_up_with_marvels_avengers_station_tickets>.

694 Sacks, Ethan. "EXCLUSIVE: Avengers S.T.A.T.I.O.N exhibit fan-tastic Blend of Props, High-Tech." *nydailynews.com*. New York Daily News. 25 May 2014. <http://www.nydailynews.com/entertainment/movies/exclusive-avengers-s-t-t-o-n-exhibit-fan-tastic-article-1.1804244 >.

695 Sacks, Ethan. "EXCLUSIVE: Avengers S.T.A.T.I.O.N exhibit fan-tastic Blend of Props, High-Tech." *nydailynews.com*. New York Daily News. 25 May 2014. <http://www.nydailynews.com/entertainment/movies/exclusive-avengers-s-t-t-o-n-exhibit-fan-tastic-article-1.1804244 >.

696 Garris, Blake. "Level Up With Marvel's Avengers S.T.A.T.I.O.N. Tickets."*marvel.com*. Marvel. 1 May 2014. Web. <http://marvel.com/news/live_events/2014/5/1/22437/level_up_with_marvels_avengers_station_tickets>.

697 NASA Jet Propulsion Laboratory. News. *NASA Helps Marvel's Avengers Exhibit Bring the Science Artist's Design Concept for an Interactive Featuring NASA's Eyes on Exoplanets John Grunsfeld, NASA's Associate Administrator for the Science Mission Directorate*. Jpl.nasa.gov. NASA, 3 June 2014. Web. 18 Oct. 2014. <http://www.jpl.nasa.gov/news/news.php?release=2014-172>.

698 NASA Jet Propulsion Laboratory. News. *NASA Helps Marvel's Avengers Exhibit Bring the Science Artist's Design Concept for an Interactive Featuring NASA's Eyes on Exoplanets John Grunsfeld, NASA's Associate Administrator for the Science Mission Directorate*. Jpl.nasa.gov. NASA, 3 June 2014. Web. 18 Oct. 2014. <http://www.jpl.nasa.gov/news/news.php?release=2014-172>.

699 Howell, Elizabeth. "Avengers Assemble! NASA Brings Real Space to NYC Marvel Exhibit." *Space.com*. Purch. 6 June 2014. Web. <http://www.space.com/26152-avengers-shield-nasa-marvel.html>.

700 Corliss, Richard. "2012 Turnaround: The Avengers Brings People Back to the Movies." *Time.com*. Time Inc. 3 January 2013. Web. <http://entertainment.time.com/2013/01/03/2012-turnaround-the-avengers-brings-people-back-to-the-movies/>.

701 Howell, Elizabeth. "Avengers Assemble! NASA Brings Real Space to NYC Marvel Exhibit." *Space.com*. Purch. 6 June 2014. Web. <http://www.space.com/26152-avengers-shield-nasa-marvel.html>.

702 King, Ledyard. "Budget Deal Would Preserve NASA's Big Missions." *Usatoday.com*. Gannett. 14 January 2014. Web. <http://www.usatoday.com/story/news/nation/2014/01/14/spending-bill-would-preserve-major-nasa-missions/4480537/>.

703 Quinn, Kevin. "Federal Budget Cuts Threaten NASA's Space Travel Plans." *Abc13.com*. ABC 13 KTRK-TV Houston. 16 May 2013. Web. <http://abc13.com/archive/9105418/>.

704 "MISSION STATEMENT," comic-con.org. San Diego Comic Convention. Web. Accessed 18 October 2014. Web. <http://www.comic-con.org/>.

705 NASA. Press Department. *NASA Updates Apollo Anniversary, Next Giant Leap Events*. Nasa.gov. NASA, 18 July 2014. Web. 18 Oct. 2014. <http://www.nasa.gov/press/2014/july/nasa-updates-apollo-anniversary-next-giant-leap-events/#.VEMFrPldV8E>.

706 NASA. Press Department. *NASA Updates Apollo Anniversary, Next Giant Leap Events*. Nasa.gov. NASA, 18 July 2014. Web. 18 Oct. 2014. <http://www.nasa.gov/press/2014/july/nasa-updates-apollo-anniversary-next-giant-leap-events/#.VEMFrPldV8E>.

707 Jennewein, Chris. "NASA Landing at Comic-Con with Panel on Mars Plans." *Timesofsandiego.com*. Times of San Diego LLC. 14 July 2014. Web.<http://timesofsandiego.com/tech/2014/07/14/nasa-landing-comic-con-panel-mars-plans/>.

708 McKinnon, Mika. "NASA Advocates for Mars Mission to a Packed Room at Comic-Con," *io9.com*. Kinja. 25 July 2014. Web. <http://space.io9.com/nasa-advocates-for-mars-mission-to-a-overfilled-room-at-1611104964>.

709 NASA e-mail to the Congressional Research Service regarding attendance at Comic Con International: San Diego, September 2014.

710 NASA e-mail to the Congressional Research Service regarding attendance at Comic Con International: San Diego, September 2014.

711 MIT. Office of Sponsored Programs, News & Events. *NASA Conference Travel Restrictions Continue*. Http://osp.mit.edu/about-osp/news/nasa-conference-

travel-restrictions-continue. Massachusetts Institute of Technology, 5 Feb. 2014. Web. 18 Oct. 2014. <http://osp.mit.edu/about-osp/news/nasa-conference-travel-restrictions-continue>.

712 Hill, Kyle. "Seth Green And Buzz Aldrin Make NASA'S Presence Known At Comic-Con." *Nerdist.com*. Nerdist, 25 July 2014. Web. http://www.nerdist.com/2014/07/seth-green-and-buzz-aldrin-make-nasas-presence-known-at-comic-con/>.

713 NASA website, accessed 2 October 2014; <http://www.nasa.gov/sites/default/files/marvel20140603b.jpg>.

714 Special Inspector General for Afghanistan Reconstruction. *Management Safety Alert Letter (K-Span ANA Facilities)*. Report No.: SIGAR SP13-3. Arlington, VA: SIGAR. 4 April 2013. Web. <http://www.sigar.mil/pdf/alerts/SIGAR%20SP%20Alert%20Letter%2013-3%20April%204%202013.pdf>. P1.

715 Special Inspector General for Afghanistan Reconstruction. *Management Safety Alert Letter (K-Span ANA Facilities)*. Report No.: SIGAR SP13-3. Arlington, VA: SIGAR. 4 April 2013. Web. <http://www.sigar.mil/pdf/alerts/SIGAR%20SP%20Alert%20Letter%2013-3%20April%204%202013.pdf>. P1.

716 Special Inspector General for Afghanistan Reconstruction. *Management Safety Alert Letter (K-Span ANA Facilities)*. Report No.: SIGAR SP13-3. Arlington, VA: SIGAR. 4 April 2013. Web. <http://www.sigar.mil/pdf/alerts/SIGAR%20SP%20Alert%20Letter%2013-3%20April%204%202013.pdf>. P2.

717 Special Inspector General for Afghanistan Reconstruction. *Management Safety Alert Letter (K-Span ANA Facilities)*. Report No.: SIGAR SP13-3. Arlington, VA: SIGAR. 4 April 2013. Web. <http://www.sigar.mil/pdf/alerts/SIGAR%20SP%20Alert%20Letter%2013-3%20April%204%202013.pdf>. P3.

718 Special Inspector General for Afghanistan Reconstruction. *Management Safety Alert Letter (K-Span ANA Facilities)*. Report No.: SIGAR SP13-3. Arlington, VA: SIGAR. 4 April 2013. Web. <http://www.sigar.mil/pdf/alerts/SIGAR%20SP%20Alert%20Letter%2013-3%20April%204%202013.pdf>.

719 Special Inspector General for Afghanistan Reconstruction. *Review: Safety of Spray Foam Insulation in ANA Facilities*. Report No.: SIGAR-14-77 SP. Arlington, VA: SIGAR. 9 July 2014. <http://www.sigar.mil/pdf/Special%20Projects/SIGAR-14-77-SP.pdf>.

720 Special Inspector General for Afghanistan Reconstruction, *Review: Safety of Spray Foam Insulation in ANA Facilities*, SIGAR-14-77 SP. Arlington, VA: SIGAR. 9 July 2014. Web. <http://www.sigar.mil/pdf/Special%20Projects/SIGAR-14-77-SP.pdf>. p6.

721 Special Inspector General for Afghanistan Reconstruction, *Review: Safety of Spray Foam Insulation in ANA Facilities*, SIGAR-14-77 SP. Arlington, VA: SIGAR. 9 July 2014. Web. <http://www.sigar.mil/pdf/Special%20Projects/SIGAR-14-77-SP.pdf>. p4.

722 Kredo, Adam. "SIGAR: Afghan Children Risk Electrocution Due to Faulty Construction." *Freebecon.com*. The Washington Free Beacon. 17 July 2013. Web. <http://freebeacon.com/issues/sigar-faulty-school-construction-in-afghanistan-putting-children-at-risk/>.

723 Kredo, Adam. "SIGAR: Afghan Children Risk Electrocution Due to Faulty Construction." *Freebecon.com*. The Washington Free Beacon. 17 July 2013. Web. <http://freebeacon.com/issues/sigar-faulty-school-construction-in-afghanistan-putting-children-at-risk/>.

724 Federal Aviation Administration. *Final Environmental Assessment Runway Safety Area Improvements: Sioux Falls Regional Airport*. Sioux Falls Airport Authority. Web. 22 July 2013. <http://www.sfairport.com/media/documents/sioux_falls_finalea_june_2013fonsirod.pdf >.

725 Federal Aviation Administration. Final Environmental Assessment Runway Safety Area Improvements: Sioux Falls Regional Airport. Sioux Falls Airport Authority. Web. 22 July 2013. <http://www.sfairport.com/media/documents/sioux_falls_finalea_june_2013fonsirod.pdf >.

726 Federal Aviation Administration. *Final Environmental Assessment Runway Safety Area Improvements: Sioux Falls Regional Airport*. Sioux Falls Airport Authority. Web. 22 July 2013. <http://www.sfairport.com/media/documents/sioux_falls_finalea_june_2013fonsirod.pdf >.

727 Federal Aviation Administration. *Final Environmental Assessment Runway Safety Area Improvements: Sioux Falls Regional Airport*. Sioux Falls Airport Authority. Web. 22 July 2013. <http://www.sfairport.com/media/documents/sioux_falls_finalea_june_2013fonsirod.pdf >.

728 Federal Aviation Administration. *Final Environmental Assessment Runway Safety Area Improvements: Sioux Falls Regional Airport*. Sioux Falls Airport Authority. Web. 22 July 2013. <http://www.sfairport.com/media/documents/sioux_falls_finalea_june_2013fonsirod.pdf >.

729 Federal Aviation Administration. *Final Environmental Assessment Runway Safety Area Improvements: Sioux Falls Regional Airport*. Sioux Falls Airport Authority. Web. 22 July 2013. <http://www.sfairport.com/media/documents/sioux_falls_finalea_june_2013fonsirod.pdf >..

730 Federal Aviation Administration. *Final Environmental Assessment Runway Safety Area Improvements: Sioux Falls Regional Airport*. Sioux Falls Airport Authority. Web. 22 July 2013. <http://www.sfairport.com/media/documents/sioux_falls_finalea_june_2013fonsirod.pdf >.

731 Federal Aviation Administration. *Final Environmental Assessment Runway Safety Area Improvements: Sioux Falls Regional Airport*. Sioux Falls Airport Authority. Web. 22 July 2013. <http://www.sfairport.com/media/documents/sioux_falls_finalea_june_2013fonsirod.pdf >.

732 Federal Aviation Administration. *Final Environmental Assessment Runway Safety Area Improvements: Sioux Falls Regional Airport*. Sioux Falls Airport Authority. Web. 22 July 2013. <http://www.sfairport.com/media/documents/sioux_falls_finalea_june_2013fonsirod.pdf >.

733 Keloland TV. "Updates Underway at Elmwood Golf Course." *Keloland.com*. Keloland TV. 9 September 2013. Web. <http://www.keloland.com/newsdetail.cfm/updates-underway-at-elmwood-golf-course/?id=152987>.

734 "Dakota Golf – Elmwood, Prairie Green and Kuehn Park Golf Course." FACEBOOK. Web. <https://www.facebook.com/dakotagolf/photos_stream?ref=page_internal>.

735 Jorgensen, Dan. "Elmwood East 9: Not Up To Par." *Keloland.com*. Keloland TV. 28 August 2013. Web. <http://www.keloland.com/newsdetail.cfm/elmwood-east-9-not-up-to-par/?id=152538>.

736 Kelley, Matt. "How Alaska Ferry Project Floated; Sen Stevens Pushed Pricey Military Test." *Usatoday.com*. Gannett. 28 September 2007. Web. <http://usatoday30.usatoday.com/printedition/news/20070928/a_ferry28.art.htm>. A 10.

737 Hollander, Zaz. "Mat-Su Borough Determined to do Something with Ferry." *And.com*. Alaska Dispatch Publishing. 12 August 2013. Web. <http://www.adn.com/article/20130812/mat-su-borough-determined-do-something-ferry>.

738 Caldwell, Suzanne. "Mat-Su Borough Offers Star Crossed M/V Susitna Ferry for Free." *adn.com*. Alaska Dispatch Publishing. 30 January 2014. Web. http://www.adn.com/article/mat-su-borough-offers-star-crossed-mv-susitna-ferry-free>.

739 Hollander, Zaz. "Mat-Su Borough Determined to do Something with Ferry." *And.com*. Alaska Dispatch Publishing. 12 August 2013. Web. <http://www.adn.com/article/20130812/mat-su-borough-determined-do-something-ferry>.

740 Hollander, Zaz. "Mat-Su Borough Determined to do Something with Ferry." *And.com*. Alaska Dispatch Publishing. 12 August 2013. Web. <http://www.adn.com/article/20130812/mat-su-borough-determined-do-something-ferry>.

741 Brehmer, Elwood. "Feds Ask Mat-Su for Ferry Grants Back." *Alaskajournal.com*. Alaska Journal of Commerce. 7 August 2014. Web. <http://www.alaskajournal.com/Alaska-Journal-of-Commerce/Breaking-News-2013/Feds-ask-Mat-Su-for-ferry-grants-back/>.

742 Brehmer, Elwood. "Feds Ask Mat-Su for Ferry Grants Back." *Alaskajournal.com*. Alaska Journal of Commerce. 7 August 2014. Web. <http://www.alaskajournal.com/Alaska-Journal-of-Commerce/Breaking-News-2013/Feds-ask-Mat-Su-for-ferry-grants-back/>.

743 Caldwell, Suzanne. "Mat-Su Borough Offers Star Crossed M/V Susitna Ferry for Free." *adn.com*. Alaska Dispatch Publishing. 30 January 2014. Web. http://www.adn.com/article/mat-su-borough-offers-star-crossed-mv-susitna-ferry-free>.

744 Zaz Hollander, "Prospective Buyers Tour Mat-Su Ferry as Federal Grant Deadline Moves Back," Alaska Dispatch News, September 2, 2014, http://www.adn.com/

article/20140903/prospective-buyers-tour-mat-su-ferry-federal-grant-deadline-moves-back

745 Matt Kelley, "How Alaska Ferry Project Floated; Sen Stevens Pushed Pricey Military Test," USA Today, September 28, 2007, A 10.

746 Hollander, Zaz. "Mat-Su Borough Determined to do Something with Ferry." *And.com*. Alaska Dispatch Publishing. 12 August 2013. Web. <http://www.adn.com/article/20130812/mat-su-borough-determined-do-something-ferry>.

747 Kelley, Matt. "How Alaska Ferry Project Floated; Sen Stevens Pushed Pricey Military Test." *Usatoday.com*. Gannett. 28 September 2007. Web. <http://usatoday30.usatoday.com/printedition/news/20070928/a_ferry28.art.htm>. A 10.

748 Caldwell, Suzanne. "Mat-Su Borough Offers Star Crossed M/V Susitna Ferry for Free." *adn.com*. Alaska Dispatch Publishing. 30 January 2014. Web. http://www.adn.com/article/mat-su-borough-offers-star-crossed-mv-susitna-ferry-free>.

749 Tobin, Dave. "Where Did the $3 Million of Federal Money Invested in Syracuse Suburban Airport, in Oswego County, Go?" *Syracuse.com*. Syracuse Media Group. 29 March 2011. Web. <http://www.syracuse.com/news/index.ssf/2011/03/where_did_the_3_million_of_fed.html>.

750 Federal Bureau of Investigation, Albany Division. Newsroom. *Jamesville Man Enters Guilty Plea to Conspiracy to Commit Bank Fraud. Fbi.gov*. U.S. Attorney's Office, Northern District of New York, 24 July 2014. Web. 18 Oct. 2014. <http://www.fbi.gov/albany/press-releases/2014/jamesville-man-enters-guilty-plea-to-conspiracy-to-commit-bank-fraud>.

751 Letter from Senator Tom Coburn to the Federal Aviation Administration Commissioner, J. Randolph Babbit, April 5, 2011.

752 Letter from Senator Tom Coburn to the Federal Aviation Administration Commissioner, J. Randolph Babbit, April 5, 2011.

753 Kenyon, Jim. "For Sale: Failed Airport in Oswego Count.," *CNYCentral.com*. Sinclair Communications, LLC. 12 September 2014. Web. <http://www.cnycentral.com/news/story.aspx?id=1095978#.VBijdqPD-id>.

754 Federal Bureau of Investigation, Albany Division. Newsroom. *Jamesville Man Enters Guilty Plea to Conspiracy to Commit Bank Fraud. Fbi.gov*. U.S. Attorney's Office, Northern District of New York, 24 July 2014. Web. 18 Oct. 2014. <http://www.fbi.gov/albany/press-releases/2014/jamesville-man-enters-guilty-plea-to-conspiracy-to-commit-bank-fraud>.

755 Tobin, Dave. "Where Did the $3 Million of Federal Money Invested in Syracuse Suburban Airport, in Oswego County, Go?" *Syracuse.com*. Syracuse Media Group. 29 March 2011. Web. <http://www.syracuse.com/news/index.ssf/2011/03/where_did_the_3_million_of_fed.html>.

756 Kenyon, Jim. "For Sale: Failed Airport in Oswego Count.," *CNYCentral.com*. Sinclair Communications, LLC. 12 September 2014. Web. <http://www.cnycentral.com/news/story.aspx?id=1095978#.VBijdqPD-id>.

757 Dr. Nafeez Ahmed, "Nasa-funded study: industrial civilisation headed for 'irreversible collapse'?" The Guardian, March 14, 2014; http://www.theguardian.com/environment/earth-insight/2014/mar/14/nasa-civilisation-irreversible-collapse-study-scientists.

758 Dr. Nafeez Ahmed, "Nasa-funded study: industrial civilisation headed for 'irreversible collapse'?" The Guardian, March 14, 2014; http://www.theguardian.com/environment/earth-insight/2014/mar/14/nasa-civilisation-irreversible-collapse-study-scientists.

759 Ahmed, Nafeez. "Nasa-funded Study: Industrial Civilisation Headed for 'Irreversible Collapse'?" *theguardian.com*. Guardian News and Media Limited. 14 March 2014. Web. <http://www.theguardian.com/environment/earth-insight/2014/mar/14/nasa-civilisation-irreversible-collapse-study-scientists>.

760 NASA Procurement Data View – Contract Number Query, NASA. <https://prod.nais.nasa.gov/cgibin/npdv/contract.cgi>.

761 Summary of NASA activity relative to agreement NNX12AD03A and the study "Human and Nature Dynamics (HANDY) Modeling Inequality and Use of Resources in the Collapse or Sustainability of Societies," NASA, March 26, 2014.

762 NASA Procurement Data View – Contract Number Query, NASA. <https://prod.nais.nasa.gov/cgibin/npdv/contract.cgi>.

763 Summary of NASA activity relative to agreement NNX12AD03A and the study "Human and Nature Dynamics (HANDY) Modeling Inequality and Use of Resources in the Collapse or Sustainability of Societies," NASA, March 26, 2014.

764 Summary of NASA activity relative to agreement NNX12AD03A and the study "Human and Nature Dynamics (HANDY) Modeling Inequality and Use of Resources in the Collapse or Sustainability of Societies," NASA, March 26, 2014.

765 Wall, Mike. "NASA Clarifies Its Role in Civilization-Collapse Study." *Space.com*. Purch. 20 March 2014. Web. <http://www.space.com/25160-nasa-statement-civilization-collapse-study.html>.

766 Wall, Mike. "NASA Clarifies Its Role in Civilization-Collapse Study." *Space.com*. Purch. 20 March 2014. Web. <http://www.space.com/25160-nasa-statement-civilization-collapse-study.html>.

767 Ahmed, Nafeez. "Nasa-funded Study: Industrial Civilisation Headed for 'Irreversible Collapse'?" *theguardian.com*. Guardian News and Media Limited. 14 March 2014. Web. <http://www.theguardian.com/environment/earth-insight/2014/mar/14/nasa-civilisation-irreversible-collapse-study-scientists>.

768 Florida Museum of Natural History. Pressroom. *UF Receives $1.97 Million NSF Grant to Develop Paleontology Network.Http://www.flmnh.ufl.edu/*. University of Florida, 10 Feb. 2014. Web. 18 Oct. 2014. <http://www.flmnh.ufl.edu/pressroom/2014/02/10/uf-receives-1-97-million-nsf-grant-to-develop-paleontology-network/>.

769 Florida Museum of Natural History. Pressroom. *UF Receives $1.97 Million NSF Grant to Develop Paleontology Network.Http://www.flmnh.ufl.edu/*. University of Florida, 10 Feb. 2014. Web. 18 Oct. 2014. <http://www.flmnh.ufl.edu/pressroom/2014/02/10/uf-receives-1-97-million-nsf-grant-to-develop-paleontology-network/>.

770 Florida Museum of Natural History. Pressroom. *UF Receives $1.97 Million NSF Grant to Develop Paleontology Network.Http://www.flmnh.ufl.edu/*. University of Florida, 10 Feb. 2014. Web. 18 Oct. 2014. <http://www.flmnh.ufl.edu/pressroom/2014/02/10/uf-receives-1-97-million-nsf-grant-to-develop-paleontology-network/>.

771 "The FOSSIL Project." FACEBOOK. <https://www.facebook.com/TheFossilProject >.

772 "The FOSSIL Project". FACEBOOK. <https://www.facebook.com/TheFossilProject >.

773 "Fossils" FACEBOOK. <https://www.facebook.com/groups/fossilfootprints>.

774 "The Fossil Forum" FACEBOOK. <https://www.facebook.com/groups/135008766530423>.

775 National Science Foundation, Award Abstract #0949416. Web. <http://nsf.gov/awardsearch/showAward?AWD_ID=0949416>.

776 Taylor, Luke. "Game Show." *Mpnews.org*. Minnesota Public Radio. 1 July 2011. Web. http://www.mprnews.org/story/2011/07/01/game-show>.

777 McClellan, Jason. "Video Game Music Composers Are The Heroes In A New Web Series." *Techtimes.com*. TECHTIMES.com. 9 September 2014. Web. <http://www.techtimes.com/articles/15166/20140909/video-game-music-composers-are-the-heroes-in-a-new-web-series.htm>.

778 "Tibbetts, Than. ""Yeah, so It's Actually Really Fun to Listen to Music without Guns after a While."." Review. Web log post. *Thandland.com*. Than Tibbetts, 7 July 2011. Web. 18 Oct. 2014. <http://thanland.com/links/top-score-the-podcast-about-video-game-soundtracks.html>.

779 Reese, Emily. "Top Score Podcast." *Top Score Podcast*. Tumblr, n.d. Web. 18 Oct. 2014. <http://topscorepodcast.tumblr.com/>.

780 "Reese, Emily. "Top Score Podcast." *Top Score Podcast*. Tumblr, n.d. Web. 18 Oct. 2014. <http://topscorepodcast.tumblr.com/>.

781 USASpending.gov, Prime Award Spending Data for Federal Award Identifier 14-3400-7088; Web. <http://www.usaspending.gov/explore?frompage=assistance&tab=By%20Prime%20Awardee&comingfrom=searchresults&federal_award_id=14-3400-7088&fiscal_year=all&typeofview=complete>.

782 Data from iTunes Store Page for "Top Score with Emily Reese."

783 Bridgman, Anne, "Budget Cuts Affect Music, Arts." *Eugeneweek.com*. Eugene Weekly. 11 April 2013. Web. <http://www.eugeneweekly.com/20130411/shortchanging-our-schools/budget-cuts-affect-music-arts>.

784 Moravian College. News and Events. *Moravian College Receives NEH Grant to Educate Teachers About Bach. Moravian.edu*. N.p., 15 Aug. 2013. Web. 18 Oct. 2014. <http://www.moravian.edu/default.aspx?pageid=6283#.VEMjRvldV8E>.

785 Binford, Hilde. "Johann Sebastian Bach: Music of the Baroque and Enlightenment: Program Description." Web. <http://home.moravian.edu/public/music/bach/letter.htm>.

786 Binford, Hilde. "Johann Sebastian Bach: Music of the Baroque and Enlightenment: Program Description." Web. <http://home.moravian.edu/public/music/bach/letter.htm>.

787 Moravian College. News and Events. *Moravian College Receives NEH Grant to Educate Teachers About Bach. Moravian.edu*. N.p., 15 Aug. 2013. Web. 18 Oct. 2014. <http://www.moravian.edu/default.aspx?pageid=6283#.VEMjRvldV8E>.

788 Moravian College. News and Events. *Moravian College Receives NEH Grant to Educate Teachers About Bach. Moravian.edu*. N.p., 15 Aug. 2013. Web. 18 Oct. 2014. <http://www.moravian.edu/default.aspx?pageid=6283#.VEMjRvldV8E>. .

789 Moravian College. News and Events. *Moravian College Receives NEH Grant to Educate Teachers About Bach. Moravian.edu*. N.p., 15 Aug. 2013. Web. 18 Oct. 2014. <http://www.moravian.edu/default.aspx?pageid=6283#.VEMjRvldV8E>.

790 Rimkunas, John. "Wild and Crazy Guys..." Weblog post. *The Bach Story*. Blogger, 15 July 2014. Web. 18 Oct. 2014. <http://johnrimkunas.blogspot.com/2014/07/wild-and-crazy-guys.html>..

791 Rimkunas, John. "Ein Feste Burge..." Weblog post. *The Bach Story*. Blogger, 8 July 2014. Web. 18 Oct. 2014. < http://johnrimkunas.blogspot.com/2014/07/ein-feste-burg.html>.

792 Rimkunas, John. "Sports News..." Weblog post. *The Bach Story*. Blogger. 14 July 2014. Web. http://johnrimkunas.blogspot.com/2014/07/sports-news.html.>

793 Satullo, Sara K.. "Moravian College Awarded Grant to Send Teachers to Germany to Study Bach." *Lehighvalleylive.com*. PennLive LLC. 1 September 2013. Web. <http://www.lehighvalleylive.com/bethlehem/index.ssf/2013/09/post_351.html>.

794 USASpending.gov. "Prime Award Spending Data: Gateway to Blues." Web. <http://www.usaspending.gov/search?form_fields=%7B%22contract_description%22%3A%22Gateway+to+Blues%22%7D>; *Gateway to the Blues Visitors Center*, Tunica Convention & Visitors Bureau,. Web. <http://www.tunicatravel.com/things-to-do/cultural-attractions/gateway>.

795 Franklin, Webster. "Gateway To The Blues Visitor Center Now Open." *Tunicatravel.com*. Tunica Convention & Visitors Bureau. 16 December 2011. Web. <http://www.tunicatravel.com/things-to-do/cultural-attractions/gateway>.

796 See Webster Franklin, *Gateway To The Blues Visitor Center Now Open*, Tunica Convention & Visitors Bureau, http://www.tunicatravel.com/blog/2011/december/gateway-to-the-blues-visitor-center-now-open.

797 See *Gateway to the Blues Visitors Center*, Tunica Convention & Visitors Bureau, http://www.tunicatravel.com/things-to-do/cultural-attractions/gateway.

798 *2013 Report Card for America's Infrastructure*, American Society of Civil Engineers, <http://www.infrastructurereportcard.org>.

799 American Road & Transportation Builders Association. "U.S. Deficient Bridges." *artba.org*. ARTBA. Web. <http://www.artba.org/economics/us-deficient-bridges/>.

800 Rockey, Sally and Francis Collins. "One Nation in Support of Biomedical Research?" *nexus.od.nih.gov*. National Institutes of Health Office of Extramural Research 24 September 2013. Web. <http://nexus.od.nih.gov/all/2013/09/24/one-nation-in-support-of-biomedical-research/>.

801 Rockey, Sally and Francis Collins. "One Nation in Support of Biomedical Research?" *nexus.od.nih.gov*. National Institutes of Health Office of Extramural Research 24 September 2013. Web. <http://nexus.od.nih.gov/all/2013/09/24/one-nation-in-support-of-biomedical-research/>.

802 USASpending. "Prime Award Spending Data." Federal Award ID: K23AT006328. *USAspending.gov*. Web. <http://www.usaspending.gov/search?form_fields=%7B%22search_term%22%3A%22K23+AT006328%22%7D>.

803 Lindahl, Jared R., Christopher T. Kaplan, Evan M. Winget, and Willoughby B. Britton. "A Phenomenology of Meditation-induced Light Experiences: Traditional Buddhist and Neurobiological Perspectives." Frontiers in Psychology 4.000973 (2014): 1-16. Proquest. Web. <http://journal.frontiersin.org/Journal/10.3389/fpsyg.2013.00973/full>.

804 Britton, Willoughby B., Jared R. Lindahl, B. Rael Cahn, Jake H. Davis, and Roberta E. Goldman. "Awakening Is Not a Metaphor: The Effects of Buddhist Meditation Practices on Basic Wakefulness." Annals of the New York Academy of Sciences 1307 (2014): 64-81. Wiley. Web. <"Awakening is not a metaphor: the effects of Buddhist meditation practices on basic wakefulness>.

805 Lindahl, Jared R., Christopher T. Kaplan, Evan M. Winget, and Willoughby B. Britton. "A Phenomenology of Meditation-induced Light Experiences: Traditional Buddhist and Neurobiological Perspectives." Frontiers in Psychology 4.000973 (2014): 1-16. Proquest. Web. <http://journal.frontiersin.org/Journal/10.3389/fpsyg.2013.00973/full>. P75

806 Britton, Willoughby B., Jared R. Lindahl, B. Rael Cahn, Jake H. Davis, and Roberta E. Goldman. "Awakening Is Not a Metaphor: The Effects of Buddhist Meditation Practices on Basic Wakefulness." Annals of the New York Academy of Sciences 1307 (2014): 64-81. Wiley. Web. <"Awakening is not a metaphor: the effects of Buddhist meditation practices on basic wakefulness>. p75

807 Britton, Willoughby B., Jared R. Lindahl, B. Rael Cahn, Jake H. Davis, and Roberta E. Goldman. "Awakening Is Not a Metaphor: The Effects of Buddhist Meditation Practices on Basic Wakefulness." Annals of the New York Academy of Sciences 1307 (2014): 64-81. Wiley. Web. <"Awakening is not a metaphor: the effects of Buddhist meditation practices on basic wakefulness>.

808 Lindahl, Jared R., Christopher T. Kaplan, Evan M. Winget, and Willoughby B. Britton. "A Phenomenology of Meditation-induced Light Experiences: Traditional Buddhist and Neurobiological Perspectives." Frontiers in Psychology 4.000973 (2014): 1-16. Proquest. Web. <http://journal.frontiersin.org/Journal/10.3389/fpsyg.2013.00973/full>..

809 Soave, Robby. "Feds Spend Millions Dressing Creepy Students Up As Fruits, Vegetables." *Dailycaller.com*. The Daily Caller. 17 March 2014. Web. <http://dailycaller.com/2014/03/17/feds-spend-millions-dressing-creepy-students-up-as-fruits-vegetables>.

810 University of TN. "About Fruved." *Fruved.com*. Web. <http://fruved.com/about/>.

811 University of TN. "About Fruved." *Fruved.com*. Web. <http://fruved.com/about/>.

812 University of TN. "About Fruved." *Fruved.com*. Web. <http://fruved.com/about/>.

813 Soave, Robby. "Feds Spend Millions Dressing Creepy Students Up As Fruits, Vegetables." *Dailycaller.com*. The Daily Caller. 17 March 2014. Web. <http://dailycaller.com/2014/03/17/feds-spend-millions-dressing-creepy-students-up-as-fruits-vegetables>.

814 Dodrill, Tara. "Get Fruved: Government Spends $4.8 Million To Get Students To Dress Up Like Fruit."*Inquisitir.com*. The Inquisitor News. 19 March 2014. Web. <http://www.inquisitr.com/1177823/get-fruved-government-spends-4-8-million-to-get-students-to-dress-up-like-fruit/>.

815 USDA. Department of Communications. *USDA Announces Support for Innovative, Sustainable Wood Building Materials to Protect Environment and Create Jobs.* *Usda.gov.* USDA, 18 Mar. 2014. Web. 18 Oct. 2014. <http://www.usda.gov/wps/portal/usda/usdahome?contentid=2014/03/0041.xml&contentidonly=true>.

816 USDA. Department of Communications. *USDA Announces Support for Innovative, Sustainable Wood Building Materials to Protect Environment and Create Jobs.* *Usda.gov.* USDA, 18 Mar. 2014. Web. 18 Oct. 2014. <http://www.usda.gov/wps/portal/usda/usdahome?contentid=2014/03/0041.xml&contentidonly=true>..

817 Website of Smartlam Technologies Group. <http://www.smartlam.com>.

818 Rodriguez, Julie M. USDA Invests $2 Million in Sustainable Wooden Skyscraper Competition." *Inhabitat.com.* Inhabitant. 24 March 2014. Web. http://inhabitat.com/usda-invests-2-million-in-sustainable-wooden-skyscraper-designs/>.

819 Hintze, Lynnette, "Builder part of White House workshop," *dailyinterlake.com.* Daily Inter Lake. 29 March 2014. Web. <http://www.dailyinterlake.com/members/builder-part-of-white-house-workshop/article_a0eb02c6-b6eb-11e3-bc6a-001a4bcf887a.html>.

820 Rodriguez, Julie M. USDA Invests $2 Million in Sustainable Wooden Skyscraper Competition." *Inhabitat.com.* Inhabitant. 24 March 2014. Web. http://inhabitat.com/usda-invests-2-million-in-sustainable-wooden-skyscraper-designs/>.

821 Fountain, Henry, "Wood That Reaches New Heights." *Nytimes.com.* The New York Times Company. 4 June 2012. Web. <http://www.nytimes.com/2012/06/05/science/lofty-ambitions-for-cross-laminated-timber-panels.html?pagewanted=all&_r=0>.

822 IT Dashboard. "Disability Case Processing System." *Itdashboard.gov.* Office of Management and Budget. Web. <https://itdashboard.gov/investment?buscid=630>.

823 IT Dashboard. "Disability Case Processing System." *Itdashboard.gov.* Office of Management and Budget. Web. <https://itdashboard.gov/investment?buscid=630>.

824 IT Dashboard. "Disability Case Processing System." *Itdashboard.gov.* Office of Management and Budget. Web. <https://itdashboard.gov/investment?buscid=630>.

825 Social Security Administration. "Independent Analysis of the Disability Case Processing System." Final Report. 3 June 2014. Web. <http://oversight.house.gov/wp-content/uploads/2014/07/DCPS-Study.compressed.pdf>.

826 Social Security Administration. "Independent Analysis of the Disability Case Processing System." Final Report. 3 June 2014. Web. <http://oversight.house.gov/wp-content/uploads/2014/07/DCPS-Study.compressed.pdf>.

827 Social Security Administration. "Independent Analysis of the Disability Case Processing System." Final Report. 3 June 2014. Web. <http://oversight.house.gov/wp-content/uploads/2014/07/DCPS-Study.compressed.pdf>.

828 Social Security Administration. "Independent Analysis of the Disability Case Processing System." Final Report. 3 June 2014. Web. <http://oversight.house.gov/wp-content/uploads/2014/07/DCPS-Study.compressed.pdf>.

829 Social Security Administration. "Independent Analysis of the Disability Case Processing System." Final Report. 3 June 2014. Web. <http://oversight.house.gov/wp-content/uploads/2014/07/DCPS-Study.compressed.pdf>.

830 Social Security Administration. "Independent Analysis of the Disability Case Processing System." Final Report. 3 June 2014. Web. <http://oversight.house.gov/wp-content/uploads/2014/07/DCPS-Study.compressed.pdf>.

831 Social Security Administration. "Independent Analysis of the Disability Case Processing System." Final Report. 3 June 2014. Web. <http://oversight.house.gov/wp-content/uploads/2014/07/DCPS-Study.compressed.pdf>.

832 Social Security Administration. "Independent Analysis of the Disability Case Processing System." Final Report. 3 June 2014. Web. <http://oversight.house.gov/wp-content/uploads/2014/07/DCPS-Study.compressed.pdf>.

833 Social Security Administration. "Independent Analysis of the Disability Case Processing System." Final Report. 3 June 2014. Web. <http://oversight.house.gov/wp-content/uploads/2014/07/DCPS-Study.compressed.pdf>.

834 Cohen, Alexander, and James Arkin. "Afghans Don't Like Tofu, Either."*foreignpolicy.* Foreign Policy. 25 July 2014. Web. <http://www.foreignpolicy.com/articles/2014/07/25/afghans_don_t_like_tofu_either_soybeans_afghanistan>.

835 "SIGAR-14-69-SP," Letter from SIGAR John Sopko to Tom Vilsack, Secretary, U.S. Department of Agriculture, 9 June 2014. Web. <http://www.sigar.mil/pdf/Special%20Projects/SIGAR-14-69-SP.pdf>.

836 Cohen, Alexander, and James Arkin. "Afghans Don't Like Tofu, Either."*foreignpolicy.* Foreign Policy. 25 July 2014. Web. <http://www.foreignpolicy.com/articles/2014/07/25/afghans_don_t_like_tofu_either_soybeans_afghanistan>.

837 "SIGAR-14-69-SP," Letter from SIGAR John Sopko to Tom Vilsack, Secretary, U.S. Department of Agriculture, 9 June 2014. Web. <http://www.sigar.mil/pdf/Special%20Projects/SIGAR-14-69-SP.pdf>.

838 Cohen, Alexander, and James Arkin. "Afghans Don't Like Tofu, Either."*foreignpolicy.* Foreign Policy. 25 July 2014. Web. <http://www.foreignpolicy.com/articles/2014/07/25/afghans_don_t_like_tofu_either_soybeans_afghanistan>.

839 *See Value-Added Producer Grants Program*, CFDA, <https://www.cfda.gov/index?s=program&mode=form&tab=core&id=49ca2743a0169877e58643ed2f7e5544>.

840 *See Value-Added Producer Grants Program*, CFDA, <https://www.cfda.gov/index?s=program&mode=form&tab=core&id=49ca2743a0169877e58643ed2f7e5544>.

841 *See Value-Added Producer Grants Program*, CFDA, <https://www.cfda.gov/index?s=program&mode=form&tab=core&id=49ca2743a0169877e58643ed2f7e5544>.

842 Ocean Spray Cranberries, Inc. *Ocean Spray Announces 2013 Financial Results.* BusinessWire. 2 December <2013. Web. http://finance.yahoo.com/news/ocean-spray-announces-2013-financial-150000572.html>.

843 Office of Congressman Bill Keating. Media Center. KEATING ANNOUNCES VALUE-ADDED PRODUCER GRANT FOR OCEAN SPRAY CRANBERRIES. Website of Congressman Bill Keating. U.S. House of Representatives, 21 Aug. 2014. Web. <http://keating.house.gov/index.php?option=com_content&view=article&id=291:ocean-spray-cranberries-grant&catid=14&Itemid=13>.

844 Blue Diamond Growers. *Company Info. Bluediamond.com.* Blue Diamond Growers. Web. <http://www.bluediamond.com/index.cfm?navid=12>.

845 US Department of Agriculture. *Value-Added Producer Grant Awards Fiscal Year 2014.* USDA Rural Development. http://www.rurdev.usda.gov/supportdocuments/RD_2014VAPGRecipients.pdf.

846 Blue Diamond Growers. *Company Info. Bluediamond.com.* Blue Diamond Growers. Web. <http://www.bluediamond.com/index.cfm?navid=12>.

847 Sunsweet. *About Us. Sunsweetfoodservice.com.* Sunsweet Growers. Web. <http://www.sunsweetfoodservice.com/about.html>.

848 *Market Access Program*, USDA Foreign Agricultural Service. Web. <http://www.fas.usda.gov/programs/market-access-program-map>.

849 *See* Tom Coburn, *Treasure Map: The Market Access Program's Bounty of Waste, Loot and Spoils Plundered from Taxpayer*, June 2012. Web. http://www.coburn.

senate.gov/public//index.cfm?a=Files.Serve&File_id=5c2568d4-ae96-40bc-b3d8-19e7a259f749>.

850 See *MAP Funding Allocations – FY 2014*, USDA (accessed Sept. 19, 2014), <http://www.fas.usda.gov/programs/market-access-program-map/map-funding-allocations-fy-2014-0>.

851 See *MAP Funding Allocations – FY 2014*, USDA (accessed Sept. 19, 2014), <http://www.fas.usda.gov/programs/market-access-program-map/map-funding-allocations-fy-2014-0>.

852 National Science Foundation, Award Abstract #1062619; http://www.nsf.gov/awardsearch/showAward?AWD_ID=1062619&HistoricalAwards=false.

853 National Science Foundation, Award Abstract #1062619; http://www.nsf.gov/awardsearch/showAward?AWD_ID=1062619&HistoricalAwards=false.

854 SAE International, SAE Clean Snowmobile Challenge: Event Sponsorship, http://students.sae.org/cds/snowmobile/event/sponsors.htm.

855 National Science Foundation, Award Abstract #1062619; http://www.nsf.gov/awardsearch/showAward?AWD_ID=1062619&HistoricalAwards=false.

855 National Science Foundation, Award Abstract #1062619;

856 Marcia Goodrich, "Kettering, McGill Win 2014 Clean Snowmobile Challenge," *Michigan Tech News*, March 10, 2014, http://www.mtu.edu/news/stories/2014/march/kettering-mcgill-win-2014-clean-snowmobile-challenge.html.

857 Alexander-Bloch, Benjamin. "St. Bernard Government Reluctantly Moves Forward With Ice House in Yscloskey." *Nola.com*. NOLA Media Group. 6 August 2014. Web. <http://www.nola.com/politics/index.ssf/2014/08/st_bernard_government_reluctan.html>.

858 Perlstein, Mike. "St. Bernard Parish Spends Hundreds of Thousands And Still Can't Get Bulk Ice to Docks." *Wwltv.com*. WWL-TV Eyewitness News, a Gannett Company. 1 July 2013. Web. <http://www.wwltv.com/news/eyewitness/mikeperlstein/St-Bernard-getting-cold-reception-on-plans-for-ice-house-213915791.html>.

859 Alexander-Bloch, Benjamin. "St. Bernard Government Reluctantly Moves Forward With Ice House in Yscloskey." *Nola.com*. NOLA Media Group. 6 August 2014. Web. <http://www.nola.com/politics/index.ssf/2014/08/st_bernard_government_reluctan.html>.

860 Alexander-Bloch, Benjamin. "St. Bernard Government Reluctantly Moves Forward With Ice House in Yscloskey." *Nola.com*. NOLA Media Group. 6 August 2014. Web. <http://www.nola.com/politics/index.ssf/2014/08/st_bernard_government_reluctan.html>.

861 Alexander-Bloch, Benjamin. "St. Bernard Government Reluctantly Moves Forward With Ice House in Yscloskey." *Nola.com*. NOLA Media Group. 6 August 2014. Web. <http://www.nola.com/politics/index.ssf/2014/08/st_bernard_government_reluctan.html>.

862 Alexander-Bloch, Benjamin. "St. Bernard Government Reluctantly Moves Forward With Ice House in Yscloskey." *Nola.com*. NOLA Media Group. 6 August 2014. Web. <http://www.nola.com/politics/index.ssf/2014/08/st_bernard_government_reluctan.html>.

863 Alexander-Bloch, Benjamin. "St. Bernard Government Reluctantly Moves Forward With Ice House in Yscloskey." *Nola.com*. NOLA Media Group. 6 August 2014. Web. <http://www.nola.com/politics/index.ssf/2014/08/st_bernard_government_reluctan.html>.

864 Alexander-Bloch, Benjamin. "St. Bernard Government Reluctantly Moves Forward With Ice House in Yscloskey." *Nola.com*. NOLA Media Group. 6 August 2014. Web. <http://www.nola.com/politics/index.ssf/2014/08/st_bernard_government_reluctan.html>.

865 Alexander-Bloch, Benjamin. "St. Bernard Government Reluctantly Moves Forward With Ice House in Yscloskey." *Nola.com*. NOLA Media Group. 6 August 2014. Web. <http://www.nola.com/politics/index.ssf/2014/08/st_bernard_government_reluctan.html>.

866 Perlstein, Mike. "St. Bernard Parish Spends Hundreds of Thousands And Still Can't Get Bulk Ice to Docks." *Wwltv.com*. WWL-TV Eyewitness News, a Gannett Company. 1 July 2013. Web. <http://www.wwltv.com/news/eyewitness/mikeperlstein/St-Bernard-getting-cold-reception-on-plans-for-ice-house-213915791.html>.

867 H. Davis Cole & Associates. "Yscloskey Ice House." *Hdaviscole.com*. H. Davis Cole & Associates, LLC. Web. <http://www.hdaviscole.com/gallery.php?action=submit&id=9>.

868 The Editorial Board, NOLA.com. "Put St. Bernard Ice House Project on Ice: Editorial." Editorial. Nola.com. NOLA Media Group, 8 Aug. 2014. Web. <http://www.nola.com/opinions/index.ssf/2014/08/put_st_bernard_ice_house_proje.html>.

869 Perlstein, Mike. "St. Bernard Parish Spends Hundreds of Thousands And Still Can't Get Bulk Ice to Docks." *Wwltv.com*. WWL-TV Eyewitness News, a Gannett Company. 1 July 2013. Web. <http://www.wwltv.com/news/eyewitness/mikeperlstein/St-Bernard-getting-cold-reception-on-plans-for-ice-house-213915791.html>.

870 Perlstein, Mike. "St. Bernard Parish Spends Hundreds of Thousands And Still Can't Get Bulk Ice to Docks." *Wwltv.com*. WWL-TV Eyewitness News, a Gannett Company. 1 July 2013. Web. <http://www.wwltv.com/news/eyewitness/mikeperlstein/St-Bernard-getting-cold-reception-on-plans-for-ice-house-213915791.html>.

871 Alexander-Bloch, Benjamin. "St. Bernard Government Reluctantly Moves Forward With Ice House in Yscloskey." *Nola.com*. NOLA Media Group. 6 August 2014. Web. <http://www.nola.com/politics/index.ssf/2014/08/st_bernard_government_reluctan.html>.

872 Alexander-Bloch, Benjamin. "St. Bernard Government Reluctantly Moves Forward With Ice House in Yscloskey." *Nola.com*. NOLA Media Group. 6 August 2014. Web. <http://www.nola.com/politics/index.ssf/2014/08/st_bernard_government_reluctan.html>.

873 "The Editorial Board, NOLA.com. "Put St. Bernard Ice House Project on Ice: Editorial." Editorial. Nola.com. NOLA Media Group, 8 Aug. 2014. Web. <http://www.nola.com/opinions/index.ssf/2014/08/put_st_bernard_ice_house_proje.html>.

874 The Editorial Board, NOLA.com. "Put St. Bernard Ice House Project on Ice: Editorial." Editorial. Nola.com. NOLA Media Group, 8 Aug. 2014. Web. <http://www.nola.com/opinions/index.ssf/2014/08/put_st_bernard_ice_house_proje.html>.

875 Alexander-Bloch, Benjamin. "St. Bernard Government Reluctantly Moves Forward With Ice House in Yscloskey." *Nola.com*. NOLA Media Group. 6 August 2014. Web. <http://www.nola.com/politics/index.ssf/2014/08/st_bernard_government_reluctan.html>.

876 H. Davis Cole & Associates. "Yscloskey Ice House." *Hdaviscole.com*. H. Davis Cole & Associates, LLC. Web. <http://www.hdaviscole.com/gallery.php?action=submit&id=9>.

877 Perlstein, Mike. "St. Bernard Parish Spends Hundreds of Thousands And Still Can't Get Bulk Ice to Docks." *Wwltv.com*. WWL-TV Eyewitness News, a Gannett Company. 1 July 2013. Web. <http://www.wwltv.com/news/eyewitness/mikeperlstein/St-Bernard-getting-cold-reception-on-plans-for-ice-house-213915791.html>.

878 National Institutes of Health, "Kiddio: Food Fight – Training Vegetable Parenting Practices," Project Number 1R44HD075521-02. Web. <http://projectreporter.nih.gov/project_info_details.cfm?aid=8789535&icde=21290453>.

879 Fresh Fruit Portal. "U.S. Researchers Developing App to Improve 'Vegetable Parenting," *FreshFruitPortal.com*. 13 July 2012. Web. <http://www.freshfruitportal.com/2012/07/13/u-s-researchers-developing-app-to-improve-vegetable-parenting/?country=united%20states>.

880 Wood, Marcia. "Getting Your Kids to Eat More Vegetables." Agricultural Research (July 2012): 12-14. Www.ars.usga.gov. U.S. Department of Agriculture. Web. <Wood, Marcia. "Getting Your Kids to Eat More Vegetables." Agricultural Research (July 2012): n. pag. Http://www.ars.usda.gov/. U.S. Department of Agriculture. Web>.

881 National Institutes of Health, "Kiddio: Food Fight – Training Vegetable Parenting Practices," Project Number 1R44HD075521-02 <http://projectreporter.nih.gov/project_info_details.cfm?aid=8789535&icde=21290453>.

882 National Institutes of Health, "Kiddio: Food Fight – Training Vegetable Parenting Practices," Project Number 1R44HD075521-02 <http://projectreporter.nih.gov/project_info_details.cfm?aid=8789535&icde=21290453>

883 Yuting, Zhang, Chao Zhou, and Seo Hyon Baik. "A Simple Change To The Medicare Part D Low-Income Subsidy Program Could Save $5 Billion." Health Affairs 33.6 (2014): 940-45. Healthaffairs.org. Project HOPE, June 2014. Web. 19 Oct. 2014. <http://content.healthaffairs.org/content/33/6/940.full>.

884 Yuting, Zhang, Chao Zhou, and Seo Hyon Baik. "A Simple Change To The Medicare Part D Low-Income Subsidy Program Could Save $5 Billion." Health Affairs 33.6 (2014): 940-45. Healthaffairs.org. Project HOPE, June 2014. Web. 19 Oct. 2014. <http://content.healthaffairs.org/content/33/6/940.full>.

885 Yuting, Zhang, Chao Zhou, and Seo Hyon Baik. "A Simple Change To The Medicare Part D Low-Income Subsidy Program Could Save $5 Billion." Health Affairs 33.6 (2014): 940-45. Healthaffairs.org. Project HOPE, June 2014. Web. 19 Oct. 2014. <http://content.healthaffairs.org/content/33/6/940.full>.

886 Yuting, Zhang, Chao Zhou, and Seo Hyon Baik. "A Simple Change To The Medicare Part D Low-Income Subsidy Program Could Save $5 Billion." Health Affairs 33.6 (2014): 940-45. Healthaffairs.org. Project HOPE, June 2014. Web. 19 Oct. 2014. <http://content.healthaffairs.org/content/33/6/940.full>.

887 Yuting, Zhang, Chao Zhou, and Seo Hyon Baik. "A Simple Change To The Medicare Part D Low-Income Subsidy Program Could Save $5 Billion." Health Affairs 33.6 (2014): 940-45. Healthaffairs.org. Project HOPE, June 2014. Web. 19 Oct. 2014. <http://content.healthaffairs.org/content/33/6/940.full>.

888 Yuting, Zhang, Chao Zhou, and Seo Hyon Baik. "A Simple Change To The Medicare Part D Low-Income Subsidy Program Could Save $5 Billion." Health Affairs 33.6 (2014): 940-45. Healthaffairs.org. Project HOPE, June 2014. Web. 19 Oct. 2014. <http://content.healthaffairs.org/content/33/6/940.full>.

889 Smith, Paul E. Townofcary.org. Rep. no. PL14-018. Http://www.townofcary.org/Town_Council/Agendas___Minutes/Staff_Reports/PL14-018_Acceptance_of_the_Section_108_Loan_from_the_U_S__Department_of_Housing_and_Urban_Development_25753.htm, 26 June 2014. Web.

890 Specht, Paul A. "The Mayton Inn Loan Gets OK for Downtown Cary." *Carynews.com*. The Cary News. 20 June 2014. Web. <http://www.carynews.com/2014/06/20/3951492/the-mayton-inn-loan-gets-ok-for.html>.

891 Kurry, Dawn. "Boutique '20s-style Hotel to Break Ground in Downtown Cary." *Bizjournals.com*. Triangle Business Journal. 18 July 2014. Web. <http://www.bizjournals.com/triangle/blog/real-estate/2014/07/boutique-20s-style-hotel-to-break-ground-in-cary.html>.

892 Kurry, Dawn. "Boutique '20s-style Hotel to Break Ground in Downtown Cary." *Bizjournals.com*. Triangle Business Journal. 18 July 2014. Web. <http://www.bizjournals.com/triangle/blog/real-estate/2014/07/boutique-20s-style-hotel-to-break-ground-in-cary.html>.

893 Specht, Paul A. "Construction to Start Soon on Downtown's Cary's The Mayton Inn." *Carynews.com*. The Cary News. 27 June 2014. Web. <http://www.carynews.com/2014/06/27/3970004/construction-to-start-soon-on.html>.

894 The Mayton Inn Website. "All Amenities." *Maytoninn.com*. Web. http://www.maytoninn.com/rooms-rates/all-amenities>.

895 Mayton Inn. "It's Official: The Mayton Inn!" Weblog post. Http://maytoninn.wordpress.com/. Wordpress, 9 Oct. 2012. Web. 19 Oct. 2014. <http://maytoninn.wordpress.com/2012/10/09/its-official-the-mayton-inn/>.

896 The Mayton Inn Website. "All Amenities." *Maytoninn.com*. Web. http://www.maytoninn.com/rooms-rates/all-amenities>.

897 Kurry, Dawn. "Boutique '20s-style Hotel to Break Ground in Downtown Cary." *Bizjournals.com*. Triangle Business Journal. 18 July 2014. Web. <http://www.bizjournals.com/triangle/blog/real-estate/2014/07/boutique-20s-style-hotel-to-break-ground-in-cary.html>.

898 Specht, Paul A. "The Mayton Inn Loan Gets OK for Downtown Cary." *Carynews.com*. The Cary News. 20 June 2014. Web. <http://www.carynews.com/2014/06/20/3951492/the-mayton-inn-loan-gets-ok-for.html>.

899 Google hotel search, conducted 22 July 2014. <https://www.google.com/hotels/?gl=US&cu_link=1#search;l=Cary,+North+Carolina;q=cary,+nc+hotel;d=2014-08-03;n=1;mf=r;ar=;rtt=600;si=55e6887a;av=r>.

900 Google hotel search, conducted 22 July 2014. <https://www.google.com/hotels/?gl=US&cu_link=1#search;l=Cary,+North+Carolina;q=cary,+nc+hotel;d=2014-08-03;n=1;mf=r;ar=;rtt=600;si=55e6887a;av=r>.

901 The Mayton Inn website. Accessed 22 July 2014. <http://www.maytoninn.com/>.

902 Stensland, Jeff. "Urban Rail Ad Campaign Under Fire." *Austin.twcnews.com*. Time Warner Cable Enterprises LLC. 2 August 2014. Web. <http://austin.twcnews.com/content/news/303685/urban-rail-ad-campaign-under-fire/>.

903 Stensland, Jeff. "Urban Rail Ad Campaign Under Fire." *Austin.twcnews.com*. Time Warner Cable Enterprises LLC. 2 August 2014. Web. <http://austin.twcnews.com/content/news/303685/urban-rail-ad-campaign-under-fire/>.

904 Stensland, Jeff. "Urban Rail Ad Campaign Under Fire." *Austin.twcnews.com*. Time Warner Cable Enterprises LLC. 2 August 2014. Web. <http://austin.twcnews.com/content/news/303685/urban-rail-ad-campaign-under-fire/>.

905 Henry, Terrence. "Why is Project Connect Handing Out This Inaccurate Urban Rail Map?" *kut.org*. KUT. 10 June 2014. Web. <http://kut.org/post/why-project-connect-handing-out-inaccurate-urban-rail-map>.

906 Henry, Terrence. "Why is Project Connect Handing Out This Inaccurate Urban Rail Map?" *kut.org*. KUT. 10 June 2014. Web. <http://kut.org/post/why-project-connect-handing-out-inaccurate-urban-rail-map>.

907 KXAN Staff. "$600M Rail Bond Will be on Ballot; Many Questions Still Loom." *Kxan.com*. LIN Television of Texas, LP. 7 August 2014. Web. <http://kxan.com/2014/08/07/city-council-set-to-vote-on-urban-rail-bond-today/>.

908 NASA OIG. Oig.nasa.gov. Rep. no. IG-14-015. NASA OIG Office of Audits, 27 Feb. 2014. Web. <http://oig.nasa.gov/audits/reports/FY14/IG-14-015.pdf>.

909 NASA OIG. Oig.nasa.gov. Rep. no. IG-14-015. NASA OIG Office of Audits, 27 Feb. 2014. Web. <http://oig.nasa.gov/audits/reports/FY14/IG-14-015.pdf>.

910 NASA OIG. Oig.nasa.gov. Rep. no. IG-14-015. NASA OIG Office of Audits, 27 Feb. 2014. Web. <http://oig.nasa.gov/audits/reports/FY14/IG-14-015.pdf>. Estimate calculated by dividing the IG's seven-month estimated cost of $679,000 into a per-month figure.

911 NASA OIG. Oig.nasa.gov. Rep. no. IG-14-015. NASA OIG Office of Audits, 27 Feb. 2014. Web. <http://oig.nasa.gov/audits/reports/FY14/IG-14-015.pdf>.

912 NASA OIG. Oig.nasa.gov. Rep. no. IG-14-015. NASA OIG Office of Audits, 27 Feb. 2014. Web. <http://oig.nasa.gov/audits/reports/FY14/IG-14-015.pdf>.

913 NASA OIG. Oig.nasa.gov. Rep. no. IG-14-015. NASA OIG Office of Audits, 27 Feb. 2014. Web. <http://oig.nasa.gov/audits/reports/FY14/IG-14-015.pdf>..

914 NASA OIG. Oig.nasa.gov. Rep. no. IG-14-015. NASA OIG Office of Audits, 27 Feb. 2014. Web. <http://oig.nasa.gov/audits/reports/FY14/IG-14-015.pdf>. p2.

915 Kaufman, Matt. "The Saga of the Lost Space Tapes" *washingtonpost.com*. The Washington Post. 31 January 2007. Web. <http://www.washingtonpost.com/wp-dyn/content/article/2007/01/30/AR2007013002065.html>.

916 Fernandez, Manny. "NASA Searchers for Loot That Traveled From Space to Another Void." *Nytimes.com*. The New York Times Company. 21 January 2012. Web. <http://www.nytimes.com/2012/01/22/science/space/nasa-tackles-problem-of-missing-moon-rocks.html?pagewanted=all&_r=0>.

917 *See generally* U.S. Environmental Protection Agency Office of Inspector General. *Early Warning Report: National Service Center for Environmental Publications in Blue Ash, Ohio, Spent $1.5 Million to Store Excess Publications*. Report No. 14-P-0132. EPA OIG. Washington, D.C. 11 Mar. 2014. Web. <http://www.epa.gov/oig/reports/2014/20140311-14-P-0132.pdf>.

918 U.S. Environmental Protection Agency Office of Inspector General. *Early Warning Report: National Service Center for Environmental Publications in Blue Ash, Ohio, Spent $1.5 Million to Store Excess Publications*. Report No. 14-P-0132. EPA OIG. Washington, D.C. 11 Mar. 2014. Web. <http://www.epa.gov/oig/reports/2014/20140311-14-P-0132.pdf>. at p3.

919 U.S. Environmental Protection Agency Office of Inspector General. *Early Warning Report: National Service Center for Environmental Publications in Blue Ash, Ohio, Spent $1.5 Million to Store Excess Publications.* Report No. 14-P-0132. EPA OIG. Washington, D.C. 11 Mar. 2014. Web. <http://www.epa.gov/oig/reports/2014/20140311-14-P-0132.pdf>. p5.

920 U.S. Environmental Protection Agency Office of Inspector General. *Early Warning Report: National Service Center for Environmental Publications in Blue Ash, Ohio, Spent $1.5 Million to Store Excess Publications.* Report No. 14-P-0132. EPA OIG. Washington, D.C. 11 Mar. 2014. Web. <http://www.epa.gov/oig/reports/2014/20140311-14-P-0132.pdf>. p7.

921 U.S. Environmental Protection Agency Office of Inspector General. *Early Warning Report: National Service Center for Environmental Publications in Blue Ash, Ohio, Spent $1.5 Million to Store Excess Publications.* Report No. 14-P-0132. EPA OIG. Washington, D.C. 11 Mar. 2014. Web. <http://www.epa.gov/oig/reports/2014/20140311-14-P-0132.pdf>.

922 U.S. Environmental Protection Agency Office of Inspector General. *Early Warning Report: National Service Center for Environmental Publications in Blue Ash, Ohio, Spent $1.5 Million to Store Excess Publications.* Report No. 14-P-0132. EPA OIG. Washington, D.C. 11 Mar. 2014. Web. <http://www.epa.gov/oig/reports/2014/20140311-14-P-0132.pdf>. p6.

923 PaymentAccuracy.gov. "About Improper Payments: The Problem." Web. 19 September 2014/ Wen/ <https://paymentaccuracy.gov/about-improper-payments>.

924 PaymentAccuracy.gov. "Improper Payment Amounts (FYs 2004-2003)." 19 September 2014. Web. <https://paymentaccuracy.gov/improper-payment-amounts>.

925 PaymentAccuracy.gov. "Supplemental Nutrition Assistance Program (SNAP)." 19 September 2014. Web. <https://paymentaccuracy.gov/tracked/supplemental-nutrition-assistance-program-snap-2013#learnmore>.

926 PaymentAccuracy.gov. "Supplemental Nutrition Assistance Program (SNAP)." 19 September 2014. Web. <https://paymentaccuracy.gov/tracked/supplemental-nutrition-assistance-program-snap-2013#learnmore>.

927 Staff Report. "11 Louisiana Residents Convicted of Public Benefits Fraud." *Shreveporttimes.com*. Gannett. 2 October 2014. Web. <http://www.shreveporttimes.com/story/news/local/2014/09/30/louisiana-residents-convicted-public-benefits-fraud/16487489/>.

928 Malinowski, W. Zachary. "Sentences Handed Down in Providence Food Stamp Fraud Case." 21 September 2014. Web. <http://www.providencejournal.com/news/courts/20140921-sentences-handed-down-in-providence-food-stamp-fraud-case.ece>.

929 WGAL News 8. "23 Sentenced for Welfare Fraud." *Wgal.com*. 16 October 2014. Web. < http://www.wgal.com/news/23-sentenced-for-welfare-fraud/29138500>.

930 Department of Defense, Office of Inspector General. *Defense Logistics Agency Aviation Potentially Overpaid Bell Helicopter for Sole-Source Commercial Spare Parts.* Rep. No. DODIG-2014-088. Alexandria, VA. 7 July 2014. Web. <http://www.dodig.mil/pubs/report_summary.cfm?id=5890>.

931 Capaccio, Tony and Salant, Jonathan D. "Pentagon Found to Pay Textron Unit $8,214 for a $445 Gear." *Bloomberg.com*. Bloomberg L.P. 9 July 2014. Web. <http://www.bloomberg.com/news/2014-07-08/pentagon-found-to-pay-textron-unit-8-124-for-a-445-gear.html>.

932 Department of Defense, Office of Inspector General. *Defense Logistics Agency Aviation Potentially Overpaid Bell Helicopter for Sole-Source Commercial Spare Parts.* Rep. No. DODIG-2014-088. Alexandria, VA. 7 July 2014. Web. <http://www.dodig.mil/pubs/report_summary.cfm?id=5890>.

933 Capaccio, Tony and Salant, Jonathan D. "Pentagon Found to Pay Textron Unit $8,214 for a $445 Gear." *Bloomberg.com*. Bloomberg L.P. 9 July 2014. Web. <http://www.bloomberg.com/news/2014-07-08/pentagon-found-to-pay-textron-unit-8-124-for-a-445-gear.html>.

934 Capaccio, Tony and Salant, Jonathan D. "Pentagon Found to Pay Textron Unit $8,214 for a $445 Gear." *Bloomberg.com*. Bloomberg L.P. 9 July 2014. Web. <http://www.bloomberg.com/news/2014-07-08/pentagon-found-to-pay-textron-unit-8-124-for-a-445-gear.html>.

935 Department of Defense, Office of Inspector General. *Defense Logistics Agency Aviation Potentially Overpaid Bell Helicopter for Sole-Source Commercial Spare Parts.* Rep. No. DODIG-2014-088. Alexandria, VA. 7 July 2014. Web. <http://www.dodig.mil/pubs/report_summary.cfm?id=5890>.

936 Capaccio, Tony and Salant, Jonathan D. "Pentagon Found to Pay Textron Unit $8,214 for a $445 Gear." *Bloomberg.com*. Bloomberg L.P. 9 July 2014. Web. <http://www.bloomberg.com/news/2014-07-08/pentagon-found-to-pay-textron-unit-8-124-for-a-445-gear.html>.

937 DHS Office of Inspector General. *U.S. Immigration and Customs Enforcement's Management of the Federal Employees' Compensation Act Program.* Rep. No. OIG-14-105.Washington, D.C. 1 July 2014. Web. <http://www.oig.dhs.gov/assets/Mgmt/2014/OIG_14-105_Jul14.pdf>. p4

938 DHS Office of Inspector General. *U.S. Immigration and Customs Enforcement's Management of the Federal Employees' Compensation Act Program.* Rep. No. OIG-14-105.Washington, D.C. 1 July 2014. Web. <http://www.oig.dhs.gov/assets/Mgmt/2014/OIG_14-105_Jul14.pdf>. p4

939 DHS Office of Inspector General. *U.S. Immigration and Customs Enforcement's Management of the Federal Employees' Compensation Act Program.* Rep. No. OIG-14-105.Washington, D.C. 1 July 2014. Web. <http://www.oig.dhs.gov/assets/Mgmt/2014/OIG_14-105_Jul14.pdf>. p4

940 Sopko, John F. "SIGAR Disposition Notification Request." Letter to The Honorable Charles T. Hagel, Secretary of Defense. 3 Oct. 2014. MS. Office of the Special Inspector General for Afghanistan Reconstruction, Arlington, VA.
Web. <http://www.sigar.mil/pdf/special%20projects/SIGAR-15-04-SP_IL_G222%20Disposition%20Notf%20Req_03Oct2014_Redacted.pdf>.

941 Department of Defense, Office of Inspector General. *Critical Information Needed to Determine the Cost and Availability of G222 Spare Parts.* Report No.: D2012-D000AT-0170.000. Alexandria, VA: DOD-OIG. 31 January 2013. Print.

942 Sopko, John F. "SIGAR Disposition Notification Request." Letter to The Honorable Charles T. Hagel, Secretary of Defense. 3 Oct. 2014. MS. Office of the Special Inspector General for Afghanistan Reconstruction, Arlington, VA.
Web. <http://www.sigar.mil/pdf/special%20projects/SIGAR-15-04-SP_IL_G222%20Disposition%20Notf%20Req_03Oct2014_Redacted.pdf>

943 Sopko, John F. "SIGAR Disposition Notification Request." Letter to The Honorable Charles T. Hagel, Secretary of Defense. 3 Oct. 2014. MS. Office of the Special Inspector General for Afghanistan Reconstruction, Arlington, VA.
Web. <http://www.sigar.mil/pdf/special%20projects/SIGAR-15-04-SP_IL_G222%20Disposition%20Notf%20Req_03Oct2014_Redacted.pdf>

944 Schogol, Jeff. "DLA Junks Multimillion Planes for Afghan Air Force, Sells Scrap for 6 Cents a Pound." *Airforcetimes.com*. Gannett. 9 October 2014. Web. <http://www.airforcetimes.com/article/20141009/NEWS/310090068/DLA-junks-multimillion-planes-Afghan-Air-Force-sells-scrap-6-cents-pound>.

945 Capaccio, Tony. "Planes Parked in Weeds in Kabul After $486 Million Spent." *Bloomberg.com*. Bloomberg L.P. 9 December 2013. Web. <http://www.bloomberg.com/news/2013-12-10/planes-parked-in-weeds-in-kabul-after-486-million-spent.html>.

946 Smith, Jada F., "Eisenhower Memorial Moves Forward," *nytimes.com*. The New York Times Company. 24 September 2014. Web. <http://www.nytimes.com/2014/09/25/us/25eisenhower.html?_r=0>.

947 Joynt, Carol Ross. "Tug of War." *Washingtonian.com*. Washington Magazine, Inc. 30 April 2014. Web. <http://www.washingtonian.com/articles/people/tug-of-war/>.

948 Smith, Jada F., "Eisenhower Memorial Moves Forward," *nytimes.com*. The New York Times Company. 24 September 2014. Web. <http://www.nytimes.com/2014/09/25/us/25eisenhower.html?_r=0>.

949 Smith, Jada F., "Eisenhower Memorial Moves Forward," *nytimes.com*. The New York Times Company. 24 September 2014. Web. <http://www.nytimes.com/2014/09/25/us/25eisenhower.html?_r=0>.

950 Zongker, Brett, "Eisenhower Memorial Approval Delayed Into 2013," ap.com. Associated Press. 16 November 2012. Web. http://bigstory.ap.org/article/eisenhower-memorial-approval-delayed-2013>.

951 Committee on Natural Resources, Majority Staff. *Five-Star Folly: An Investigation into the Cost Increases, Construction Delays, and Design Problems That Have Been a Disservice to the Effort to memorialize Dwight D. Eisenhower.* U.S. House of Representatives. Web. http://naturalresources.house.gov/uploadedfiles/oversightreport-113-eisenhowermemorial.pdf>.

952 Smith, Jada F., "Eisenhower Memorial Moves Forward," *nytimes.com.* The New York Times Company. 24 September 2014. Web. <http://www.nytimes.com/2014/09/25/us/25eisenhower.html?_r=0>.

953 Clift, Eleanor. "The Strange Fight Over the Eisenhower Memorial. *Thedailybeast.com.* The Daily Beast Company LLC. 3 September 2014. Web. <http://www.thedailybeast.com/articles/2014/09/03/the-strange-fight-over-the-eisenhower-memorial.html>.

954 Shubow, Justin. "It's Time to Bury Frank Gehry's Eisenhower Memorial." *Rollcall.com* CQ Roll Call. 3 February 2014. Web. <http://www.rollcall.com/news/its_time_to_bury_frank_gehrys_eisenhower_memorial_commentary-230612-1.html>.

955 Committee on Natural Resources, Majority Staff. *Five-Star Folly: An Investigation into the Cost Increases, Construction Delays, and Design Problems That Have Been a Disservice to the Effort to memorialize Dwight D. Eisenhower.* U.S. House of Representatives. Web. http://naturalresources.house.gov/uploadedfiles/oversightreport-113-eisenhowermemorial.pdf>.

956 Roche, Sam. "It You Like Ike, Start Over With His Memorial." *Wsj.com.* Dow Jones & Company. 4 August 2014. Web. http://online.wsj.com/articles/sam-roche-if-you-like-ike-start-over-with-his-memorial-1407195093>.

957 Rosiak, Luke, "Uncertain Future Troubles Eisenhower Memorial Commission and its Insular Staff." *Washingtonexaminer.com.* Washington Examiner. 15 April 2014. Web. <http://washingtonexaminer.com/uncertain-future-troubles-eisenhower-memorial-commission-and-its-insular-staff/article/2547245>.

958 Rosiak, Luke, "Uncertain Future Troubles Eisenhower Memorial Commission and its Insular Staff." *Washingtonexaminer.com.* Washington Examiner. 15 April 2014. Web. <http://washingtonexaminer.com/uncertain-future-troubles-eisenhower-memorial-commission-and-its-insular-staff/article/2547245>.

959 Boyle, Katherine. "Planning Commission Goes to War with Gehry Partners Over Eisenhower Memorial." *Washingtonpost.com.* The Washington Post. 3 April 2014. Web. http://www.washingtonpost.com/entertainment/museums/planning-commission-goes-to-war-with-gehry-partners-over-eisenhower-memorial-design/2014/04/03/b7351f14-bb6c-11e3-9c3c-311301e2167d_story.html>.

960 Smith, Jada F., "Eisenhower Memorial Moves Forward," *nytimes.com.* The New York Times Company. 24 September 2014. Web. <http://www.nytimes.com/2014/09/25/us/25eisenhower.html?_r=0>.

961 Brooks, Mike. "Native Americans Turning Butterflies Into Businesses." *Okcfoc.com.* KOKH FOX 25. 14 August 2014. Web. <http://www.okcfox.com/story/26286223/native-americans-turning-butterflies-into-businesses>.

962 Brooks, Mike. "Native Americans Turning Butterflies Into Businesses." *Okcfoc.com.* KOKH FOX 25. 14 August 2014. Web. <http://www.okcfox.com/story/26286223/native-americans-turning-butterflies-into-businesses>.

963 Lobosco, Katie. "Butterfly Farm is a Surprising Job Creator." *CNN.COM.* CNN. 19 August 2014. Web. <http://money.cnn.com/2014/08/14/smallbusiness/butterfly-farm-jobs/>.

964 Lobosco, Katie. "Butterfly Farm is a Surprising Job Creator." *CNN.COM.* CNN. 19 August 2014. Web. <http://money.cnn.com/2014/08/14/smallbusiness/butterfly-farm-jobs/>.

965 Habib, Nour. "Thlopthlocco Tribal Town Receives $500,000 Grant for Butterfly Farming." *Tulsaworld.com.* BH Media Group Holdings, Inc. 4 August 2014. Web. <http://www.tulsaworld.com/news/local/thlopthlocco-tribal-town-receives-grant-for-butterfly-farming/article_82cf4f0f-e374-57c0-a625-4239c80e79b6.html?mode=jqm>.

966 Rutland, Amanda. "Muscogee (Creek) Tribal Town Receives Federal Grant." *Muscogeenation-nsn.gov.* Muscogee (Creek) Nation. 14 September 2014. Web. <http://www.muscogeenation-nsn.gov/Pages/Articles/14Sep/butterflygrant.html>.

967 Habib, Nour. "Thlopthlocco Tribal Town Receives $500,000 Grant for Butterfly Farming." *Tulsaworld.com.* BH Media Group Holdings, Inc. 4 August 2014. Web. <http://www.tulsaworld.com/news/local/thlopthlocco-tribal-town-receives-grant-for-butterfly-farming/article_82cf4f0f-e374-57c0-a625-4239c80e79b6.html?mode=jqm>.

968 Habib, Nour. "Thlopthlocco Tribal Town Receives $500,000 Grant for Butterfly Farming." *Tulsaworld.com.* BH Media Group Holdings, Inc. 4 August 2014. Web. <http://www.tulsaworld.com/news/local/thlopthlocco-tribal-town-receives-grant-for-butterfly-farming/article_82cf4f0f-e374-57c0-a625-4239c80e79b6.html?mode=jqm>.

969 Habib, Nour. "Thlopthlocco Tribal Town Receives $500,000 Grant for Butterfly Farming." *Tulsaworld.com.* BH Media Group Holdings, Inc. 4 August 2014. Web. <http://www.tulsaworld.com/news/local/thlopthlocco-tribal-town-receives-grant-for-butterfly-farming/article_82cf4f0f-e374-57c0-a625-4239c80e79b6.html?mode=jqm>.

970 Habib, Nour. "Thlopthlocco Tribal Town Receives $500,000 Grant for Butterfly Farming." *Tulsaworld.com.* BH Media Group Holdings, Inc. 4 August 2014. Web. <http://www.tulsaworld.com/news/local/thlopthlocco-tribal-town-receives-grant-for-butterfly-farming/article_82cf4f0f-e374-57c0-a625-4239c80e79b6.html?mode=jqm>.

971 Thlopthlocco Tribal Town of Oklahoma website, Accessed 18 October 2014. <http://tttown.org/>.

972 Habib, Nour. "Thlopthlocco Tribal Town Receives $500,000 Grant for Butterfly Farming." *Tulsaworld.com.* BH Media Group Holdings, Inc. 4 August 2014. Web. <http://tulsaworld.com/news/local/thlopthlocco-tribal-town-receives-grant-for-butterfly-farming/article_82cf4f0f-e374-57c0-a625-4239c80e79b6.html?mode=jqm>.

973 Brooks, Mike. "Native Americans Turning Butterflies Into Businesses." *Okcfoc.com.* KOKH FOX 25. 14 August 2014. Web. <http://www.okcfox.com/story/26286223/native-americans-turning-butterflies-into-businesses>.

974 Lobosco, Katie. "Butterfly Farm is a Surprising Job Creator." *CNN.COM.* CNN. 19 August 2014. Web. <http://money.cnn.com/2014/08/14/smallbusiness/butterfly-farm-jobs/>.

975 Lobosco, Katie. "Butterfly Farm is a Surprising Job Creator." *CNN.COM.* CNN. 19 August 2014. Web. <http://money.cnn.com/2014/08/14/smallbusiness/butterfly-farm-jobs/>.

976 Lobosco, Katie. "Butterfly Farm is a Surprising Job Creator." *CNN.COM.* CNN. 19 August 2014. Web. <http://money.cnn.com/2014/08/14/smallbusiness/butterfly-farm-jobs/>.

977 Habib, Nour. "Thlopthlocco Tribal Town Receives $500,000 Grant for Butterfly Farming." *Tulsaworld.com.* BH Media Group Holdings, Inc. 4 August 2014. Web. <http://www.tulsaworld.com/news/local/thlopthlocco-tribal-town-receives-grant-for-butterfly-farming/article_82cf4f0f-e374-57c0-a625-4239c80e79b6.html?mode=jqm>.

978 "Board of Directors Meeting Agenda." *Psta.net.* Pinellas Suncoast Transit Authority. 14 December 2011. Web. <http://www.psta.net/PDF/BM%20Agenda%2012-14-11.pdf>.

979 "Eva," Pinellas Suncoast Transit Authority, July 19, 2013, https://www.youtube.com/watch?v=FR2kGChlisw&list=UUdnSqkMP59ilSL_v_GtcNTQ, accessed August 4, 2014.

980 http://greenlightpinellas.com/about/the-greenlight-pinellas-plan

981 Kroft, Steve. "Biggest IRS Scam Around: Identity Tax Refund Fraud." 21 September 2014. Web. <http://www.cbsnews.com/news/irs-scam-identity-tax-refund-fraud-60-minutes/>.

982 White, James R. *Identity Theft: Additional Actions Could Help IRS Combat the Large, Evolving Threat of Refund Fraud*. Report No.: GAO-14-633. Report to Congressional Requesters. Governmental Accountability. August 2014. Web. <http://www.gao.gov/assets/670/665368.pdf >.

983 Treasury Inspector General for Tax Administration. *There are Billions of Dollars in Undetected Tax Refund Fraud Resulting From Identity Theft*. Report No. 2012-42-080. Washington, D.C.: TIGTA. 19 July 2012. Web. <http://www.treasury.gov/tigta/auditreports/2012reports/201242080fr.pdf>.

984 White, James R. *Identity Theft: Additional Actions Could Help IRS Combat the Large, Evolving Threat of Refund Fraud*. Report No.: GAO-14-633. Report to Congressional Requesters. Governmental Accountability. August 2014. Web. <http://www.gao.gov/assets/670/665368.pdf >.

985 White, James R. *Identity Theft: Additional Actions Could Help IRS Combat the Large, Evolving Threat of Refund Fraud*. Report No.: GAO-14-633. Report to Congressional Requesters. Governmental Accountability. August 2014. Web. <http://www.gao.gov/assets/670/665368.pdf >.

986 Kroft, Steve. "Biggest IRS Scam Around: Identity Tax Refund Fraud." 21 September 2014. Web. <http://www.cbsnews.com/news/irs-scam-identity-tax-refund-fraud-60-minutes/>.

987 Kroft, Steve. "Biggest IRS Scam Around: Identity Tax Refund Fraud." 21 September 2014. Web. <http://www.cbsnews.com/news/irs-scam-identity-tax-refund-fraud-60-minutes/>.

988 White, James R. *Identity Theft: Additional Actions Could Help IRS Combat the Large, Evolving Threat of Refund Fraud*. Report No.: GAO-14-633. Report to Congressional Requesters. Governmental Accountability. August 2014. Web. <http://www.gao.gov/assets/670/665368.pdf >.

989 UNC Morehead Planetarium and Science Center, *Call for Event Submissions*, 12 December 2013. <http://moreheadplanetarium.org/blog/index.php?cat=5>.

990 UNC Morehead Planetarium and Science Center, *Call for Event Submissions*. 12 December 2013, Web. <http://moreheadplanetarium.org/blog/index.php?cat=5>.

991 National Science Foundation, *Award Abstract #14223004*. <http://www.nsf.gov/awardsearch/showAward?AWD_ID=1423004>; National Science Foundation, *Award Abstract #1423050*. <http://www.nsf.gov/awardsearch/showAward?AWD_ID=1423050>.

992 Science Festival Alliance, *About the Science Festival Alliance*, http://sciencefestivals.org/about/about-the-science-festival-alliance.

993 National Science Foundation, *Award Abstract #14223004*. <http://www.nsf.gov/awardsearch/showAward?AWD_ID=1423004>; National Science Foundation, *Award Abstract #1423050*. <http://www.nsf.gov/awardsearch/showAward?AWD_ID=1423050>.

994 National Science Foundation, *Award Abstract #14223004*. <http://www.nsf.gov/awardsearch/showAward?AWD_ID=1423004>; National Science Foundation, *Award Abstract #1423050*. <http://www.nsf.gov/awardsearch/showAward?AWD_ID=1423050>.

995 Oliver, Becky. "Investigation: Trouble at the Job Corps." *Myfoxfw.com*. KDFW Fox 4. 4 August 2014. Web. <http://www.myfoxdfw.com/story/26195573/investigation-trouble-at-the-job-corps>.

996 Tate, Kristin. "Government-Funded Youth Program Allegedly Ridden with Corruption, Rape, Drug Abuse." *Breitbart.com*. Brietbart. 23 July 2014. Web. <http://www.breitbart.com/Breitbart-Texas/2014/07/23/Government-Funded-Youth-Program-Allegedly-Ridden-with-Corruption-Rape-Drug-Abuse>.

997 Oliver, Becky. "Investigation: Trouble at the Job Corps." *Myfoxfw.com*. KDFW Fox 4. 4 August 2014. Web. <http://www.myfoxdfw.com/story/26195573/investigation-trouble-at-the-job-corps>.

998 Oliver, Becky, "Investigation: Trouble at the Job Corps, part 2." *Myfoxfw.com*. KDFW Fox4. 6 August 2014, <http://www.myfoxdfw.com/story/26206562/trouble-at-the-job-corps-part-2>.

999 Oliver, Becky, "Investigation: Trouble at the Job Corps, part 2." *Myfoxfw.com*. KDFW Fox4. 6 August 2014, <http://www.myfoxdfw.com/story/26206562/trouble-at-the-job-corps-part-2>.

1000 Oliver, Becky, "Investigation: Trouble at the Job Corps, part 2." *Myfoxfw.com*. KDFW Fox4. 6 August 2014, <http://www.myfoxdfw.com/story/26206562/trouble-at-the-job-corps-part-2>.

1001 Oliver, Becky, "Investigation: Trouble at the Job Corps, part 2." *Myfoxfw.com*. KDFW Fox4. 6 August 2014, <http://www.myfoxdfw.com/story/26206562/trouble-at-the-job-corps-part-2>.

1002 Fahrenthold, David A., "Great Society at 50: LBJ's Job Corps will cost taxpayers $1.7 billion this year. Does it work?" *washingtonpost.com*. The Washington Post. 19 May 2014. Web. <http://www.washingtonpost.com/politics/jobs-corps-benefits-lead-to-questions-on-programs-costs/2014/05/19/80136056-db86-11e3-8009-71de85b9c527_story.html>. According to the Department of Labor, the Treasure Island is scheduled to close.

1003 Fahrenthold, David A. "Job Corps Closing Troubled Center in Oklahoma. 28 August 2014. Web. <http://www.washingtonpost.com/blogs/federal-eye/wp/2014/08/28/job-corps-closing-troubled-center-in-oklahoma/>.

1004 Fahrenthold, David A., "Great Society at 50: LBJ's Job Corps will cost taxpayers $1.7 billion this year. Does it work?" *washingtonpost.com*. The Washington Post. 19 May 2014. Web. <http://www.washingtonpost.com/politics/jobs-corps-benefits-lead-to-questions-on-programs-costs/2014/05/19/80136056-db86-11e3-8009-71de85b9c527_story.html>.

1005 Oliver, Becky, "Investigation: Trouble at the Job Corps, part 2." *Myfoxfw.com*. KDFW Fox4. 6 August 2014, <http://www.myfoxdfw.com/story/26206562/trouble-at-the-job-corps-part-2>.

1006 Fahrenthold, David A., "Great Society at 50: LBJ's Job Corps will cost taxpayers $1.7 billion this year. Does it work?" *washingtonpost.com*. The Washington Post. 19 May 2014. Web. <http://www.washingtonpost.com/politics/jobs-corps-benefits-lead-to-questions-on-programs-costs/2014/05/19/80136056-db86-11e3-8009-71de85b9c527_story.html>.

1007 Fahrenthold, David A., "Great Society at 50: LBJ's Job Corps will cost taxpayers $1.7 billion this year. Does it work?" *washingtonpost.com*. The Washington Post. 19 May 2014. Web. <http://www.washingtonpost.com/politics/jobs-corps-benefits-lead-to-questions-on-programs-costs/2014/05/19/80136056-db86-11e3-8009-71de85b9c527_story.html>.

1008 Information provided by the Department of the Navy.

1009 Bendick, John, Brian Kettl, and Jen Thran. "NAVSUP Updates the Buy It Green Guide." *Currents* spring 2014: 69+. *Greenfleet*. U.S. Navy. Web. <http://greenfleet.dodlive.mil/files/2014/05/Spr14_NAVSUP_Buy_It_Green.pdf>.

1010 Turner, Katherine, and Ashely Tolbert. "CNO Recognizes Awards Winners for Exceptional Environmental Stewardship." *Currents* summer 2014: 7+. *Greenfleet*. U.S. Navy. Web. <http://greenfleet.dodlive.mil/files/2014/08/Sum14_CNO__Awards_Winners.pdf>.

1011 Office of the Secretary of the Navy. "Great Green Fleet." Web. <http://greenfleet.dodlive.mil/energy/great-green-fleet/>.

1012 Information provided by the Department of the Navy.

1013 Information provided by the Department of the Navy.

1014 National Science Foundation. "Collaborative Research: Wikipedia and the Democratization of Academic Knowledge." Award No. 1322934 and Award No. 1322971. Web. <http://www.nsf.gov/awardsearch/showAward?AWD_ID=1322934>. <http://www.nsf.gov/awardsearch/showAward?AWD_ID=1322971>.

1015 National Science Foundation. "Collaborative Research: Wikipedia and the Democratization of Academic Knowledge." Award No. 1322934 and Award No. 1322971. Web. <http://www.nsf.gov/awardsearch/showAward?AWD_ID=1322934>. <http://www.nsf.gov/awardsearch/showAward?AWD_ID=1322971>.

1016 National Science Foundation. "Collaborative Research: Wikipedia and the Democratization of Academic Knowledge." Award No. 1322934 and Award No. 1322971. Web. <http://www.nsf.gov/awardsearch/showAward?AWD_ID=1322934>. <http://www.nsf.gov/awardsearch/showAward?AWD_ID=1322971>.

Harrington, Elizabeth. "Government-Funded Study: Why is Wikipedia Sexist?." *Freebeacon.com.* The Washington Free Beacon. 30 July 2014. Web. http://freebeacon.com/issues/government-funded-study-why-is-wikipedia-sexist/>.

1017 Filipacchi, Amanda. "Wikipedia's Sexism Toward Female Novelists." *Nytimes.com.* The New York Times Company. 24 April 2013. Web. <http://www.nytimes.com/2013/04/28/opinion/sunday/wikipedias-sexism-toward-female-novelists.html>.

1018 MacDonald, Heather. "Wikipedia Is Male-Dominated. That Doesn't Mean It's Sexist." *Slate.com* The Slate Group, The Washington Post Company. 9 February 2011. Web. <http://www.slate.com/articles/double_x/doublex/2011/02/wikipedia_is_maledominated_that_doesnt_mean_its_sexist.2.html>.

1019 National Science Foundation. "Collaborative Research: Wikipedia and the Democratization of Academic Knowledge." Award No. 1322934 and Award No. 1322971. Web. <http://www.nsf.gov/awardsearch/showAward?AWD_ID=1322934>. <http://www.nsf.gov/awardsearch/showAward?AWD_ID=1322971>.

1020 Transportation for America. *The Fix We're In For: The State of Our Nation's Bridges 2013.* Transportation for America. Web. <http://t4america.org/docs/bridgereport2013/2013BridgeReport.pdf>.

1021 Bridgers, Leslie, "Portland to Install Traffic-slowing Devices on 10 Streets." *Pressherald.com.* Maine Today Media, Inc. 28 June 2014. Web. http://www.pressherald.com/2014/06/28/portland-to-install-traffic-slowing-devices-on-10-streets/>.

1022 WMTW ABC 8. "Traffic Calming Coming to Portland Neighborhoods." *Wmtw.com.* Hearst Properties, Inc. 1 August 2014. Web. <http://www.wmtw.com/news/traffic-calming-coming-to-portland-neighborhoods/27270340>.

1023 WMTW ABC 8. "Traffic Calming Coming to Portland Neighborhoods." *Wmtw.com.* Hearst Properties, Inc. 1 August 2014. Web. <http://www.wmtw.com/news/traffic-calming-coming-to-portland-neighborhoods/27270340>.

1024 Harry, David. "2 Portland Neighborhoods to Get Traffic-calming Measures." *Theforecaster.net.* The Forecaster. 24 June 2014. Web. <http://www.theforecaster.net/news/print/2014/06/24/2-portland-neighborhoods-get-traffic-calming-measu/202619>.

1025 U.S. Economic Development Administration. Public Affairs Department. U.S. Department of Commerce Invests $1.5 Million to Support Mixed-Use Development of Thompson's Point in Portland, Maine. Eda.gov. Department of Commerce, 20 Sept. 2012. Web. 19 Oct. 2014. <http://www.eda.gov/news/press-releases/2012/09/20/portland_me.htm>.

1026 Harry, David. "2 Portland Neighborhoods to Get Traffic-calming Measures." *Theforecaster.net.* The Forecaster. 24 June 2014. Web. <http://www.theforecaster.net/news/print/2014/06/24/2-portland-neighborhoods-get-traffic-calming-measu/202619>.

1027 "WMTW ABC 8. "Traffic Calming Coming to Portland Neighborhoods." *Wmtw.com.* Hearst Properties, Inc. 1 August 2014. Web. <http://www.wmtw.com/news/traffic-calming-coming-to-portland-neighborhoods/27270340>.

1028 Website of the City of Portland, Maine, News Release, "Traffic Calming Measures Coming to Libbytown & Rosemont." 30 June 2014. Web. <http://www.portlandmaine.gov/CivicAlerts.aspx?AID=230>.

1029 Harry, David. "2 Portland Neighborhoods to Get Traffic-calming Measures." *Theforecaster.net.* The Forecaster. 24 June 2014. Web. <http://www.theforecaster.net/news/print/2014/06/24/2-portland-neighborhoods-get-traffic-calming-measu/202619>.

1030 Harry, David. "2 Portland Neighborhoods to Get Traffic-calming Measures." *Theforecaster.net.* The Forecaster. 24 June 2014. Web. <http://www.theforecaster.net/news/print/2014/06/24/2-portland-neighborhoods-get-traffic-calming-measu/202619>.

1031 U.S. Senator Tom Coburn M.D. Wastebook 2013. < http://www.coburn.senate.gov/public//index.cfm?a=Files. Serve&File_id=d204730e-4a24-4711-b1db-99bb6c29d4b6>.

1032 U.S. Department of Justice, Justice Management Division, Procurement Services Staff. Brand Name Justification. file:///C:/Users/ca42886/Downloads/Brand_Name_Justification%20(2).pdf>.

1033 U.S. Department of Justice, Justice Management Division, Procurement Services Staff. Brand Name Justification.

1034 U.S. Attorney General Eric Holder. *Memorandum For All Department of Justice Employees: Budget Implications for the Department of Justice Workforce.* 21 January 2011. Washington, DC: Department of Justice January 21, 2011. <http://abcnews.go.com/images/Politics/AG%20Memo%20re%20Budget%20Implications%20for%20the%20DOJ%20Workforce.pdf>.

1035 Department of Justice. Office of Public Affairs. *Attorney General Holder Announces Justice Department to Lift Hiring Freeze. Justice.gov.* DOJ, 10 Feb. 2014. Web. 18 Oct. 2014. <http://www.justice.gov/opa/pr/attorney-general-holder-announces-justice-department-lift-hiring-freeze>.

Bureau of Labor and Statistics. Economic News Releases. *Employment Situation Summary. Bls.gov.* U.S. Department of Labor, 3 Oct. 2014. Web. 18 Oct. 2014. <http://www.bls.gov/news.release/empsit.nr0.htm>.

1037 National Association for Law Placement. "Employment for the Class of 2012-Selected Findings." *Nalp.org.* 2013 Web. <http://www.nalp.org/uploads/Classof2012SelectedFindings.pdf>.

1038 Dorsewitz, Michael. "DOJ Spending Over Half Million to 'EnhanceProfile' on LinkedIn." *Bizpacreview.com.* BizPac Review. 3 January 2014. Web. < http://www.bizpacreview.com/2014/01/03/doj-spending-over-half-million-to-enhance-profile-on-linkedin-91908>.

1039 U.S. Department of Justice, Justice Management Division, Procurement Services Staff. Brand Name Justification. file:///C:/Users/ca42886/Downloads/Brand_Name_Justification%20(2).pdf>.

U.S. Department of Justice, Justice Management Division, Procurement Services Staff. Brand Name Justification. file:///C:/Users/ca42886/Downloads/Brand_Name_Justification%20(2).pdf>.

1041 Gullo, Karen. "LinkedIn Sues Unknown Hackers Over Fakes Profiles." *Bloomberg.com* Bloomberg L.P. 7 January 2014. Web. <http://www.bloomberg.com/news/2014-01-07/linkedin-sues-unknown-hackers-over-thousands-of-fake-accounts.html>.

1042 Martosko, David. "Expensive 'Choices': U.S. Taxpayers Spent $55,000 on Travel Expenses for Hillary Clinton's BOOK TOUR in Paris and Berlin – Including Her $3,668-a-night Hotel Suite." *Dailymail.co.uk* Associated Newspapers Ltd. 11 August 2014. Web. <http://www.dailymail.co.uk/news/article-2722178/Expensive-Choices-US-taxpayers-spent-55-000-travel-expenses-Hillary-Clintons-BOOK-TOUR-Paris-Berlin.html>.

1043 Martosko, David. "Expensive 'Choices': U.S. Taxpayers Spent $55,000 on Travel Expenses for Hillary Clinton's BOOK TOUR in Paris and Berlin – Including Her $3,668-a-night Hotel Suite." *Dailymail.co.uk* Associated Newspapers Ltd. 11 August 2014. Web. <http://www.dailymail.co.uk/news/article-2722178/Expensive-Choices-US-taxpayers-spent-55-000-travel-expenses-Hillary-Clintons-BOOK-TOUR-Paris-Berlin.html>.

1044 Martosko, David. "Expensive 'Choices': U.S. Taxpayers Spent $55,000 on Travel Expenses for Hillary Clinton's BOOK TOUR in Paris and Berlin – Including Her $3,668-a-night Hotel Suite." *Dailymail.co.uk* Associated Newspapers Ltd. 11 August 2014. Web. <http://www.dailymail.co.uk/news/article-2722178/Expensive-Choices-US-taxpayers-spent-55-000-travel-expenses-Hillary-Clintons-BOOK-TOUR-Paris-Berlin.html>.

1045 Martosko, David. "Expensive 'Choices': U.S. Taxpayers Spent $55,000 on Travel Expenses for Hillary Clinton's BOOK TOUR in Paris and Berlin – Including Her $3,668-a-night Hotel Suite." *Dailymail.co.uk* Associated Newspapers Ltd. 11 August 2014. Web. <http://www.dailymail.co.uk/news/article-2722178/Expensive-Choices-US-taxpayers-spent-55-000-travel-expenses-Hillary-Clintons-BOOK-TOUR-Paris-Berlin.html>.

1046 Martosko, David. "Expensive 'Choices': U.S. Taxpayers Spent $55,000 on Travel Expenses for Hillary Clinton's BOOK TOUR in Paris and Berlin – Including Her $3,668-a-night Hotel Suite." *Dailymail.co.uk* Associated Newspapers Ltd. 11 August 2014. Web. <http://www.dailymail.co.uk/news/article-2722178/Expensive-Choices-US-taxpayers-spent-55-000-travel-expenses-Hillary-Clintons-BOOK-TOUR-Paris-Berlin.html>.

1047 Martosko, David. "Expensive 'Choices': U.S. Taxpayers Spent $55,000 on Travel Expenses for Hillary Clinton's BOOK TOUR in Paris and Berlin – Including Her $3,668-a-night Hotel Suite." *Dailymail.co.uk* Associated Newspapers Ltd. 11 August 2014. Web. <http://www.dailymail.co.uk/news/article-2722178/Expensive-Choices-US-taxpayers-spent-55-000-travel-expenses-Hillary-Clintons-BOOK-TOUR-Paris-Berlin.html>.

1048 Martosko, David. "Expensive 'Choices': U.S. Taxpayers Spent $55,000 on Travel Expenses for Hillary Clinton's BOOK TOUR in Paris and Berlin – Including Her $3,668-a-night Hotel Suite." *Dailymail.co.uk* Associated Newspapers Ltd. 11 August 2014. Web. <http://www.dailymail.co.uk/news/article-2722178/Expensive-Choices-US-taxpayers-spent-55-000-travel-expenses-Hillary-Clintons-BOOK-TOUR-Paris-Berlin.html>.

1049 Martosko, David. "Expensive 'Choices': U.S. Taxpayers Spent $55,000 on Travel Expenses for Hillary Clinton's BOOK TOUR in Paris and Berlin – Including Her $3,668-a-night Hotel Suite." *Dailymail.co.uk* Associated Newspapers Ltd. 11 August 2014. Web. <http://www.dailymail.co.uk/news/article-2722178/Expensive-Choices-US-taxpayers-spent-55-000-travel-expenses-Hillary-Clintons-BOOK-TOUR-Paris-Berlin.html>.

1050 Smith Emily and Ian Mohr. "Page Six: Execs on Notice After Hillary's Book Sales Tank." *Pagesix.com*. NYP Holdings, Inc. 8 July 2014. Web. <http://pagesix.com/2014/07/08/execs-on-notice-after-hillarys-book-sales-tank/>.

1051 Nicholas, Peter. "Hillary Clinton Faces Heat Over Paid Speeches; UNLV Students Want $225,000 Fee for Upcoming Appearance Donated." *Wsj.com*. Dow Jones & Company. 27 June 2014. Web. <http://online.wsj.com/articles/hillary-clinton-faces-heat-over-paid-speeches-1403894283>.

1052 Welch, Laurie, "Burley's Airport Fails Standards; Could Lose FAA Funding." *Magicvalley.com*. Twin Falls Times-News. 13 July 2014. Web. **<http://magicvalley.com/news/local/mini-cassia/burley-s-airport-fails-standards-could-lose-faa-funding/article_e437bce4-0a48-11e4-99c8-0019bb2963f4.html>**.

1053 Welch, Laurie, "Burley's Airport Fails Standards; Could Lose FAA Funding." Magicvalley.com. Twin Falls Times-News. 13 July 2014. Web. <http://magicvalley.com/news/local/mini-cassia/burley-s-airport-fails-standards-could-lose-faa-funding/article_e437bce4-0a48-11e4-99c8-0019bb2963f4.html>.

1054 Welch, Laurie, "Burley's Airport Fails Standards; Could Lose FAA Funding." Magicvalley.com. Twin Falls Times-News. 13 July 2014. Web. <http://magicvalley.com/news/local/mini-cassia/burley-s-airport-fails-standards-could-lose-faa-funding/article_e437bce4-0a48-11e4-99c8-0019bb2963f4.html>.

1055 Welch, Laurie, "Burley's Airport Fails Standards; Could Lose FAA Funding." Magicvalley.com. Twin Falls Times-News. 13 July 2014. Web. <http://magicvalley.com/news/local/mini-cassia/burley-s-airport-fails-standards-could-lose-faa-funding/article_e437bce4-0a48-11e4-99c8-0019bb2963f4.html>.

1056 Welch, Laurie, "Burley's Airport Fails Standards; Could Lose FAA Funding." Magicvalley.com. Twin Falls Times-News. 13 July 2014. Web. <http://magicvalley.com/news/local/mini-cassia/burley-s-airport-fails-standards-could-lose-faa-funding/article_e437bce4-0a48-11e4-99c8-0019bb2963f4.html>.

1057 Welch, Laurie, "Burley's Airport Fails Standards; Could Lose FAA Funding." Magicvalley.com. Twin Falls Times-News. 13 July 2014. Web. <http://magicvalley.com/news/local/mini-cassia/burley-s-airport-fails-standards-could-lose-faa-funding/article_e437bce4-0a48-11e4-99c8-0019bb2963f4.html>.

1058 Welch, Laurie, "Burley's Airport Fails Standards; Could Lose FAA Funding." Magicvalley.com. Twin Falls Times-News. 13 July 2014. Web. <http://magicvalley.com/news/local/mini-cassia/burley-s-airport-fails-standards-could-lose-faa-funding/article_e437bce4-0a48-11e4-99c8-0019bb2963f4.html>.

1059 Lenkersdorfer, Jay. "City Approves Final Airport Site Study." *Minicassia.com*. News Journal. 11 July 2014. Web. <http://www.minicassia.com/news/article_89150fd0-0942-11e4-b38f-001a4bcf6878.html>.

1060 Welch, Laurie, "Burley's Airport Fails Standards; Could Lose FAA Funding." Magicvalley.com. Twin Falls Times-News. 13 July 2014. Web. <http://magicvalley.com/news/local/mini-cassia/burley-s-airport-fails-standards-could-lose-faa-funding/article_e437bce4-0a48-11e4-99c8-0019bb2963f4.html>.

1061 Welch, Laurie, "Burley's Airport Fails Standards; Could Lose FAA Funding." Magicvalley.com. Twin Falls Times-News. 13 July 2014. Web. <http://magicvalley.com/news/local/mini-cassia/burley-s-airport-fails-standards-could-lose-faa-funding/article_e437bce4-0a48-11e4-99c8-0019bb2963f4.html>.

1062 Lenkersdorfer, Jay. "City Approves Final Airport Site Study." *Minicassia.com*. News Journal. 11 July 2014. Web. <http://www.minicassia.com/news/article_89150fd0-0942-11e4-b38f-001a4bcf6878.html>.

1063 Welch, Laurie, "Burley's Airport Fails Standards; Could Lose FAA Funding." Magicvalley.com. Twin Falls Times-News. 13 July 2014. Web. <http://magicvalley.com/news/local/mini-cassia/burley-s-airport-fails-standards-could-lose-faa-funding/article_e437bce4-0a48-11e4-99c8-0019bb2963f4.html>.

1064 Welch, Laurie, "Burley's Airport Fails Standards; Could Lose FAA Funding." Magicvalley.com. Twin Falls Times-News. 13 July 2014. Web. <http://magicvalley.com/news/local/mini-cassia/burley-s-airport-fails-standards-could-lose-faa-funding/article_e437bce4-0a48-11e4-99c8-0019bb2963f4.html>.

1065 Welch, Laurie, "Burley's Airport Fails Standards; Could Lose FAA Funding." Magicvalley.com. Twin Falls Times-News. 13 July 2014. Web. <http://magicvalley.com/news/local/mini-cassia/burley-s-airport-fails-standards-could-lose-faa-funding/article_e437bce4-0a48-11e4-99c8-0019bb2963f4.html>.

1066 Welch, Laurie, "Burley's Airport Fails Standards; Could Lose FAA Funding." Magicvalley.com. Twin Falls Times-News. 13 July 2014. Web. <http://magicvalley.com/news/local/mini-cassia/burley-s-airport-fails-standards-could-lose-faa-funding/article_e437bce4-0a48-11e4-99c8-0019bb2963f4.html>.

1067 Welch, Laurie, "Burley's Airport Fails Standards; Could Lose FAA Funding." Magicvalley.com. Twin Falls Times-News. 13 July 2014. Web. <http://magicvalley.com/news/local/mini-cassia/burley-s-airport-fails-standards-could-lose-faa-funding/article_e437bce4-0a48-11e4-99c8-0019bb2963f4.html>.

1068 "Burley Municipal Airport to Magic Valley Regional Airport." Google Maps. Web. <https://www.google.com/maps/dir/Burley+Municipal+Airport,+Burley,+ID+83318/Magic+Valley+Regional+Airport,+492+Airport+Loop,+Twin+Falls,+ID+83301/@42.5607097,-114.6795824,9z/data=!4m14!4m13!1m5!1m1!1s0x54ab3680b39d19d 5:0x5fc3d5e1 fb36d509!2m2!1d-113.771545!2d42.542603!1m5!1m1!1s0x54acbadbeb372657:0x3e21d634f7e0af24!2m2!1d-114.486048!2d42.481968!3e0>.

1069 Welch, Laurie, "Burley's Airport Fails Standards; Could Lose FAA Funding." Magicvalley.com. Twin Falls Times-News. 13 July 2014. Web. <http://magicvalley.com/news/local/mini-cassia/burley-s-airport-fails-standards-could-lose-faa-funding/article_e437bce4-0a48-11e4-99c8-0019bb2963f4.html>.

1070 The total grant amount since 2012 is $674,590. National Institute of Health, Research Portfolio Online Reporting Tools, "Project Information: 5R34AA021502-02 Tailored Mobile Text Messaging to Reduce Problem Drinking," http://projectreporter.nih.gov/project_info_description.cfm?aid=8530120&icde=20687239.

1071 National Institute of Health, Research Portfolio Online Reporting Tools. "Tailored Mobile Text Messaging to Reduce Problem Drinking." Project Number 5R34AA021502-02. Web. <http://projectreporter.nih.gov/project_info_description.cfm?aid=8530120&icde=20687239>.

1072 Harrington, Elizabeth. "NIH Spent $480,500 to Text Message Drunks." *Freebeacon.com*. The Washington Free Beacon. 12 June 2014. Web. <http://freebeacon.com/issues/nih-spent-480500-to-text-message-drunks/>.

1073 National Institute of Health, Research Portfolio Online Reporting Tools. "Tailored Mobile Text Messaging to Reduce Problem Drinking." Project Number 5R34AA021502-02. Web. <http://projectreporter.nih.gov/project_info_description.cfm?aid=8530120&icde=20687239>.

1074 Research Foundation for Mental Hygiene, Inc. "Tailored Mobile Text Messaging to Reduce Problem Drinking." *ClinicalTrials.gov.* U.S. National Institute of Health. Identifier Number: NCT01885312. Web. http://clinicaltrials.gov/ct2/show/NCT01885312>.

1075 Research Foundation for Mental Hygiene, Inc. "Tailored Mobile Text Messaging to Reduce Problem Drinking." *ClinicalTrials.gov.* U.S. National Institute of Health. Identifier Number: NCT01885312. Web. http://clinicaltrials.gov/ct2/show/NCT01885312>.

1076 National Institute of Health, Research Portfolio Online Reporting Tools. "Tailored Mobile Text Messaging to Reduce Problem Drinking." Project Number 5R34AA021502-02. Web. <http://projectreporter.nih.gov/project_info_description.cfm?aid=8530120&icde=20687239>.

1077 Research Foundation for Mental Hygiene, Inc. "Tailored Mobile Text Messaging to Reduce Problem Drinking." *ClinicalTrials.gov.* U.S. National Institute of Health. Identifier Number: NCT01885312. Web. http://clinicaltrials.gov/ct2/show/NCT01885312>.

1078 U.S. Department of Agriculture, Rural Development Assistance. "Value-Added Producer Grant Awards Fiscal Year 2014." *Rurdev.usda.gov.* 2014. Web. <http://www.rurdev.usda.gov/supportdocuments/RD_2014VAPGRecipients.pdf>.

1079 *Dairy Store*, Reed's Dairy <http://www.reedsdairy.com/dairystore/>.

1080 U.S. Department of Agriculture, Rural Development Assistance. "Value-Added Producer Grant Awards Fiscal Year 2014." *Rurdev.usda.gov.* 2014. Web. <http://www.rurdev.usda.gov/supportdocuments/RD_2014VAPGRecipients.pdf>.

1081 U.S. Department of Agriculture, Rural Development Assistance. "Value-Added Producer Grant Awards Fiscal Year 2014." *Rurdev.usda.gov.* 2014. Web. <http://www.rurdev.usda.gov/supportdocuments/RD_2014VAPGRecipients.pdf>.

1082 Vermillion, Allecia. "Kurt Timmermeister Is Opening a Shop on Capitol Hill." *Seatttlemet.com.* SagaCity Media company. 3 March 2014. Web. http://www.seattlemet.com/eat-and-drink/nosh-pit/articles/kurt-timmermeister-is-opening-february-2014>.

1083 U.S. Department of Agriculture, Rural Development Assistance. "Value-Added Producer Grant Awards Fiscal Year 2014." *Rurdev.usda.gov.* 2014. Web. <http://www.rurdev.usda.gov/supportdocuments/RD_2014VAPGRecipients.pdf>.

1084 U.S. Department of Agriculture, Rural Development Assistance. "Value-Added Producer Grant Awards Fiscal Year 2014." *Rurdev.usda.gov.* 2014. Web. <http://www.rurdev.usda.gov/supportdocuments/RD_2014VAPGRecipients.pdf>.

1085 U.S. Department of Agriculture, Rural Development Assistance. "Value-Added Producer Grant Awards Fiscal Year 2014." *Rurdev.usda.gov.* 2014. Web. <http://www.rurdev.usda.gov/supportdocuments/RD_2014VAPGRecipients.pdf>.

1086 U.S. Department of Agriculture, Rural Development Assistance. "Value-Added Producer Grant Awards Fiscal Year 2014." *Rurdev.usda.gov.* 2014. Web. <http://www.rurdev.usda.gov/supportdocuments/RD_2014VAPGRecipients.pdf>.

1087 Genger, Tamar. "Living on the Wedge: A Brave New World of Kosher Cheese."*joyofkosher.com.* Kosher Media Network. 1 May 2010. Web. <http://www.joyofkosher.com/2010/05/living-wedge-brave-world-kosher-cheese/>.

1088 Genger, Tamar. "Living on the Wedge: A Brave New World of Kosher Cheese."*joyofkosher.com.* Kosher Media Network. 1 May 2010. Web. <http://www.joyofkosher.com/2010/05/living-wedge-brave-world-kosher-cheese/>.

1089 Serenity Acres Farm & Goat Dairy. "Soap & Body: About Our Goat Milk Soap." Web. <http://www.serenityfarmfl.com/soap-and-body.cfm>.

1090 "Large" NEOs were originally those with diameters greater than 1 kilometer. In 2005, Congress required NASA to track objects as small as 140 meters in diameter.

1091 NASA. "FY 2015 PRESIDENT'S BUDGET REQUEST SUMMARY." *Nasa.gov.* Web. <http://www.nasa.gov/sites/default/files/files/508_2015_Budget_Estimates.pdf>.

1092 Information provided by the Congressional Research Service.

1093 Dunn, Marcia. "NASA Inspector Blasts Asteroid Protection Program." *Ap.org.* The Associated Press. 15 September 2014. Web. http://bigstory.ap.org/article/nasa-inspector-blasts-asteroid-protection-program>.

1094 Dunn, Marcia. "NASA Inspector Blasts Asteroid Protection Program." *Ap.org.* The Associated Press. 15 September 2014. Web. http://bigstory.ap.org/article/nasa-inspector-blasts-asteroid-protection-program>.

1095 National Aeronautics and Space Administration, Office of Inspector General. *NASA's Efforts to Identify Near-Earth Objects and Mitigate Hazards.* Rep. No. IG-14-03. Washington, D.C.: NASA-OIG. September 2014. Web. <http://oig.nasa.gov/audits/reports/FY14/IG-14-030.pdf>.

1096 National Aeronautics and Space Administration, Office of Inspector General. *NASA's Efforts to Identify Near-Earth Objects and Mitigate Hazards.* Rep. No. IG-14-03. Washington, D.C.: NASA-OIG. September 2014. Web. <http://oig.nasa.gov/audits/reports/FY14/IG-14-030.pdf>.

1097 National Aeronautics and Space Administration, Office of Inspector General. *NASA's Efforts to Identify Near-Earth Objects and Mitigate Hazards.* Rep. No. IG-14-03. Washington, D.C.: NASA-OIG. September 2014. Web. <http://oig.nasa.gov/audits/reports/FY14/IG-14-030.pdf>.

1098 Colello, Kirsten and Scott Talaga. *Who Pays for Long-Term Services and Supports? A Fact Sheet.* Rep. No. R43483. Washington, D.C.: Congressional Research Service. 16 April 2014.Web. <http://www.crs.gov/pages/Reports.aspx?PRODCODE=R43483&Source=search> . p2

1099 Mitchel, Alison. *Medicaid Provider Taxes.* Rep. No. RS22843. Washington, D.C.: Congressional Research Service. 10 January 2013. Web. <http://www.crs.gov/pages/Reports.aspx?PRODCODE=RS22843&Source=search>.

1100 The National Commission on Fiscal Responsibility and Reform. *The Moment of Truth.* Washington, D.C.: The White House. December 2010 Web. <http://www.fiscalcommission.gov/sites/fiscalcommission.gov/files/documents/TheMomentofTruth12_1_2010.pdf>. p 39. The Commission noted the 10-year cost of ending the use of provider taxes is $44 billion.

1101 Date, S.V. "Why Are We Hauling Pennsylvania Coal All the Way to Germany?" *npr.org.* National Public Radio. 22 March 2014. Web. <http://www.npr.org/blogs/itsallpolitics/2014/03/14/290238727/long-dead-congressmans-earmark-lives-on-in-europe>.

1102 H.R. 2397, 113th Cong. §8054 (2014); S.1429, 113th Cong. §8054 (2014)

1103 Date, S.V. "Why Are We Hauling Pennsylvania Coal All the Way to Germany?" *npr.org.* National Public Radio. 22 March 2014. Web. <http://www.npr.org/blogs/itsallpolitics/2014/03/14/290238727/long-dead-congressmans-earmark-lives-on-in-europe>.

1104 H.R. 2397, 113th Cong. §8054 (2014); S.1429, 113th Cong. §8054 (2014)

1105 Slade, David. "German Mayor Tours Coal Site." *Mcall.com.* The Morning Call. 5 June 2002. Web. <http://articles.mcall.com/2002-06-05/news/3404410_1_anthracite-military-bases-coal>.

1106 S Date, S.V. "Why Are We Hauling Pennsylvania Coal All the Way to Germany?" *npr.org.* National Public Radio. 22 March 2014. Web. <http://www.npr.org/blogs/itsallpolitics/2014/03/14/290238727/long-dead-congressmans-earmark-lives-on-in-europe>.

1107 Date, S.V. "Why Are We Hauling Pennsylvania Coal All the Way to Germany?" *npr.org.* National Public Radio. 22 March 2014. Web. <http://www.npr.org/blogs/

itsallpolitics/2014/03/14/290238727/long-dead-congressmans-earmark-lives-on-in-europe>.

1108 H.R. 2397, 113th Cong. §8054 (2014); S.1429, 113th Cong. §8054 (2014)

1109 Date, S.V. "Why Are We Hauling Pennsylvania Coal All the Way to Germany?" *npr.org*. National Public Radio. 22 March 2014. Web. <http://www.npr.org/blogs/itsallpolitics/2014/03/14/290238727/long-dead-congressmans-earmark-lives-on-in-europe>.

1110 U.S. Energy Information Administration. "Total Energy: Annual Energy Review." *Eia.gov*. 27 September 2012. Web <http://www.eia.gov/totalenergy/data/annual/showtext.cfm?t=ptb0709>. This is based on 2011 coal prices, but does not include the cost to ship the anthracite coal from Pennsylvania to Germany

1111 Williams, Drew. "Chippewa Valley Regional Airport Receives Federal Marketing Grant." *Weau.com*. Gray Digital Media. 2 October 2014. Web. <http://www.weau.com/home/headlines/Chippewa-Valley-Regional-Airport-receies-federal-marketing-grant-277825941.html>.

1112 Williams, Drew. "Chippewa Valley Regional Airport Receives Federal Marketing Grant." *Weau.com*. Gray Digital Media. 2 October 2014. Web. <http://www.weau.com/home/headlines/Chippewa-Valley-Regional-Airport-receies-federal-marketing-grant-277825941.html>.

1113 Williams, Drew. "Chippewa Valley Regional Airport Receives Federal Marketing Grant." *Weau.com*. Gray Digital Media. 2 October 2014. Web. <http://www.weau.com/home/headlines/Chippewa-Valley-Regional-Airport-receies-federal-marketing-grant-277825941.html>.

1114 Source: www.kayak.com, as of October 2, 2014.

1115 Source: www.kayak.com, as of October 2, 2014.

1116 WormPower, "Grant Summary." Web. <http://www.wormpower.net/research/grant-summary/#.VC1ztfnF8do>.

1117 The LCN Staff. "Schumer fights for Worm Power." *Thelcn.com*. The Livingston County News. June 2014. Web. 16 October 2014. Web. <http://www.thelcn.com/news/schumer-fights-for-worm-power/article_cd4d0134-7bdf-5861-a254-fed534142c92.html?mode=jqm>.

1118 Butler, Virginia. "Worm Power in Avon Expands 800 Percent." *Twcnews.com*. Time Warner Cable Enterprises LLC. 4 April 2010. Web. <http://rochester.twcnews.com/content/news/500655/worm-power-in-avon-expands-800-percent/>.

1119 U.S. Department of Agriculture. "Vermicomposted Dairy Manure as a Disease Suppressive Seed Treatment." NIFA. *Research, Education and Economics Information System*. Web. <http://portal.nifa.usda.gov/web/crisprojectpages/1003067-vermicomposted-dairy-manure-as-a-disease-suppressive-seed-treatment.html>.

1120 USASpending.gov. "Prime Award Spending Data, RT Solutions, LLC." Federal Award Identifier: 20143361021927.1. Web. <http://usaspending.gov/explore?frompage=assistance&tab=By%20Prime%20Awardee&comingfrom=searchresults&federal_award_id=20143361021927.1&fiscal_year=all&typeofview=complete>.

1121 U.S. Department of Agriculture. "Vermicomposted Dairy Manure as a Disease Suppressive Seed Treatment." NIFA. *Research, Education and Economics Information System*. Web. <http://portal.nifa.usda.gov/web/crisprojectpages/1003067-vermicomposted-dairy-manure-as-a-disease-suppressive-seed-treatment.html>.

1122 Butler, Virginia. "Worm Power in Avon Expands 800 Percent." *Twcnews.com*. Time Warner Cable Enterprises LLC. 4 April 2010. Web. <http://rochester.twcnews.com/content/news/500655/worm-power-in-avon-expands-800-percent/>.

1123 WormPower e-store. <http://shop.wormpower.net/>.

1124 The LCN Staff. "Schumer fights for Worm Power." *Thelcn.com*. The Livingston County News. June 2014. Web. 16 October 2014. Web. <http://www.thelcn.com

Made in the USA
San Bernardino, CA
16 November 2014